D1236789

JOHN F. KENNEDY

→ ←

AND THE MISSILE GAP

To John McNay,
A good friend and
trusted advisor. I am
privileged to have gotten
to know you at Temple,
and hope we can remain
friends for a long time.

JOHN F. KENNEDY

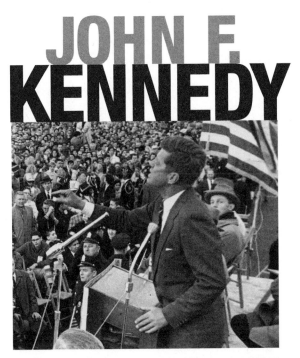

AND THE MISSILE GAP

Christopher A. Preble

NORTHERN ILLINOIS
UNIVERSITY
PRESS
DeKalb

Published by the Northern Illinois University Press, DeKalb, Illinois 60115

Manufactured in the United States using acid-free paper

All Rights Reserved

Design by Julia Fauci

Library of Congress Cataloging-in-Publication Data

Preble, Christopher A.

John F. Kennedy and the missile gap / Christopher A. Preble.

  p.   cm.

Includes bibliographical references and index.

ISBN 0-87580-332-6 (alk. paper)

1. Nuclear weapons—Government policy—United States—History—
20th century. 2. Nuclear weapons—Economic aspects—United States—
History—20th century. 3. Kennedy, John F. (John Fitzgerald), 1917–1963—
Views on national security. 4. United States—Military policy. 5. United States—
Foreign relations—Soviet Union. 6. Soviet Union—Foreign relations—United
States. 7. United States—Politics and government—1953–1961. 8. United
States—Politics and government—1961–1963. 9. National security—United
States—History—20th century. 10. Cold War. I. Title.

UA23.P6824 2004

355'.033073'09046—dc22

2004004280

Title page image courtesy of Urban Archives, Temple University, Philadelphia,
Pennsylvania.

To Krista,

with thanks and love.

Contents

Preface   *ix*

Introduction   *3*

1—Eisenhower, the New Look, and Their Critics   *19*

2—A Senator Finds His Voice   *52*

3—The Presidential Election of 1960 and the
Politics of National Security   *102*

4—The New Frontier and the Closing of the Missile Gap   *147*

Epilogue—The Legacy of Cold War Military Spending   *182*

Notes   *191*

Works Cited   *223*

Index   *235*

Preface

I began studying the story of John F. Kennedy and the missile gap as a graduate student at Temple University in 1994. I discussed my findings with my faculty advisers and my fellow graduate students, then tested my theories at academic conferences. Encouraged by positive feedback, I became more and more intrigued by the topic, and I threw myself into researching and writing this book. I have never regretted that decision.

I remain fascinated by the missile gap because the mistaken belief in it had a profound impact on U.S.–Soviet relations. The Soviets' deception convinced many Americans, including John Kennedy, that the United States was at a disadvantage vis-à-vis the Soviet Union. This mistaken belief contributed to Americans' doubts about their capacity for world leadership and, in turn, weakened the resolve of U.S. allies.

John Kennedy—both the reality of his brief but spectacular political career, and the mythology that surrounds his memory—similarly fascinates me. Few would remember his name, however, had he not won the closely contested presidential election of 1960. And his political ascendancy is attributable in large measure to the so-called missile gap.

Kennedy and the missile gap are inextricably connected. The doubts about America's strategic standing relative to the Soviet Union and the fears of military and political weakness on a global stage shook the confidence of millions of Americans. Kennedy's own fervent belief in the missile gap and his skill at communicating his concerns to his fellow citizens enabled him to advance his political career.

Although Eisenhower himself was not running for office in 1960, Kennedy's narrow electoral victory represented a defeat for Eisenhower's policies and signaled a new willingness on the part of Americans to make the sacrifices necessary to defeat the nation's adversaries. This willingness to "bear any burden" was translated into an accommodation with higher military spending. Thus, Kennedy's pledge to close the missile gap marks an important step along the road to the permanent war economy that lasted until the final days of the Cold War.

Therefore, in all that I have studied and written, I have found that the story of Kennedy and the missile gap is crucial in helping us to understand the political and economic dynamics of the Cold War. The missile gap was a critique of the strategic and economic foundations of the New Look and a political critique of the Eisenhower presidency. A study of any one of these three elements—the strategic, the economic, the political—cannot, standing alone, completely explain the history of the missile gap. A study of all three elements taken together not only explains a single episode in U.S. history but helps to explain the entire history of the Cold War.

This book is drawn from a body of research and writing compiled over nearly nine years. The work would not have been possible were it not for the kindness and generosity of countless friends, relatives, and good-hearted strangers.

First and foremost I thank Richard H. Immerman of Temple University. Dr. Immerman's devotion to the study of history and to all of his graduate and undergraduate students is boundless. It is a credit to him that he manages his many responsibilities with grace and good humor.

I also thank James W. Hilty, Susan Wolcott, Gregg Herken, David Alan Rosenberg, and Aaron L. Friedberg. Thanks also to the faculty and staff of the Department of History at Temple University; Sharon Kelly at the Kennedy Library; Bill Burr at the National Security Archive; and countless other librarians, archivists, and volunteers at the many research facilities that I have visited during the last nine years. Special thanks are in order for Fred Greenstein, emeritus professor of politics at Princeton University. Dr. Greenstein began the process of collecting materials related to the missile gap many years ago. A box containing those materials ultimately wound up in my possession, and these documents became the starting point for this project. I am grateful for the financial and research assistance I received from the Department of History at Temple University, the John F. Kennedy Library Foundation, and the Center for the Study of Force and Diplomacy at Temple.

Thanks also to Campbell Craig, Chris DeRosa, Roger Dingman, Robert Divine, Jeffrey Engel, Marc Frey, Alexandra Friedrich, Raymond Garthoff, Francis Gavin, Irwin Gellman, Jessica Gienow-Hecht, Peter Karsten, Brian Linn, John McNay, G. E. "Jerry" Miller, Howard Reiter, Steven Schwartzberg, Katherine Sibley, Tom Sisk, Kevin Soutor, Steven

Teles, and Marc Trachtenberg for their helpful comments on my work; to Ted Galen Carpenter, vice president of defense and foreign policy studies at the Cato Institute, and Leo P. Ribuffo, my senior thesis adviser at George Washington University, for their advice and counsel throughout my professional career; and to Craig Principe and Feliz Ventura, who offered invaluable assistance during the final stages of this project. Although this book could never have been completed without their help, any errors or omissions are my responsibility alone.

Thanks and love go out to my parents, Charles and Mary-Jane Preble, and to my sister, Lynn. Each in a different way convinced me that all things are possible regardless of the many obstacles that life places in one's path, provided that one has the courage and the persistence to see things through to completion. This book is tangible proof of that objective truth.

Finally, none of this would have been possible were it not for the loving guidance, patient encouragement, and welcome companionship of my wife, Krista. She has been with me every step of the way. This book, which represents another important step in our long and wonderful journey together, is dedicated to her.

JOHN F. KENNEDY

AND THE MISSILE GAP

Introduction

In August 1957 the Soviet Union launched the world's first intercontinental ballistic missile (ICBM). Then, on 4 October 1957, the Soviets
launched *Sputnik,* the world's first Earth-orbiting satellite. With its
Cold War adversary's technological prowess on public display, the
United States seemed to be marching in place—or going backward.
Journalists, politicians, and military leaders began to speak of a "missile gap"—a perceived strategic disparity between the two superpowers
brought on by the Soviet Union's gains in the production of rockets,
missiles and nuclear weapons.

Public anxiety remained high through the remainder of the 1950s and
into the early 1960s. The sense of security that Americans had known for
much of the nation's history was shattered as millions contemplated life
under the shadow of a nuclear Armageddon. Beset by doubt, Americans
came to question their nation's capacity for world leadership.

John F. Kennedy made effective use of the uncertainty about the
nation's international standing in order to challenge, and ultimately
supplant, Dwight D. Eisenhower's New Look with a new military strategy known as Flexible Response. Senator Kennedy rose to national
prominence during the missile gap years by calling for changes to national security policy and corresponding changes in the structure of
the military forces that would enable the United States to rectify the
potentially dangerous and destabilizing inferiority represented by the
presumed gap. Then, in the presidential election of 1960, Kennedy realized his crowning political achievement when he defeated Vice President Richard Nixon to become the nation's thirty-fifth president. The
missile gap was a central theme in Kennedy's campaign to get the
country moving again.

The strategic and economic critiques of the New Look, encompassed in the late 1950s by concerns about the missile gap, were based on valid concerns about U.S. security. The missile gap itself, however, was a fiction. At no time did the Soviets have a qualitative or quantitative superiority in nuclear weapons technology over the United States. The U.S. nuclear arsenal, dispersed among military bases worldwide, was never in danger of being incapacitated by a surprise Soviet attack.

Official intelligence estimates suggesting that there was no missile gap had been made available to lawmakers, including Senator Kennedy, as early as January 1960, but Kennedy chose instead to believe unofficial estimates, promulgated by journalists and maverick military officers, that inflated Soviet missile strength. After he assumed the presidency in early 1961, Kennedy privately conceded that there was no gap. Embarrassed to learn that he had been so badly mistaken, however, for nearly ten months Kennedy refused to declare publicly that the fictional gap had been closed. During this period, Kennedy used the lingering concerns over the missile gap to make the changes to the nation's military that he deemed necessary. This issue had a central role in Kennedy's rise to political immortality and in his policies as president. The question addressed here is how and why Kennedy used the gap to achieve his political ends.

Eisenhower and the New Look

The missile gap had its origins in the earliest days of the Eisenhower administration. Dwight D. Eisenhower's national security policy, articulated in National Security Council Paper NSC 162/2 and later dubbed the New Look by outside observers, called for significant cuts in military spending. The debate over the wisdom or folly of Eisenhower's fiscal restraint, which contributed to his alleged overreliance on nuclear weapons, had begun immediately after the New Look strategy was first revealed. These criticisms sharpened in late 1957 after the twin shocks of the Soviet ICBM test and the launch of *Sputnik*. Critics were further emboldened when the contents of a secret report detailing the anticipated shortcomings of the U.S. missile program were leaked to the media in late December 1957.

The missile gap became convenient shorthand for all of these troubling revelations, and it was, therefore, incorporated into the building debate over the New Look. Eisenhower's efforts during his second term to refine the New Look to meet the new threats posed by Soviet technological gains were not immediately apparent to those who criticized the "delicate balance of terror" upon which U.S. security policy was based.[2] Meanwhile, those individuals who had strained for years against the budgetary ceilings imposed by Eisenhower's New Look became increasingly vocal during his second term. Using the missile gap as their battle cry, many political and military leaders stepped forward to question the adequacy of the nation's defenses. Their public criticisms became more persistent during the late stages of Eisenhower's second term, when personnel changes within his administration forced the president to become a more active defender of his national security program.

Eisenhower bristled at the public criticism, particularly that directed at him by his former military colleagues. Although he was determined to keep a revolt of the generals out of the headlines by resolving internal disputes over national security policy in private, the president ultimately could not keep a lid on the service chiefs' competing points of view. When congressional hearings highlighted the doubts and the disagreements between the president and the military, the general-turned-president became embroiled in a controversy that would buffet his administration for the remainder of his second term.

John F. Kennedy and Flexible Response

The national security strategies of Eisenhower and Kennedy reflected each man's view of the proper balance between nuclear weapons and conventional forces. These strategies also reflected their economic philosophies. The size and structure of the two presidents' military budgets relative to the domestic economy revealed what each executive perceived to be the appropriate balance between public spending (both military and nonmilitary) and private consumption. Therefore, it is unwise—indeed it is impossible—to separate economic from military and strategic considerations when comparing and contrasting the New Look and Flexible Response.

Kennedy's missile gap rhetoric explicitly combined a military/strategic critique of the New Look with an economic critique of Eisenhower's fiscal policies. On both levels Kennedy spoke of very real concerns, even though the missile gap itself never existed. Economic growth in the United States had slowed in the 1950s, and valid questions were being raised about the ways in which the federal government might boost the domestic economy. It was not apparent that, as Eisenhower had consistently argued, military spending might crowd out more productive forms of public and private spending. Meanwhile, the critics of the New Look raised valid questions about the efficacy of nuclear deterrence in an era of approaching nuclear parity between the two superpowers. Moreover, on the international front the perception of a decline in U.S. prestige was spreading—and perception was reality.

With respect to national security, Kennedy's references to a missile gap addressed the presumed vulnerability of the entire defense establishment, not simply that of the nation's missile and rocket forces. Borrowing liberally from the writings of some of the Eisenhower administration's most vocal critics, including Henry Kissinger, retired army generals James Gavin and Maxwell Taylor, and nationally syndicated newspaper columnist Joseph Alsop, Kennedy argued that the nuclear deterrence on which the New Look was based would not be effective during the years of the missile gap. Accordingly, he called for a more diversified military establishment that would retain the means to respond to international crises with either conventional or nuclear weapons; such a force, Kennedy reasoned, would provide a more credible deterrent against nonnuclear military threats. Meanwhile, Kennedy identified with the economic policies articulated by men such as Walter Heller, John Kenneth Galbraith, James Tobin, and other leading proponents of the so-called New Economics—a philosophy that placed new faith in the government's ability to fine-tune the domestic economy with the goal of achieving maximum economic growth with low unemployment and modest inflation.

The confusion over the state of the nation's defenses and the health of the economy was thrown into the cauldron of presidential politics. John F. Kennedy was there to stir the pot. Kennedy's probable Republican opponent, Vice President Richard Nixon, harbored doubts about Eisenhower's economic measures. Like Kennedy, he was committed to expanding the nation's defenses. Kennedy knew, however, that the vice president would be reluctant to criticize the still-popular chief executive, who was his most important political asset. The senator intended to turn Eisenhower's defense program into Nixon's primary political liability. When Kennedy declared his candidacy for the presidency in January 1960, he specifically jabbed at the Eisenhower administration's national security strategy, as he had been doing for several years. He called its most recent military budget too low by "a substantial margin," and he alleged that the Soviet Union would have a significant "missile lead."[3] Less than two months later, Kennedy called for the nation to increase funding for a number of missile programs in order to "cover the current gap as best we can."[4]

Kennedy's views on the missile gap were well-known by the time he secured his party's nomination for the presidency at the Democratic

National Convention in July 1960. According to Kennedy, the missile gap threatened the nation's survival. Only concerted action by the president, including more spending on defense, could close the gap. Kennedy promised to bring that about if he was elected in November. The military/strategic and economic elements of Kennedy's missile gap rhetoric enabled him to tie foreign policy to domestic issues while he was on the stump. The most persistent theme of his campaign speeches was the nation's declining prestige. The country, Kennedy said, could not be strong abroad if it was not strong at home. Unused industrial capacity, regional unemployment, poorly distributed surpluses, and the missile gap were all, in Kennedy's stump speeches, signs of a nation in decline. Kennedy repeated this message over and over again, and it propelled him to the White House.

The Political Economy of the Missile Gap

Kennedy intended his message tying foreign policy and national security to domestic economic issues to resonate particularly well with one group of voters: defense workers. Many communities that were home to defense firms felt the economic pinch during the Eisenhower years as the New Look attempted to constrain defense spending and shifted a finite number of dollars among competing weapon systems. First, conventional weapons gave way to nuclear weapons. Then missiles supplanted airplanes. Later, solid-fueled rockets replaced the less stable first-generation, liquid-fueled ICBMs. Throughout this process, companies that had done business with the military found themselves in an uncertain situation. Some defense contracts were scaled back; others were terminated outright. Thousands of men and women lost their jobs, including nearly eight thousand at a single Bell Aircraft plant in upstate New York, another eight thousand in two factories near Detroit, and tens of thousands more who had been employed in the manufacturing sector in Southern California. The full weight of this economic hardship began to be felt in the late 1950s after the emergence of the supposed missile gap. Nationwide employment in the aviation parts and aircraft manufacturing industry had peaked at 896,000 in 1957. By 1960 nearly a quarter of these jobs had been eliminated, a reduction driven largely by the decline in purchases of military aircraft.[5]

Eisenhower was not ignorant of the economic ramifications of his military decisions. Nor was he oblivious or insensitive to the hardships caused by these employment losses. He presumed, however, that comparable jobs would be created in other industries. Eisenhower hoped that companies would return to the nation's historical pattern: producing consumer goods in times of peace and weapons in times of war. The perceived need to rein in defense spending, therefore, was a major consideration within his overarching national strategy.

By contrast, John F. Kennedy believed that military spending could be used to boost regional economic development. He explicitly appealed for support from defense workers who had been adversely affected by the economics of the New Look. When Kennedy promised to boost spending on the very weapon systems needed to close the missile gap, the men and women responsible for building those weapons understood precisely what such a policy meant for them. More defense spending meant more jobs, higher incomes, and a better future for them and their families.

The missile gap was a major element of Kennedy's presidential campaign because it had been a political winner for Kennedy and his fellow Democrats in the late 1950s. The gap provided for a powerful one-two punch against the popular Eisenhower. On the one hand, Eisenhower was charged with indifference to Soviet gains and U.S. decline. On the other hand, he was blamed for throwing hundreds of thousands out of work because of his alleged defense cuts.

Eisenhower's critics in the mid- to late 1950s had accused him of selling out the nation's security in the name of shortsighted and outdated economic principles. Many of these critics attacked the New Look's alleged inadequacies by implicitly rejecting Eisenhower's view that the U.S. economy could not sustain the high level of expenditures necessary to support a diversified military establishment that included both conventional forces and nuclear weapons. Kennedy carried these critiques to the next level by arguing explicitly that the profound threat posed by the missile gap necessitated far greater defense spending.

Kennedy followed through on his campaign promise to spend more on defense during the spring and summer of 1961. His choice of which weapons and programs to expand demonstrates the extent to which the missile gap critique had always been about more than missiles. Kennedy did increase the size of the nuclear deterrent force that he had inherited from his predecessor. But he also pushed ahead with a conventional arms buildup that resulted in a considerable realignment of the individual services' budgets during the early 1960s. Kennedy made these changes because he agreed with those critics of the New Look who had argued, long before the appearance of the supposed missile gap, that nuclear deterrence was not an effective foundation for the nation's grand strategy. Many New Look critics actually feared the deterrent effects of nuclear weapons: They argued that a condition of nuclear parity between the United States and the Soviet Union would deter the United States from responding to military offensives waged with conventional weapons. Others worried about the coercive effects of both conventional and nuclear weapons in Europe and elsewhere—that if the Soviets were no longer fearful of U.S. nuclear retaliation, they would use the threat of attack (whether nuclear or conventional) to bend other nations to their will.

The larger issue separating Kennedy from Eisenhower, and implicitly Nixon, however, had always been economic. The economic state of the nation, and the appropriate means for altering the status quo, changed in January 1961 with the new administration. These changes, combined with the broader military/strategic critique of the missile gap, opened the door for Maxwell Taylor's, and ultimately John F. Kennedy's, Flexible Response strategy, which promised more spending on defense in general and on conventional forces in particular. Kennedy was more willing than his predecessor had been to entertain the notion of using government spending, and particularly military spending, to boost the domestic economy. He was encouraged in this belief by the coterie of economists—Heller, Tobin, Galbraith, and others—who had shaped the military and economic debates of the late 1950s.

Key Questions

General Maxwell Taylor recorded that President Kennedy once turned to his National Security Council and asked, "Who ever believed in the missile gap?" This question is easily answered: Millions of Americans believed in the missile gap, and they wanted it closed. Likewise, John F. Kennedy had believed in the missile gap, and he had promised to close it.

But the missile gap was a myth. It was, in the words of Arnold Horelick and Myron Rush, a sustained effort "to deceive the West regarding the pace and scope of the Soviet Union's program for building and deploying ICBMs."[6] Why was the Soviet Union's deception so effective? Why did knowledgeable people, including John F. Kennedy, come to believe in the missile gap despite Eisenhower's repeated and persistent attempts to set the record straight?[7] An examination of the way in which someone as well-informed and well-connected as Kennedy came to believe in the missile gap reveals how millions of less-informed Americans also came to believe in it.

Still, the answer to the question of how and why so many came to believe in the missile gap cannot explain the significance of the gap in Kennedy's rise to national prominence. Nor can it convey the importance of the missile gap critique in the restructuring of U.S. national security policy under Kennedy. Three more questions are relevant here: First, why did the missile gap succeed as a critique of the New Look where other critiques, such as the bomber gap, had failed? Second, why and how did Kennedy use the missile gap to achieve political success? And third, why did Kennedy expand weapon systems that were ostensibly intended to close the missile gap even after he learned that there was no gap?

The missile gap succeeded as a critique of the New Look because of a coalescing of economic and national security concerns that became particularly acute in 1958. The political economy of the missile gap reflected the interests of a number of different groups, including representatives of government, industry, labor unions, and local civic organizations. The activities of these interest groups were often inextricably connected to their perceptions of how their economic interests were tied to defense spending. Put simply, members of a community or group tended to support a particular weapon system if they stood to gain economically from its development and manufacture, and they were often inclined to support politicians who backed such projects. This occasionally translated into support for a specific military strategy that was tied to a particular weapon or product. The New Look had its share of supporters within this framework, but there were also many detractors. Because it provided for a critique of the New Look, the missile gap was a useful tool for eliciting the support of hundreds of thousands of men and women who had been displaced because of the Eisenhower's spending priorities.

The political economy of defense spending during the Cold War was a concern for all communities in the United States, even those that were not directly involved in the manufacture and deployment of military hardware. In periods of widespread insecurity, such as that of the late 1950s, particularly that of the post-*Sputnik* period after October 1957, citizens who do not have direct economic ties to a particular weapon system or national security strategy are nonetheless concerned about national defense on a more abstract level. The entire nation's sense of security was shaken during the missile gap period, and taxpayers were generally more inclined than they had been during Eisenhower's first term to bear a greater economic burden for defense in order to close that gap.

The missile gap was a new and more sensational representation of the prevailing critiques of Eisenhower's New Look military strategy. These critiques had raged for several years, but their political effect had been relatively limited. Other controversies over the readiness or vulnerability of U.S. military forces had arisen and subsided during Eisenhower's presidency, but few people had questioned the president's strategic judgment. By the late 1950s, however, the missile gap had gained traction as a political issue where earlier critiques of the New Look had failed. With Soviet satellites in space and the U.S. economy in a slump, the missile gap came to symbolize all that was wrong with the United States.

In other words, the debate over the New Look did not become a major public issue until Americans began to fear for their own survival. These fears rose when a growing number of military leaders and strategic thinkers claimed that the nation's nuclear deterrence strategy was flawed, and they rose still further when journalists began to speak of a looming missile gap. The debate did not become an economic issue until the ramifications of Eisenhower's defense economics began to take their toll, particularly within communities that had become dependent upon defense spending during the early 1950s. Once both of these things had happened, the debate over the New Look became a political issue. Suddenly politicians and policy makers who had criticized Eisenhower's fiscal restraint on philosophical grounds for years had a more tangible political issue with which to attack the president and his policies. The missile gap became their rallying cry. And John F. Kennedy cried early and often.

Kennedy used the missile gap to achieve political success because he recognized the underlying political and economic factors that contributed to its unique salience as a political issue. In the late 1950s he became a leading political figure, but he was not yet the most important of his era. He was not the first person to refer to a missile gap, nor was he the only politician to use the issue for political gain. And yet Kennedy's political ascendancy neatly coincided with the rise of the missile gap as he used the issue persuasively during the presidential campaign of 1960.

The missile gap continued to factor into Kennedy's policy making even after he had achieved his ultimate political success and even after he was told that there was no gap. Why? Again, we must look to the political economy of the missile gap for answers. Two distinct forces characterized this political economy: the security concerns and personal motivations of military leaders and defense analysts, and the economic concerns of defense workers, their families, and their communities. These concerns had led Kennedy the candidate to advocate programs and policies that were necessary for rectifying the potentially dangerous and destabilizing inferiority represented by the presumed missile gap. The same considerations enabled Kennedy to implement changes to the nation's military after he became president.

Even though the missile gap provided political cover for the administration's spending requests before Congress, the changes to the nation's military that were implemented by the Kennedy administration were not predicated on the existence of a gap. Well before the emergence of the missile gap myth, critics of the New Look had objected to the primacy Eisenhower's policies placed on nuclear deterrence. Therefore, even in the wake of the discovery that there was no missile gap, Kennedy sought a more varied military structure, with more men in uniform and new counterinsurgency forces for the army, newer aircraft and missiles for the air force, and more ships and submarines for the navy. All of these changes were designed to improve the nation's ability to respond to both nuclear and nonnuclear threats.

The Scholarly Context

The literature on the missile gap is vast and varied. Several excellent works detail the ways in which the Soviets attempted to exploit the presumed strategic advantage created by the mythical gap.[8] Other studies examine how relations between the United States and the Soviet Union changed following the Kennedy administration's public revelation that there was no gap, with several works suggesting that the Cuban missile crisis, the most dangerous episode of the Cold War, was tied to the disappearance of the gap.[9] This book examines the phenomenon of the missile gap itself by focusing on Kennedy's experience with the issue throughout the entire missile gap period, from late 1957 to the time of his assassination.[10]

Many of the dozens of biographies of Kennedy and Nixon ignore the deeper economic and military/strategic issues associated with the missile gap debate. This is a serious oversight given that the missile gap and its political economy provide scholars with a unique opportunity to examine the complex interaction of a number of competing and divergent forces within the national security policy bureaucracy— the military services, intelligence agencies, congressional and presidential politics, and the media. Although bureaucracies exert tremendous influence over the formulation and execution of national security policy, external factors also affect policy outcomes. The missile gap is particularly instructive in helping scholars to understand the influence of these forces because the gap myth was largely created and perpetuated by individuals acting outside of official channels.

Many of Kennedy's defense decisions in early 1961 were made with undue haste because they were not based upon an accurate understanding of the nature of the strategic balance.[11] Accordingly, this study focuses primarily on understanding why Kennedy came to believe in the missile gap and on how this mistaken belief factored into his behavior, first as a senator, later as a presidential candidate, and finally as president. Several other studies have sought to explain the missile gap myth by focusing on the weaknesses of U.S. intelligence during the late 1950s. Some have argued that interservice rivalries generated pressures to build weapon systems that served each service's parochial interests because the threat of the missile gap seemed to argue for a considerable expansion of many different weapon systems. Still others have interpreted the missile gap as primarily a partisan political phenomenon. Eisenhower deemed the gap an "imaginative creation of irresponsibility" and a "useful piece of political demagoguery" intended to advance the causes and candidates of the Democratic Party.[12] Physicist and Pentagon science adviser Herbert York agreed, concluding that the missile gap disappeared after Kennedy's election because "the term had been pretty much taken over by the Democrats as a campaign criticism of the Eisenhower Administration, and the political utility of such charges disappeared with the election of the new Administration."[13]

While the present study confirms that all of these factors—political posturing, military rivalry, and intelligence inadequacies—should be considered in an examination of the missile gap, it also shows that the missile gap myth was driven primarily by economic considerations, or more precisely, by the competition between the economic philosophies of Eisenhower and those of the proponents of the New Economics. People on both sides of the debate believed in the hostility of the Soviet regime and believed that, if left unchecked, the Soviets would extend their domination of Eastern Europe to other regions and other regimes, but they differed over the proper means for deterring Soviet aggression. To those who warned about a missile gap, it was better to risk spending too much money on defense to counter a threat that might ultimately prove illusory. To those who argued that there was no missile gap—or, more accurately, that any such gap was militarily insignificant—it was foolish to spend countless billions of dollars building unnecessary weapons when the true nature of the threat was unclear. It was better, they argued, to maintain an arsenal that would be sufficient for retaliation even after a surprise attack, but not one so large as to place undue burdens on the domestic economy.

The two leading politicians of the late 1950s and early 1960s articulated these competing positions. Eisenhower—alone at times even within his own administration—placed his faith in his own capacity to judge the nature of the Soviet threat and to determine the appropriate amount of money to spend on defense. He was most conscious of the limits to be placed on defense spending, limits that he imposed on a restless military. John Kennedy believed otherwise. Allying himself with some of the most outspoken critics of Eisenhower's fiscal restraint, an eclectic band of liberal economists and politicians, defense intellectuals, and both uniformed and retired military officers, who all railed against the New Look's massive-retaliation nuclear policy, Kennedy implemented changes in the structure of the nation's military forces that ultimately provided him and his successors with a greater range of military options—options that were used to disastrous ends in Southeast Asia and elsewhere in the mid- to late 1960s.[14]

The Political Economy of National Security

The development and manufacture of military technology and hardware and the formulation of military strategy are conducted within the context of diverse political and economic forces. The story of John F. Kennedy and the missile gap is a metaphor for many aspects of the Cold War military-industrial complex because it acknowledges the pervasive relationships among economics, politics, and national security.

The study of the political economy of national security is concerned with the manner in which industry and labor cooperate with political and military leaders in order to design, develop, and manufacture implements of warfare.[15] The study of this cooperation within liberal-democratic political systems is particularly interesting because democratic governments have a limited ability to compel businesses to manufacture certain products. Likewise, except in times of great crisis, liberal democracies cannot require individuals to work in particular places or within particular industries. The planning and distribution of economic resources for warfare is tied, therefore, to the physical abilities and limitations of industry specifically and of the entire economy generally. Governments cannot dictate that military hardware will be produced without also considering the necessary trade-offs within the civilian economy. Therefore, government and industry cooperate with one another in a liberal political system in order to achieve a balance between the needs of national security and the desires of citizens and consumers.

Within this loose system business leaders apply direct pressure to military leaders and politicians on behalf of their products. Still, their individual political influence should not be overstated. Those studies that focus solely on the actions of business leaders paint an inaccurate picture of the dynamics of the political economy of national security within democracies. A single business owner has, after all, only one vote to cast. One can only begin to appreciate the true nature of the political power of industry by considering how the economic interests of a single business owner coincide with those of hundreds, or perhaps thousands, of individuals who work to design, manufacture, and market the business's product. Politicians become involved not solely at the behest of individual business owners, but rather to maximize the well-being of the greatest number of their constituents, while also ensuring that the military needs of the nation are met.

The formulation of national security policy is both an economic and a political phenomenon; that is not to say, however, that political and economic considerations alone drove military strategy and weapons acquisition during the Cold War. Rather, the U.S. arms buildup of the Cold War was conducted in response to legitimate security threats. Although there may have been discrete incidents during the Cold War period that were exacerbated by misunderstandings, the Cold War itself was based on deep ideological differences between the two poles of power. The Soviet Union posed both a military and political danger to U.S. allies and interests in Europe and Asia during the late 1940s and early 1950s, and by late 1957, once they had developed a functioning ICBM, the Soviets' military capabilities also threatened citizens in the United States.

This study adopts a favorable view of the efficacy and rectitude of U.S. Cold War strategy, particularly that component of the strategy that was predicated on nuclear deterrence, but internal political and economic factors generated by a considerable and sustained military buildup may have prolonged the Cold War. Although the military buildup was justified and legitimate in light of the ideological and military threat posed by the Soviet Union, it might have been harmful to long-term economic development in the United States. A national security strategy constrained by a greater appreciation for economic limits—such as that envisioned by Eisenhower's New Look—would have been less burdensome for American taxpayers and less likely to have led to a protracted ground war in Southeast Asia. It also would have been less threatening to the Soviet Union. Underlying this discussion of the missile gap as a largely economic phenomenon, therefore, is a conviction that Eisenhower was correct on two counts: the first military/strategic, the second economic.

First of all, the New Look was a sensible strategy on strictly military grounds because Eisenhower was right to believe that a Flexible Response strategy that emphasized the capability to wage limited, conventional wars was likely to lead to full-scale nuclear war. Under the New Look, threats to peripheral interests did not warrant overt military action, although they might have and did occasionally warrant covert action. Because Eisenhower emphasized that only threats to vital national interests would justify the use of the ultimate weapon, the New Look became the primary vehicle for avoiding war during the 1950s.[16]

The New Look was a superior national security strategy also because it was mindful of the potentially harmful economic effects of military spending. Eisenhower's economic philosophy, which held that public expenditures must be controlled, forced his political and military subordinates to make sometimes difficult decisions about what to keep and what to cut. Maxwell Taylor, who served as army chief of staff for several years during Eisenhower's presidency, complained that the determination of military strategy had become no more than an "incidental by-product of the administrative processes of the defense budget."[17]

Notwithstanding Taylor's grousing, we now know that Eisenhower's use of the defense budget to shape strategy and force structure did not weaken the United States militarily. Rather, by emphasizing military spending's potentially harmful effects on the domestic economy over the long term, Ike's national security policies contributed to the ultimate victory of the United States over the Soviet Union in the Cold War.[18]

Millions of Eisenhower's contemporaries did not view his national security policies in such a favorable light. Kennedy's policies were predicated on a different reading of the economic effects of military spending, with some advisers believing that such spending was an efficient vehicle for spurring the economy. When the Nobel Foundation awarded their annual prize in economics to James Tobin in 1981, the economist looked back on his career and on the economic lessons of the twenty years since he had been made the youngest member of Kennedy's Council of Economic Advisers. Tobin celebrated the principles of the council's 1962 economic report, a document that can be characterized as a manifesto of the New Economics. According to Tobin, the council's advice "gradually gained a large measure of acceptance, and by the end of 1965, our basic macroeconomic goals were achieved." "Alas," he went on to lament, "these victories were lost during the Vietnam war and the stagflation of the 1970s."[19]

Tobin and other proponents of the New Economics must share the blame for both the quagmire in Vietnam and the stagflation of the 1970s. The economic philosophy underlying the New Frontier and

Flexible Response opened the door to questionable military actions, including a deepening of the U.S. commitment in Southeast Asia. Relieved of the burden of justifying military expenditures according to narrowly defined national security needs, the Kennedy and Johnson administrations pursued several peripheral military engagements that would have been, and indeed were, deemed unessential during the Eisenhower years.

Other authors also have argued that a lack of appreciation for economic limits encouraged policy makers to pursue peripheral engagements in the mid- to late 1960s. Richard Aliano faults Kennedy for failing to "define the limits of the United States' commitments and responsibilities." By adopting an activist economic policy, Aliano writes, Kennedy "bequeathed to Lyndon Johnson a commitment limited neither by his own conception of the nature of the cold war nor by the versatility of the military establishment."[20]

John Gaddis makes a similar argument in his classic work *Strategies of Containment*. He explains how variations in the implementation of containment can be traced to economic theory. "The ultimate danger," Gaddis warns, "was what the United States might do to itself to meet obligations it itself had established." This danger became apparent only during Vietnam. The problem was a poverty of plenty—or what Gaddis calls the problem of perceived means. "The mechanism that has most often forced the consideration of unpalatable options . . . has been budgetary," he writes. "When one knows one has only limited resources to work with, then distinctions between what is vital and peripheral, between the feasible and unfeasible, come more easily, if not less painfully."[21]

Whereas Eisenhower worried about defense spending in excess of 10 percent of gross national product (GNP), many of the proponents of the New Economics professed to be unconcerned by a defense budget twice that large, although many hoped that public monies being diverted to the military might ultimately be redirected to peaceful purposes. John Kennedy—less constrained than was his predecessor by concerns over the burden of military spending on the domestic economy—advocated a military strategy and military force structure that would have consumed a far greater share of the nation's finite resources over the course of the Cold War.

The missile gap stands as one of the enduring legacies of the Cold War, and the political economy of the missile gap helps us to understand the political and economic nature of the military buildup throughout the era. My research confirms that the economics of defense spending were a pervasive concern. So long as the Cold War continued, there would be jobs for the millions of Americans employed in the defense industry and for the millions more who worked and lived in communities where defense firms were located. But the story of the missile gap is much more than a mere metaphor for the political economy of the Cold War. The story itself is inherently interesting, involving colorful personalities, dramatic political events, and freshly relevant insights into the nature of U.S. political and economic development during the past fifty years. The missile gap may have been a short-term phenomenon with relatively limited long-term effects; by contrast, however, the political economy of the Cold War—of which the political economy of the missile gap was one important element—was a pervasive element of the domestic political landscape and the economy of the United States during the entire Cold War. By tapping into these deep and enduring political and economic themes, Kennedy's missile gap rhetoric helped to propel him into immortality.

CHAPTER ONE

Eisenhower, the New Look, and Their Critics

"A program for rapidly building up strength . . . will be costly. Budgetary considerations will need to be subordinated to the stark fact that our very independence as a nation is at stake."
—from NSC 68, April 1950[1]

"To amass military power without regard to our economic capacity would be to defend ourselves against one kind of disaster by inviting another."
—President Dwight D. Eisenhower, January 1954[2]

"Recent economic policies . . . have cost the United States its world leadership and gravely threatened its survival as a nation. . . . It is time to base economic policy on the evidence of history rather than on imaginary future catastrophes."
—James Tobin, March 1958[3]

Scholars have identified crucial differences among the national security strategies of the Truman, Eisenhower, and Kennedy administrations. Cost was one determining factor in these divergent strategies. The first three presidents of the nuclear era differed with each other primarily in their perception of the level of taxation and spending that could be supported by the U.S. economy. Throughout the 1950s and early 1960s, as at other times during the Cold War, each of these commanders-in-chief asked himself the crucial questions: How much is enough? And how much is too much?

Many of the contemporary critiques of Eisenhower's New Look strategy focused on Eisenhower's belief that the domestic economy could not support the expenditures necessary to field a modern conventional army large enough to deter the Soviet Union from launching a conventional attack on U.S. allies in Europe and, to a lesser extent, in Asia. Eisenhower's national security strategy depended instead on a robust, forward-deployed nuclear force intended to deter would-be adversaries from unleashing an attack upon the United States or upon its allies and vital interests around the world. Such a nuclear deterrent force, Eisenhower reasoned, would be far less costly than a more diversified military capable of fighting and winning conventional as well as nuclear wars. Furthermore, Eisenhower believed that any conflict, even one that started out as a strictly conventional engagement, would quickly escalate to a nuclear war. He was determined, therefore, to completely prevent the outbreak of military conflict because any conflict at all was likely to spiral into World War III.[4]

Eisenhower's intentions on this score were not always clear to his contemporaries, however. As often as not, his overwhelming desire to prevent a global thermonuclear war was masked by his more general concern for limiting the burdens of defense spending on the domestic economy. Kennedy did not share Eisenhower's concern about the economic effects of military spending. Indeed, Kennedy believed that such spending could provide an economic boost, particularly to distressed regions that seemed to have been left behind by the prosperity of the 1950s. And when he was forced to confront the grim reality of the potential for nuclear Armageddon after he took his place in the Oval Office, Kennedy concluded, as his predecessor had, that such a conflagration could in no way serve U.S. national interests.

But such concerns were far from Kennedy's mind when he embarked upon his political journey from senatorial obscurity to national celebrity. The critique of Eisenhower's strategy that enabled his rise focused especially on Eisenhower's reluctance to spend more on defense, which, Kennedy charged, had allowed the Soviet Union to open the missile gap.

National Security under Truman

Eisenhower was not the first president to confront the dilemmas of rising defense costs and expanding security threats. Eisenhower's predecessor, Harry S. Truman, had drastically cut military expenditures immediately after the end of World War II on the presumption that the nation's preponderant military and economic power would serve as a deterrent to Soviet aggression. Truman feared that a burdensome military budget would fundamentally alter the nature of the U.S. political and economic system.

As the Cold War deepened and as U.S. national security commitments around the globe began to strain military resources, Truman initially resisted efforts to increase the size of the defense budget. Louis Johnson, who had replaced James Forrestal as secretary of defense in March 1949, backed Truman in his cost-cutting crusade. He battled with the military chiefs who were feeling overextended during the late 1940s and who were seeking greater funding for their respective services. The most famous—or notorious—of these battles became known as the Revolt of the Admirals, a bitter public fight precipitated when Johnson abruptly canceled construction of the navy's first supercarrier in a move to cut costs.[5]

Other fiscal conservatives in the Truman administration, including Edwin Nourse, chair of the Council of Economic Advisers, joined Johnson in his battle against rising defense expenditures. There were competing voices, however. Several of Truman's more liberal economic advisers, including council members John Clark and Leon Keyserling, adopted a dramatically different view of the economy and of the wisdom of restraining military spending during sluggish economic times. Less troubled by temporary federal deficits and modest inflation than by the specter of an economy operating below its full potential, Clark and Keyserling argued that the economy could "sustain—in fact must be subjected to policies which *make it able to sustain*—such military outlays as are vital" for the maintenance of national security.[6] Events in the late summer and early fall of 1949 forced this debate over the proper relationship between the domestic economy and the nation's security to the surface and placed new pressures on President Truman to increase the defense budget.

Leon Keyserling's ascension to the position of chair of the Council of Economic Advisers in May 1950 represented an important turning point in Truman's defense policies because Keyserling rejected Nourse's argument that defense spending in excess of 6–7 percent of gross national product could cause undue harm to the domestic economy. Indeed, Keyserling believed that the economy could easily sustain defense expenditures that consumed as much as 20 percent of GNP. Following Nourse's departure in October 1949, Keyserling immediately embraced a vast increase in defense expenditures when he played a role in the drafting of NSC 68, a document that mapped out a new military and economic strategy for fighting and winning the Cold War. Keyserling may not have had a direct hand in the composing of NSC 68, but his views permeated all levels of government in late 1949 and early 1950.

Into this philosophical and intellectual milieu stepped Paul Nitze, the principal drafter of NSC 68. A forty-three-year-old with over ten years of experience in Washington, D.C., Nitze became the head of the State Department's Policy Planning Staff on 1 January 1950, replacing the legendary George F. Kennan. By this time Nitze was already well on his way to becoming a legend in his own right; it was a role for which he had been well groomed.[7]

Paul H. Nitze was born in Amherst, Massachusetts, but he spent much of his early childhood in Chicago. After attending the University of Chicago High School, Nitze traveled east to attend the Hotchkiss School, an elite preparatory school in Connecticut, and then Harvard, where he graduated in 1928. He joined the New York investment firm of Dillon, Read and Company in 1929 and became a vice president of the prestigious firm in 1937, at the age of thirty.

Nitze first arrived in Washington, D.C., in June 1940 as an aide to James Forrestal, the former president of Dillon, Read. During World War II he worked on the newly formed U.S. Strategic Bombing Survey (USSBS).[8] In this capacity, he was one of the first Americans to witness firsthand the destruction and devastation wrought by the atomic bombings of Hiroshima and Nagasaki, Japan. He observed that the effects of the bombings were horrific but not paralyzing and concluded that nuclear weapons alone would not determine winners and losers in future conflicts. The key to survival was preparedness. Mindful of these lessons but chastened by the announcement in August 1949 that the Soviets also had an atomic bomb, Nitze set out— at the behest of Secretary of State Dean Acheson and with the tacit support of Keyserling and others—to remake U.S. national security strategy for the Cold War.[9]

Truman reacted cautiously when the recommendations of NSC 68 were presented to him in April 1950. Though the original document advanced no precise cost estimates, they were expected to be high.[10] But the shock of the Korean War, the ascendancy of communism in China, and recent advances in the Soviet nuclear weapons program ultimately convinced Truman of the need to dramatically increase the size of the defense budget.

Truman's approval of NSC 68 as official policy in September 1950 reflected a marked shift in the government's attitude toward defense spending and economic growth. The authors of NSC 68 had noted that the concerted military buildup called for in the document would be costly and might require sacrifices in the form of either higher taxes or reductions in other areas of government spending. The document stressed, however, that "Budgetary considerations will need to be subordinated to the stark fact that our very independence as a nation may be at stake."[11] And while the text offered up these sobering and dramatic warnings, it held out hope that the increased defense spending would help to grow the U.S. economy.

Noting that the Soviet Union was dedicating nearly 14 percent of its available resources to defense and another 25 percent to "investment," much of which was in "war-supporting industries," NSC 68 maintained that the United States was limited more by "the decision on the proper allocation of resources" than by its ability to produce additional military hardware. Noting that total U.S. output had declined from 1948 to 1949, NSC 68 pointed to the president's Economic Report of January 1950, which had argued that progress toward the goal of expanding the nation's economy "would permit, and might itself be aided by, a buildup of the economic and military strength of the United States and the free world."[12]

According to Aaron Friedberg, NSC 68 was "a battering ram with which its authors hoped to shatter the existing budget ceiling."[13] The cost estimates for the military proposals associated with the document, promulgated after the outbreak of war in Korea, envisioned a defense budget of as much as $40 billion, an increase of nearly 300 percent. Projected expenditures under NSC 68 of as much as $50 billion would constitute approximately 15 percent of total national output and would not, the document implied, impose an undue burden on the economy.[14]

Although scholars have debated the long-term impact of NSC 68 on U.S. policy and strategy, they are in agreement that the document signaled an opening for substantial increases in military spending. As Paul Pierpaoli observes, whereas governments had once determined the aggregate budget and then adjusted programs to fit into that budget, "the opposite became the rule after 1950: policy makers determined national security requirements first and then adjusted aggregate fiscal policy to meet security demands."[15]

Truman appears to have settled on this approach with some reluctance. Evidence of the president's backsliding on the question of using defense spending to boost the economy was clear in early 1951. In February of that year he requested $10 billion in additional taxes to pay for increases in defense spending, with the intention that the Korean mobilization would be conducted on a pay-as-you-go basis. However, after the midterm elections of November 1950, Truman faced an increasingly hostile Congress dominated by Republicans and conservative Democrats. This new Congress pressured Truman to reduce spending in other areas and to hold taxes steady or reduce them.[16]

There were other signs that the Keyserling position on defense spending and economic growth was in retreat in the later stages of Truman's second term. After the Bureau of the Budget projected a deficit of $10 billion for FY 1951 and $12 billion for FY 1952, Truman requested a reappraisal of NSC 68. More than a year later, in the summer of 1952, the NSC issued Charles Bohlen's study "The Bases of Soviet Action." Truman approved the report as NSC 135/3 on 25 September 1952. Bohlen attacked many of the views expressed in NSC 68, chiefly taking issue with Nitze's interpretation of the aggressiveness of Soviet foreign policy. Unlike Nitze, Bohlen believed that the Soviet leadership would not take aggressive actions that were likely to threaten the regime. He also dismissed Nitze's notion of a year of maximum danger, believing instead that Soviet moves would be cautious and confined largely to the exploitation of opportunities in areas of Western weakness on the periphery. Given Bohlen's determination that Soviet aims were likely to be circumscribed, NSC 135/3 advised against an aggressive "rollback" strategy that might aggravate international tensions.[17] The study also found that U.S. forces were badly overextended. Accordingly, the report called for a reappraisal of current spending programs to determine whether scarce resources might be better allocated for purposes of national defense.

A follow-up study called for by the Bohlen document and later dubbed NSC 141 concluded that in spite of the reassessment of the Soviet threat current spending programs were still inadequate. Approved on Truman's last day in office, 19 January 1953, NSC 141 departed from many of the specific conclusions and policy recommendations of previous reports, but it largely reaffirmed and extended the economic assumptions underlying NSC 68, arguing that national security programs could be accelerated or expanded without damaging the U.S. economy. Both NSC 135/3 and NSC 141 emphasized one clear point: military budget cuts were unwise and unwarranted. Both documents called for still more spending on a diversified defense establishment, although the latter made no specific cost estimates. Truman's military budget for FY 1953 dedicated nearly 14 percent of the GNP to defense, the highest proportion of the post–World War II era. Truman's final budget, submitted in January 1953, projected total defense spending of $45.5 billion for FY 1954, or just under 13 percent of projected GNP.[18]

Truman appeared to adopt the softer language inherent in the later reports when he eschewed talk of rollback in his farewell address. However, the general direction of U.S. military planning at the end of the Truman years suggested the need to prepare for a number of near-term contingencies in order to respond to Soviet threats throughout the globe—in Europe, the Middle East, and the Far East.[19] With his words and with his actions, Truman bequeathed to his successor a national security strategy based largely on the economic principles of Leon Keyserling and Paul Nitze. These principles, articulated in NSC 68, held that the economy could sustain expenditures that were necessary for the maintenance of national security and that security must take precedence over budgetary considerations.

Eisenhower's National Security Strategy

The incoming Eisenhower administration responded with a different national security strategy, which was ultimately delineated in NSC 162/2 and dubbed the New Look by contemporary observers. Whereas the authors of NSC 68 had argued that the nation's means could—indeed must—be expanded to fit its perceived security interests, Eisenhower believed that the nation's economy could not sustain the level of expenditures envisioned by the authors of Truman's NSC 68 and NSC 141, and he intended to establish a balance between military needs and the capabilities of the domestic economy.[20]

Eisenhower had formed these views long before he became president. In 1947, he had explained to his longtime friend and adviser Walter Bedell ("Beetle") Smith that there was "very obviously a definite limit to our resources." He feared "internal deterioration through the annual expenditure of unconscionable sums on a program of indefinite duration, extending far into the future." Strategists, Eisenhower concluded, must recognize that "national security and national solvency are mutually dependent"; otherwise, the U.S. economy might crumble under the "crushing weight of military power."[21]

Eisenhower repeated this theme time and time again. In testimony before Congress in 1951, he stressed that the United States must maintain its military strength in the face of competition from the Soviet Union but emphasized that this must be done within the reasonable constraints of the domestic economy. "Our system," Eisenhower said, "must remain solvent, as we attempt a solution of this great problem of security. Else we have lost the battle from within that we are trying to win from without."[22] Eisenhower reiterated this philosophy in his State of the Union address in 1954: "Our problem," he said, "is to achieve adequate military strength within the limits of endurable strain upon our economy. To amass military power without regard to our economic capacity would be to defend ourselves against one kind of disaster by inviting another."[23]

Eisenhower was convinced that the level of spending envisioned by the authors of NSC 68 and NSC 141 might fundamentally alter the relationship between the citizen and the state. His concern grew out of his long-standing belief that overly burdensome defense spending—in his view, spending in excess of 10 percent of GNP—would create a so-called garrison state.[24] He envisioned national security as a product of both military strength and economic strength, in a relationship that was part of what he referred to as the Great Equation. "Spiritual force, multiplied by economic force, multiplied by military force is roughly equal to security," he explained. "If one of these factors falls to zero, or near zero, the resulting product does likewise."[25]

Eisenhower's belief that the nation's means were finite shaped his perception of interests. Eisenhower was decidedly not an isolationist, but he recognized the lure of isolationism, and he feared that the American people would drift in that direction if the burdens of inter-nationalism became too great—indeed, some within the Republican Party already envisioned a return to such a posture. In June 1953 Eisenhower noted that the public's appetite for sacrifice would be sorely tested by the limited and inconclusive wars that would become more and more prevalent in the nuclear age.[26]

Eisenhower had no intention of involving the United States in an-other Korea-style conventional war. Accordingly, he justified signifi-cant cuts in conventional forces—in the army and navy especially—with his faith in nuclear deterrence. Eisenhower may have doubted the efficacy of nuclear weapons—he once warned against seeing them as a "cheap way to solve things"[27]—but while he voiced such concerns privately, the public pronouncements of his administration implied an affinity for nuclear weapons that horrified many contemporary ob-servers. After Secretary of State John Foster Dulles declared in January 1954 that the United States would deter aggression by responding "at places and with means of its own choosing" with "massive retaliatory power," the most memorable phrase from his speech became synony-mous with Eisenhower's overarching national security strategy. For the next seven years, debate would revolve around the wisdom or folly of the New Look's apparent overreliance on nuclear deterrence and around the related question of the economic burdens of defense spending.

Eisenhower's Economic Philosophy

Although he was generally skeptical of politicians playing an active part in the economy, Eisenhower accepted the president's role—to borrow a term from John Sloan—as manager of prosperity. This role had been developed during the New Deal, but Eisenhower, according to Sloan, "imbued it with a Cold War perspective" by relating the challenges of the domestic economy to the contest between the

United States and the Soviet Union. In this context the president pledged to dedicate the full resources of the nation, both public and private, to ensuring that there would never be another depression. A dramatic economic downturn, Eisenhower reasoned, would represent a victory for the Soviet Union.[28]

Many critics assumed that Eisenhower's attitude toward government spending, taxes, and a balanced budget reflected a reactionary or old-fashioned understanding of economic policy. But there was more to Eisenhower's economic philosophy than a simple aversion to government spending and a slavish devotion to a balanced budget. His administration included academic economists, such as Arthur Burns and Raymond Saulnier, who were willing to use government spending to boost the economy. In practice Ike exhibited a willingness to use government spending that was often ignored by contemporary critics and has often been understated by scholars. He championed two enormous public works projects, the interstate highway system and the St. Lawrence Seaway; refused to roll back most major New Deal programs and expanded Social Security; increased foreign aid; and submitted to Congress only three balanced budgets out of eight.[29]

In his excellent study of Eisenhower's economic policy making, John Sloan concludes that modern observers now credit Eisenhower with compiling a solid economic record. "Nevertheless," he writes, "as he left office in January 1961 Eisenhower was seriously criticized because of the three recessions and the sluggish rate of growth during his second term." Eisenhower was especially frustrated and disappointed by the lack of political support for his willingness to fight the occasionally unpopular battle against inflation.[30]

But stable prices were not sufficient in the post–World War II era. The public's expectations had risen during the 1950s. Although Eisenhower's critics, including many liberal Democrats and other proponents of Keynesian economics, conceded that the administration had achieved some success, they argued that it was possible to achieve much more given the knowledge of economic conditions that was available to policy makers in the postwar period. Specifically, these critics believed that less concern with a balanced budget and a less restrictive monetary policy would have produced faster economic growth and less unemployment during Eisenhower's terms as president.[31] Notwithstanding occasional economic ups and downs during which governmental action was clearly warranted, Eisenhower hoped to contain rising federal spending. In this respect he did differ with Truman, but he especially differed with the more liberal advisers within his predecessor's administration.

Defense Spending and the Economy

Inflation, a balanced budget, and the relative merits of public versus private spending were not the only issues that separated Eisenhower and his detractors. Eisenhower also differed with his critics on the potential detrimental economic effects of military spending. As much as he pursued any other endeavor, the former military officer fought hard to reduce defense expenditures during his two terms in office. In NSC discussions, for example, he frequently staked out a middle ground between the budget-minded members of his administration—such as Treasury Secretary George Humphrey and Budget Director Joseph Dodge, who argued for more cuts in defense spending—and military leaders who argued for more money.[32]

National security and economic security were inextricably connected during the Cold War. As an explicit policy goal the federal government pursued the use of military spending to boost employment, particularly during periods of economic downturn and in chronically depressed regions of the country. This faith in the efficacy of defense spending for counteracting economic distress was not confined to a single political party and was not limited by ideology. Even an avowedly conservative political leader such as Eisenhower called upon the federal power to authorize defense spending during his presidency. For example, during the early stages of an economic downturn in late 1953, Eisenhower told chairman of the Joint Chiefs of Staff Admiral Arthur Radford that the nation should "take the same approach to military production that we do to public works. . . . In other words, you put the heat on this production when we face an economic depression and take off the heat when the economy is going at full tilt." Four years later, in the midst of the recession of 1957–1958, Eisenhower pushed a package of government spending initiatives that included an acceleration of defense contract awards.[33]

Despite Eisenhower's apparent willingness to alter the distribution and timing of defense contracts during recessionary periods, he was generally less inclined to use this discretionary spending power in better economic times. Casual observers might characterize Eisenhower's attitude toward the economic displacement associated with changing defense needs as callous or indifferent, but to do so would be misleading. In Eisenhower's view military spending diverted finite resources from the domestic economy, and because Eisenhower believed that military spending was inherently wasteful and unproductive, he strenuously opposed any major shift in the balance between military and domestic priorities.

Eisenhower clearly stated his attitude toward the necessary trade-offs between defense and domestic spending very early in his first term. In March 1953 journalist Samuel A. Lubell recommended that Eisenhower reach an agreement with the Soviets to limit defense expenditures. Although the president questioned the feasibility of verifying such an agreement, he was intrigued by Lubell's proposal. In the next few weeks, Eisenhower worked with the staff of his new administration to convey the concept of choosing "butter over guns." The result of these efforts was Ike's famous "Chance for Peace" speech, delivered before the American Society of Newspaper Editors on 16 April 1953.[34]

In the speech Eisenhower explained the parameters of the Cold War in stark terms. The worst to be feared, he said, was atomic war. The best to be hoped for was "a life of perpetual fear and tension; a burden of arms draining the wealth and the labor of all peoples; a wasting of strength that defies the U.S. system or the Soviet system or any system to achieve true abundance and happiness for the peoples of this earth." He continued:

> Every gun that is made, every warship launched, every rocket fired signifies, in the final sense, a theft from those who hunger and are not fed, those who are cold and are not clothed.
> This world in arms is not spending money alone. It is spending the sweat of its laborers, the genius of its scientists, the hopes of its children.
> The cost of one modern heavy bomber is this: a modern brick school in more than 30 cities. It is two electric power plants, each serving a town of 60,000 population. It is two fine, fully equipped hospitals. It is some fifty miles of concrete pavement.
> We pay for a single fighter plane with a half million bushels of wheat.
> We pay for a single destroyer with new homes that could have housed more than 8,000 people.[35]

In short, the nation's resources are finite. Eisenhower believed that private enterprise could make more efficient use of scarce resources than could government. Therefore, spending by individuals and businesses was better than spending by government. He believed that it was particularly unwise to use military spending as an economic stimulus.

Despite Eisenhower's concerns, real reductions in the size and scope of the military budget during his two terms in office were modest and largely transitory. Conventional forces were significantly reduced during the 1950s, but these cuts were partially offset by increases for the air force. Total national security expenditures, excluding veterans' benefits, fell to $40.2 billion in 1955 from a high of $50.4 billion in 1953, but rose again to $46.6 billion in 1959.[36] Even though Eisenhower did not achieve his objective of substantially and permanently reducing military expenditures, many communities that were home to firms that produced equipment for the military suffered economic distress because the New Look's spending priorities altered the mix of weapons and other military hardware purchased by the government.

The geographic distribution of manufacturing jobs changed dramatically during the 1950s. When the government purchased fewer of a certain product, for example, wheeled vehicles, regional economic shocks followed. Or conversely, when the government increased the purchase of new technologies, some regions that specialized in the manufacture of such items enjoyed an economic boost. In FY 1953 tanks, conventional weapons, and ammunition constituted 50 percent of all military hard goods ordered by the government. In FY 1961 these same items accounted for only 12 percent of government military hard goods purchases. By contrast, missiles, which accounted for less than 0.5 percent of military hard goods expenditures in FY 1953, consumed 33 percent of such spending in FY 1961.[37]

Although new jobs were created throughout the 1950s, unemployment remained stubbornly fixed at 5 percent nationwide, and pockets of particular distress did not improve at all. The disparity in job growth between different geographic regions was dramatic. In 1961 one of every six new nonfarm jobs in the country was located in one of just three states—California, Texas, or Florida. The transition toward new defense technologies—especially missiles, rockets, and advanced electronics—had disproportionately benefited a few communities, especially in southern California, which was ten or more years ahead of the Midwest in the manufacture of such products.[38]

Eisenhower was unmoved when critics, including some members of his own administration, pressed him to spend more on defense, and especially to do so in a way that would mitigate the economic effects of changing defense needs. He was not indifferent to the hardships faced by the tens of thousands of men and women who were thrown out of work as a result of the New Look's spending priorities; rather, as he had clearly explained in his "Chance for Peace" speech, he genuinely believed that these individuals would find more productive work elsewhere. Workers who had once built tanks could now build automobiles. Engineers who had once designed airplanes could now design homes or schools or bridges. Men who had once worked as soldiers and sailors could now work as doctors to care for the sick, or farmers to grow food to feed the hungry, or in any number of other occupations dedicated to serving the needs of the general public as opposed to the relatively narrow needs of the military.

Contemporary Critiques of the New Look

Military and Strategic Critique

During Eisenhower's eight years as president, a host of critics challenged his belief in the necessity of balancing military and domestic spending. Democrats, still stinging from Republican charges of weakness leveled during the early days of the Cold War, turned the tables on the GOP in the mid- to late 1950s by charging time and time again that Eisenhower was selling out the nation's security in the name of outdated economic principles. Also, because the forces needed to fight conventional, nonnuclear wars would be far more expensive than nuclear weapons and because Eisenhower's countervailing New Look strategy appeared to be aimed at achieving more bang for the buck, many of these critics questioned both the wisdom and the efficacy of nuclear deterrence.

One of the earliest and most comprehensive published critiques of the New Look and of the strategic doctrine of massive retaliation appeared in William W. Kaufmann's *Military Policy and National Security.* Published in 1956, the book is a collection of essays by respected scholars, including Kaufmann, Roger Hilsman, Morton Kaplan, and Gordon A. Craig, who discuss national security issues from both a theoretical and a practical perspective. Perhaps the most influential essay in the volume was Kaufmann's own "The Requirements of Deterrence." In it Kaufmann, then an associate professor at Princeton University, noted that nuclear deterrence had important practical limitations. Of particular concern was so-called extended deterrence, whereby the U.S. nuclear arsenal was expected to deter the Soviets from launching an attack on Europe—even an attack limited to the use of conventional weapons. The expansion of the Soviet Union's ability to inflict a nuclear attack on the United States, argued Kaufman, increasingly eroded the credibility of the U.S. threat to retaliate against Soviet aggression because extended deterrence was coming to be equated with the implausible pledge to commit suicide.[39] This argument would become increasingly prevalent in the latter half of the 1950s.

Henry Kissinger also questioned the utility of extended nuclear deterrence. In his widely read book *Nuclear Weapons and Foreign Policy,* published in 1957, Kissinger argued that nuclear weapons had rendered warfare nearly obsolete because there appeared to be no legitimate causes that would justify the use of such weapons. This stalemate had effectively paralyzed U.S. strategy "because the consequences of our weapons technology are so fearsome" and because the U.S. had "not found it easy to define a *casus belli* which would leave no doubt concerning our moral justification to use force." Kissinger viewed deterrence as an inherently passive strategy. "If the Soviet bloc can present its challenges in less than all-out form," Kissinger postulated, "it may gain a crucial advantage. Every move on its part will then pose the appalling dilemma of whether we are willing to commit suicide to prevent encroachments." Accordingly, the Soviets would seek to make small gains that did not meet the criteria of the U.S. all-or-nothing strategy.[40]

Kissinger likened the U.S. situation in 1957 to that of France of 1936. In the tense years before World War II, the French had based their military strategy on a series of defensive fortifications known as the Maginot Line. The failures of that strategy were dramatically displayed in the summer of 1940. Just as the French had failed to keep pace with strategic realities in the late 1930s as they hung behind their Maginot Line, Kissinger contended, the United States was pursuing a strategy that did not align with realistic threats. As the power of modern weapons grew, the threat of all-out war would lose its credibility and its effectiveness. Therefore, limited war had become the only form of conflict that would enable the United States to derive the greatest strategic advantage from its industrial potential. Kissinger also argued that the nuclear stalemate forced a reconsideration of earlier conceptions of strategic deterrence. "The best strategic posture for an all-out war," he charged, depended "on the proper 'mix' of offensive and defensive capabilities."[41]

Writing in 1957, Kissinger argued that the Soviets would be unable to achieve complete surprise and that therefore their capability for delivering a knockout blow was extremely limited. Nonetheless, the devastation on both sides would be great, regardless of who struck first. Consequently, the "only outcome of an all-out war will be that *both* contenders must lose." Kissinger did envision, however, that technological change could alter the balance and that because "the stalemate for all-out war is inherently precarious," it would "require a tremendous effort" by the United States "simply to stay even."[42]

Kissinger was not alone in his characterization of the risks and limitations of a nuclear deterrent strategy that presupposed an all-out war. In his book *Limited War*, also published in 1957, Robert E. Osgood stressed how the very nature of nuclear weapons, and the tendency of nuclear warfare to become total, necessitated the adoption of an alternative strategy that would substitute limited, conventional warfare for global thermonuclear holocaust.[43] The cost for maintaining a capability for conventional war was great. Kissinger noted, for example, Army Chief of Staff General Maxwell Taylor's estimation that twenty-eight modern divisions were necessary to meet foreseeable dangers.[44] President Eisenhower reported to the National Security Council "that he 'had nearly fainted' on hearing" Taylor's recommendation.[45] Eisenhower's underlying fear of the garrison state and his attention to the "Great Equation"—that is the balancing of "requisite military strength with healthy economic growth"—would ensure that proposals such as Kissinger's, Osgood's, and Taylor's never became policy during his administration.[46] The president's detractors knew that their policy proposals were based in part on an implicit rejection of Eisenhower's economic views, but this did nothing to forestall their criticisms. If anything, they were emboldened to discredit what they perceived to be the president's outdated philosophies.

Sputnik and the Gaither Report

Critiques of the New Look generally failed to arouse popular concern during Eisenhower's first term. Then, in the latter of half of 1957, men and women who had not previously questioned Eisenhower's strategic judgment began to harbor doubts about the state of the nation's defenses. This shift in attitudes was prompted by three successive revelations related to the Cold War nuclear arms race that raised the anxiety level of millions of Americans.

In July 1957, syndicated columnist Stewart Alsop revealed that the Soviet Union had successfully launched an intercontinental ballistic missile; he characterized the event as one of "grave international significance."[47] In that same month, he disclosed that Secretary of Defense Charles Wilson intended to hold U.S. expenditures for missiles to less than 10 percent of the total military budget. The sentiments Stewart Alsop expressed in a sarcastic note to Joseph, his brother and business partner, encapsulate those of many of the president's critics in the late 1950s: "It is nobody's business, of course, if the administration decides to let the Soviets beat us to the ICBM, in order to cut taxes in the next election year."[48] On 26 August 1957, the Soviets confirmed that they possessed an ICBM, and in September, after U.S. sensors observed a second successful launch, U.S. officials—who had initially dismissed the story as an elaborate bluff—conceded that the Soviets, and the Alsops, were telling the truth.[49]

Then, on 4 October 1957, the Soviet Union launched *Sputnik*, the world's first earth-orbiting satellite. Hailed by scientists as a tremendous achievement for humankind, *Sputnik* measured just twenty-two inches in diameter and weighed 184 pounds. Less than a month later, on 3 November the Soviets launched a second satellite. *Sputnik II* weighed more than 1,100 pounds and carried a living creature into space, a dog named Laika. The engineers of the U.S. space program had intended to launch a much smaller satellite, *Vanguard,* in early 1958, but prompted by the Soviet achievements, Eisenhower promised to launch a rocket into space before the end of the year. Ominously, the first test of *Vanguard* crashed on the launch pad at Cape Canaveral, Florida, on 6 December. Suddenly, casual observers in the United States, who had taken U.S. technological leadership for granted, feared that the United States had fallen behind the Soviets in the space race.

This growing perception of technological inferiority vis-à-vis the Soviets was reinforced when the contents of a secret report detailing the anticipated shortcomings of the U.S. nuclear weapons program were leaked to the media in December 1957. The *Sputnik* launches had attracted considerable attention among the general public; now the findings of the Security Resources Panel generated anxiety among lawmakers and policy makers in Washington about the state of the nation's defenses.

President Eisenhower had charged the panel, initially chaired by H. Rowan Gaither and since that time known as the Gaither Committee, with studying the nation's civil defense needs, but the committee members soon went beyond this narrow mission to consider all aspects of the nation's defenses. The panel's report was written by Paul Nitze, the principal author of NSC 68, and retired army colonel George Lincoln, a professor at West Point with a long and distinguished career as a military planner and adviser to senior officials in Washington.[50] The Gaither Report echoed the increasingly pessimistic attitude of the late 1950s. "We have found no evidence," the introduction stated, "to refute the conclusion that USSR intentions are expansionist." Consequently, the Gaither panelists warned of "an increasing threat which may become critical in 1959 or early 1960" and went on to highlight the widening disparity between the U.S. and Soviet weapons programs. The report concluded by advocating an acceleration of U.S. programs, at an estimated cost of an additional $44 billion, in order to close the gap.[51]

Given Nitze's central role in drafting both the Gaither Report and NSC 68, it is perhaps not surprising that much of the language in the Gaither Report is similar to that of the earlier document. What is striking, however, is that Nitze's views were given so prominent a place within Eisenhower's administration. Nitze seized this forum with relish, repeating almost verbatim many of the recommendations that were part of NSC 68. For example, the Gaither Report stressed that the following two years would be "critical," whereas NSC 68 foresaw a year of maximum danger on the horizon. Failure to act "at once" to address the deficiencies in the nation's security program would be "unacceptable," the Gaither panelists warned.[52]

Further, the Gaither Report, like NSC 68 before it, argued that the U.S. economy could easily support and sustain—and might even be helped by—the spending necessary to provide for an expanded national security program. The report noted that current spending on all national security programs constituted less than 10 percent of the nation's total production, whereas 41 and 14 percent of GNP had been dedicated to defense programs during World War II and the Korean War respectively. The total spending envisioned by the report, the panelists explained, would still be less than what was required during the Korean War.

To support the Gaither Report's defense spending proposals, its authors called for tax hikes, cuts in other government expenditures, an increase in the debt limit, and curbs on inflation. But these measures notwithstanding, the authors maintained that "The demands of such a program . . . on the nation's economic resources would not pose significant problems." Rather, the "increased defense spending" was expected to have positive economic effects that would help to sustain production and employment during a moderate recession.[53]

Eisenhower disagreed with the committee's findings and objected to the high costs of the Gaither Report's proposals. He did not believe, as the panelists argued, that the economic effects of a dramatically expanded military and national security infrastructure would have no harmful effect on, and might even boost, the nation's economy. Given these and other concerns, Eisenhower directed that the report be kept secret. The contents, however, were widely leaked. By late December 1957 journalists were speaking openly of the "secret" NSC report.[54]

In January of the following year the Rockefeller Brothers Fund published a series of reports that repeated and refined many of the criticisms of the Eisenhower administration's national security policies. Written under the direction of Henry Kissinger, the report on international security claimed that the United States was "rapidly losing its lead in the race of military technology" and urged immediate action to reverse the trend. In this context, the nation's security needs transcended "normal budgetary considerations," and the economy could "afford the necessary measures." The panelists hoped that the "recent

Soviet advances in the field of earth satellites . . . will serve to spark a deep review of the basic attitudes and policies affecting the security of our country and of the free world." Finally, the authors viewed the U.S. lag in missile development and space exploration as "a symptom and not a cause" of the "national complacency over the past dozen years."[55]

The report argued that the U.S. military establishment must be both capable of deterring general war and prepared to react to limited aggression. It also asserted, as had the Gaither Report and Kissinger's earlier work, that more effective civil defense measures must be part of the nation's overall strategic posture. Other specific recommendations included modernization of aircraft procurement, acceleration of the development and deployment of intermediate-range ballistic missiles (IRBMs) and ICBMs, improved readiness for the Strategic Air Command, and expedited development and deployment of submarine-launched ballistic missiles (SLBMs). The additional costs for such programs were estimated at approximately "$3 billion each year for the next several fiscal years."[56]

Essentially dismissing concerns about the burden that an expanded military program would impose upon the economy, the panelists asserted that current military expenditures could not meet the needs of even the current force levels, let alone those of the increased level of forces called for in their report. They conceded that the price for ensuring the nation's survival would not be low, but they were "convinced . . . that the increases in defense expenditures are essential and fully justified." "We can afford," the authors concluded, "to survive."[57]

Desmond Ball observes that the Gaither and Rockefeller reports were "invariably mentioned together" during the defense debates of the late 1950s. "Their findings and recommendations were very similar," he writes, "and there were half a dozen members common to both groups," including Colonel George Lincoln, James Fisk, and James Killian. Other prominent foreign policy experts, including Roswell A. Gilpatric, a principal author of the Rockefeller Report, advised Democratic politicians in the late 1950s. Ball therefore contends that "the Rockefeller report was . . . often regarded as something like an unclassified version of the Gaither report."[58]

Eisenhower may have objected to many of the findings of these two reports, but he did not dismiss the recommendations out of hand. In fact, during the late 1950s he presided over a substantial expansion of the U.S. nuclear weapons programs, and many of these changes were initiated before the missile gap emerged as a political issue. For example, in the two years before *Sputnik,* the nation's nuclear stockpile expanded dramatically, growing from 2,110 weapons in 1955 to 5,420 in 1957. The destructive force of these weapons expanded to an even greater degree—from a mere 154 megatons in 1955 to over 16,000 megatons in 1957.[59] Eisenhower failed to rein in this overkill, despite his growing belief that the arsenal had come to be far larger than strategic requirements dictated.[60]

It became even harder to hold back these increases in the midst of the political firestorm of the late 1950s, when the strategic nuclear stockpile tripled in size in just two years, from six thousand weapons in 1958 to eighteen thousand in 1960.[61] Eisenhower's decisions to move forward with a number of new weapon systems in the late 1950s were not significantly influenced by the Gaither and Rockefeller reports. Much of the work to diversify the nuclear deterrent force and to stabilize its security had begun years earlier, though Eisenhower did accelerate the purchase of some strategic weapons.

In the final years of his presidency Ike placed particular emphasis on accelerating ICBM programs, as well as production of the Polaris SLBM. Polaris was a medium-range nuclear missile that could be launched from submarines. The Minuteman was an ICBM deployed in hardened underground silos. These second-generation solid-propellant missiles were more stable than the liquid-fueled Titan and Atlas rockets that were projected to form the foundation of the U.S. nuclear missile force in the late 1950s. Second-generation missiles were also less susceptible to a surprise attack than bombers. Improvements to the nuclear deterrent force initiated during Eisenhower's tenure moved the United States considerably closer to its goal of achieving a survivable second-strike capability even in the event of a massive surprise attack, fundamentally changing the dynamics of the nuclear arms race.[62]

Many of these efforts were not immediately apparent to Eisenhower's critics, who, often for political gain, focused on the highly visible signs of U.S. decline relative to the Soviet Union. Some might conclude that these attacks on Eisenhower's policy were entirely political, but the Rockefeller Fund was hardly the exclusive preserve of liberal Democrats. Participants included Arthur Burns, Eisenhower's former chair of the Council of Economic Advisers; Henry R. Luce, a lifelong Republican; and James Fisk and James Killian, both of whom had advised Eisenhower on science and technology issues. Eisenhower himself had created the committee that produced the Gaither Report. By the early spring of 1958 critics of the president were emerging on many fronts and in many quarters. The attack on the New Look was broad-based and bipartisan.

The New Look versus the New Economics

The combined shocks of *Sputnik* and the findings of the Gaither and Rockefeller reports occurred within the context of a slowing economy. As the economy slipped still further into recession in late 1957 and early 1958, critics attacked the economic theory that underlay the New Look with increasing fervor, and economists and public policy analysts stepped forward with their own views of the proper balance between national security "needs" and domestic "wants." In contrast to the businessmen and conservative economists of Eisenhower's cabinet, many of the president's critics had served during earlier Democratic administrations, and they vigorously disputed Eisenhower's charge that excessive government spending and high taxes were depressing business activity and causing inflation.

One such critic was Walter Heller, a leading liberal economist from the University of Minnesota who was credited with coining the phrase *New Economics*. Heller's early writings were generally confined to economics textbooks and scholarly journals, and he did not play a particularly public role in framing the economic debate in the early 1950s. He would play an increasingly important role in the late 1950s, however, and he became an influential adviser within the Democratic Party during this period. In 1966, looking back on the Eisenhower years, Heller criticized the former president for failing to realize "the economy's great and growing potential." According to Heller, the "continued fear of inflation kept policy thinking in too restrictive a mold in the late 1950s."[63]

Seymour Edwin Harris, one of the most prolific economics writers of his day, was another proponent of the New Economics. Named chair of the Department of Economics at Harvard in 1955, he had earlier served on Harry Truman's Council of Economic Advisers, and he was an economic adviser to Adlai Stevenson from 1954 to 1956. A self-described liberal Democrat, Harris consistently criticized Eisenhower's economic philosophy. In the waning days of the 1956 presidential campaign, he wondered whether the president and his academic advisers had learned any lessons from the previous twenty years about the proper relationship between tax policy, government spending, and economic growth. In particular, he questioned whether the true reason the GOP was reluctant to boost spending was that theirs was a "businessman's administration" that shared the "prejudice of businessmen against public spending." One form of public spending that had fallen victim to the budget cutters' axe was defense spending; Harris criticized the Eisenhower administration's $10 billion in military spending cuts as a "major but questionable" achievement.[64]

Harris explained that the Republicans would take credit for balancing the budget, reducing taxes, and lessening government spending, and the Democrats, by contrast, would stress that "some things are more important than finance." Along these lines, Adlai Stevenson had declared that "drastic cuts in military spending to provide resources for cutting taxes had proved costly in the loss of prestige abroad."[65] These arguments persisted long after Eisenhower's overwhelming victory over Stevenson in the election of 1956, and they were sharpened in late 1957 and early 1958.

For example, the former chairman of Truman's Council of Economic Advisers, Leon Keyserling, stepped forward in early 1958 to attack Eisenhower's policies. In the span of two months, Keyserling penned three essays emphasizing the importance of achieving higher levels of economic growth. In the *New Republic*, he argued that growth in the United States must average about 4.5 percent, but that growth in the period from 1953 to 1957 had averaged only slightly more than 2.5 percent, and growth in 1957 had fallen to only 2 percent. He charged that the Eisenhower administration's economic policies had "not only failed to modify these trends" but had actually "augmented them." Federal spending had bought "far less national security and domestic programs than we needed and could afford," and as a whole the federal budget had "pulled us downward" instead of giving us a lift." Further, Keyserling asked why spending for national security had declined "despite the rising international threat."[66]

Foreseeing that coming economic conditions would be "characterized . . . by a dangerously inadequate rate of growth in output and income, a consequent long-term rise in unemployment, and the resumption of price inflation in a retarded economy," Keyserling contrasted the U.S. economy with that of the Soviet Union. "The Russians," he wrote in a letter to the editor of the *New Republic*, "are expanding their production by 7–10 percent a year. They are 'affording' what they think they need; while we think we 'cannot afford' what we know we need."[67]

A new generation of economists also stepped forward in the late 1950s to attack Eisenhower's economic philosophy, particularly as it related to national security spending. One of these young economists was James Tobin, a professor of economics at Yale University. Born and raised in Champaign-Urbana, Illinois, Tobin had received a full scholarship to attend Harvard, where he earned his undergraduate degree in 1939. After serving in the navy during World War II, Tobin returned to Harvard to study economics under Seymour Harris and Alvin Hansen. He earned his Ph.D. in Economics in 1947.[68]

During his sophomore year at Harvard in 1936, Tobin had been introduced to the works of John Maynard Keynes, and Keynesianism formed the foundation for Tobin's largely economic critique of the Eisenhower administration's national security policy. In an essay in the *Yale Review* published in the spring of 1958, Tobin criticized the administration for reducing defense spending "at a time when the world situation cried out for accelerating and enlarging our defense effort." In Tobin's view, the fear of large federal budget deficits and high inflation and an aversion to high taxes and more generous government spending were forcing "Uncle Sam" to fight "with one hand tied behind his back."[69]

Central to Tobin's message was his belief that public needs outweigh private indulgence. "A nation on the edge of starvation might of necessity be on the edge of insecurity," he wrote, but "the United States has no private uses of resources so compelling that they justify keeping the Western World in . . . a precarious position." Later he reiterated and reinforced this theme: "The unfilled needs of defense are great and they are urgent. Whether we wish to try to meet them depends on how we weigh . . . the urgency of these defense needs against the urgency of those private uses of resources that would have to be sacrificed." Anyone with an awareness of "the luxury standard of living of the United States" would "strike the balance only one way," he argued, preferring "to save our lives rather than our leisure" and valuing "freedom over fashion."[70]

Tobin directed the weight of his argument against the classical economic philosophy of those who believed that the expansion of the federal government and the burden of taxation would drain the nation's productive strength and stifle economic growth. Arguing that "American businessmen have striven as earnestly and diligently as ever" in recent years in spite of relatively high levels of taxation, Tobin declared that "it is time to base economic policy on the evidence of history rather than on imaginary future catastrophes."[71]

Tobin used harsh and bold language in his effort to bring his readers out of their complacent faith in American ingenuity. "Military strength is not achieved by making civilian goods," he warned. "Let us not fool ourselves . . . that the use of talent and other resources to design, say, more automatic and more powerful automobiles is contributing to our national strength." The Soviets had "overtaken the United States" even though their "overall productive capacity" still fell far short, Tobin explained, because "in the grim calculus of relative military strength, much of our vast production is just thrown away, while they have concentrated on building the capacity and advancing the technology of military strength."[72]

In stark contrast to Eisenhower's philosophy as expressed in the Chance for Peace speech, Tobin's belief was that government itself was the key to the growth of the nation's productive power. He denigrated the ideology of those who believed that "dollars spent by governments are *prima facie* unproductive" and "dollars spent by private individuals and firms productive." Tobin was particularly disdainful of what was, in his view, the misallocation of resources in the private sphere. He wrote: "Government dollars spent for such things as fire and police protection, education, postal service, highways, parks, hospitals, libraries, sanitation, and flood control, need have no inferiority complex with respect to private dollars spent for steaks, television, freezers, alcohol, horse racing, gasoline, comic books, and golf."[73]

Conservatives had "greatly overestimated the weight of considerations that oppose defense spending and other governmental programs," Tobin explained, and "the president's budget for 1958–59" demonstrated "the continuing force of this tragic overestimate." By refusing to consider the "possibility that many private uses of resources might be much more logical candidates for sacrifice than governmental programs," the president had left "the way clear for *all* of the growing capacity of the economy to be channeled into still further elevation of our standards of luxury."[74] A wise person, Tobin wrote, would immediately sacrifice private luxury and leisure in order to support national security programs.

John Kenneth Galbraith, a professor of economics at Harvard and a leading liberal intellectual during the 1950s, also played a prominent role in framing the intellectual debate around the New Look and the New Economics in the late 1950s. Born in Ontario, Canada, in 1908, Galbraith earned his Ph.D. in economics in 1934 from the University of California and joined the Harvard faculty in 1948. His theories of the proper balance between private desires and public needs echoed many of Tobin's sentiments. Galbraith's most influential work, *The Affluent Society,* published in the spring of 1958, drove home the point that Eisenhower's economic policies had enabled some to prosper while others were mired in poverty.[75]

Galbraith was serving at that time as chairman of the economic advisory group within the Democratic Advisory Council. Created in late 1956 after Eisenhower's commanding reelection victory over Adlai Stevenson, the advisory council revealed a dispute within the Democratic Party over the proper political strategy to be used against Eisenhower and the GOP. Legislative leaders such as Lyndon Johnson and Sam Rayburn had generally cooperated with the popular president. Other Democrats, including Stevenson, Leon Keyserling, Hubert

Humphrey, and Estes Kefauver, disagreed with this approach. The members of the advisory council generally favored confrontation with the president, including critiques of Eisenhower's policies on ideological grounds. Eventually other rising stars within the Democratic Party, including Stuart W. Symington of Missouri and John F. Kennedy of Massachusetts, joined this influential group of liberal Democrats.[76]

In *The Affluent Society* Galbraith consistently attacked "the conventional wisdom" that had not adapted itself to the new economic realities of prosperity. The world had known only poverty for most of its history, and economics had concerned itself with the problem of scarcity, privation, and want. In the late 1950s the United States was experiencing a rare period of affluence, Galbraith explained, but economic policy was still "guided, in part, by ideas that are relevant to another world."[77] Galbraith then set out to attack the conventional wisdom he had just discredited.

One key element of the conventional wisdom, the goal of achieving a balanced budget, had gradually changed and adapted in the 1930s and 1940s, a development Galbraith attributed to the work of John Maynard Keynes. After the publication of Keynes's *The General Theory of Employment, Interest, and Money* in 1936, Galbraith asserted, "the conventional insistence on the balanced budget under all circumstances and at all levels of economic activity was in retreat."[78]

The conventional wisdom may have been in retreat during the Great Depression, but it had not been defeated. In this vein, one of Galbraith's longest chapters addresses "The Illusion of National Security." In a far-ranging discussion, Galbraith assailed the notion that military needs must compete with consumer needs in times of crisis. For decades, he explained, most observers had assumed that the size of a nation's economy was directly related to its capacity to wage war. Galbraith pointed to the fallacy of that view. Echoing Tobin's sentiments, he questioned the Eisenhower administration's balance between public and private spending.

Galbraith was particularly dismissive of the notion that military power is "a function of economic output." "Our wealth is a valuable weapon," he noted, but "as things now stand it is largely unavailable, and to the extent that it is available its usefulness is gravely impaired." For example, in the midst of the most recent military crisis—in Korea—the civilian economy and the effort to maintain the "standard of living," Galbraith argued, "became an immediate and clear-cut threat to the effective prosecution of the war." "The efforts of consumers to sustain . . . what persuasion had caused them to regard as a minimum standard of living effectively pre-empted the total output of the economy and more."[79] Galbraith was equally skeptical of Eisenhower's contention that military spending should be limited because overburdensome defense spending might have harmful economic effects. Galbraith concluded his work with a discussion of "security and survival," explaining that he returned to this theme in the closing chapter of his book because it had been nearly two years since he had drafted his earlier chapter on national security. "At that time," he wrote, "it seemed hard to believe that people might soon be persuaded that crude increases in production had little to do with national defense and that the attitude that stressed such calculations was positively damaging." Since then, he continued, the Soviet Union had "revealed a breath-taking series of scientific and technical advances." Such gains, he noted, were not handicapped by limited means. Rather, it had become evident that the U.S. failure to match the Soviets' achievement "was the result of its failure to concentrate the requisite resources on the desired ends."[80]

While many had blamed poor decision making, interservice rivalry, and inadequate administration for the decline of the U.S. technological position relative to the Soviets, Galbraith saw a far deeper cause: "that our economy, and the economic theory that explains and rationalizes its behavior, immobilizes all but a minor fraction of the product in private and, from the standpoint of national security, irrelevant production." "Our hope for survival, security, and contentment," he concluded, depended upon the direction of "resources to the most urgent ends."[81]

Eisenhower and his advisers had not dismissed the conventional wisdom, but they had not embraced it entirely either. Galbraith himself had praised the Eisenhower administration in January 1955 for showing "considerable grace and ease in getting away from the clichés of a balanced budget and the unspeakable evils of deficit financing." He commended the administration for showing "a remarkable flexibility of mind in the speed with which it has moved away from these slogans."[82]

In the wake of *Sputnik*, however, and following the findings of the Gaither and Rockefeller reports, the political and economic circumstances had changed and Galbraith was far less willing to give Eisenhower credit for his economic achievements. Instead, by the spring of 1958 he viewed Eisenhower as simply a guardian of the status quo, a narrow-minded adherent to the conventional wisdom that had been discredited by events and by theory. Galbraith was not alone, but was joined by Tobin, Heller, Harris, and Keyserling. These economists helped to establish the parameters of the economic debate for the remainder of the decade, and the battle over Eisenhower's national security policy—predicated as it was on his economic philosophy—intensified.

The Revolt of the Generals

The intellectual milieu surrounding the belief in the missile gap continued to develop in the late 1950s. While the writings of many critics appeared only in classified reports or obscure scholarly journals, a number of critiques of the New Look reflecting the practical perspectives of senior military officers received popular attention. The first of these works was Matthew Ridgway's *Soldier,* published in 1956.

Ridgway's memoir blends recollections from his long military career with a series of pointed criticisms of the direction of U.S. military policy. Ridgway appreciated the importance of civilian control over the military, but he also stressed his obligation, in the interest of national security, to represent the needs of the armed services. In particular, Ridgway criticized the interservice wrangling that had been driven by Eisenhower's economy measures. He contended that the army unfairly bore the brunt of the budget cuts: uniformed troops had been reduced from a high of 1.5 million during the Korean War to 1 million in 1956, and the army's budget had been slashed from $16.2 billion to $8.9 billion.

A letter Ridgway submitted to Secretary of Defense Charles Wilson in June of 1955, only three days before officially resigning from the army, reprinted in full in the appendix to the book, provides a useful summary of the concerns of many army officers during the era of massive retaliation. In the letter Ridgway discussed the nature of the Soviet threat and the strategies the Soviets would be likely to use in the event of general war. He also proposed a strategy for the United States that was designed to meet these challenges. Ridgway emphasized that the Soviets were committed to an offensive strategy and that they and their allies retained the initiative in engaging in conflicts worldwide. He also asserted that the circumstances of "nuclear plenty" had effectively cancelled out the advantages of nuclear deterrence. In light of this, he questioned the wisdom of continuing to base U.S. strategy on the threat to use nuclear weapons. "Since national objectives could not be realized solely by the possession of nuclear capabilities," he wrote, "no nation could regard nuclear capabilities alone as sufficient, either to prevent, or to win a war." Accordingly, Ridgway called for an "immediately available mobile joint military force . . . in which the versatility of the whole is emphasized and the preponderance of any one part is de-emphasized."[83]

Ridgway's book was reviewed in a number of prominent national publications and major newspapers, including the *New York Herald Tribune,* the *New York Times,* the journal *Foreign Affairs,* and weeklies such as the *New Yorker* and *Saturday Review*. One reviewer in the *Chicago Sunday Tribune* argued that "there are honest men who will not agree with Ridgway, but none will dispute the sincerity" of his memoir. Another review in the *Christian Science Monitor* argued that Ridgway's "honest and forthright appraisal of our military situation deserves careful reading."[84]

Ridgway was one of the first senior military officers to publicly criticize Eisenhower's national security strategy, but he was hardly the last. Two years after the publication of Ridgway's *Soldier* and in the wake of *Sputnik* and the Gaither and Rockefeller reports, retired army general James M. Gavin published *War and Peace in the Space Age*. Gavin was one of the first army officers to consider the long-term strategic and tactical ramifications of nuclear weapons on the army as an institution. For much of the late 1940s and early 1950s, however, Gavin's thoughts on the subject had been afforded little weight.[85]

After being named the army's chief of research and development in 1955, the outspoken general increasingly found himself on the losing side of a series of contentious military debates. As he became more vocal in his criticism of the administration's spending priorities and of the operations of the Joint Chiefs of Staff, he came into conflict with many of his superiors. In November 1957, only a few weeks after the launch of *Sputnik,* Gavin boldly called for an expansion of the army's missile programs to meet the new challenge posed by the Soviets' space satellite and ICBMs. These recent successes, according to Gavin, were evidence "of what informed Americans have long known: that the Soviets are making rapid progress in adapting missiles to their national needs—and the international situation."[86]

Then in early January 1958 Gavin abruptly announced his intention to retire. Having rejected Secretary of the Army Wilbur Brucker's offer of a promotion to four stars and the choice of a major assignment, Gavin explained in a special interview with the *New York Times* that he believed he could "do more on the outside for national defense than on the inside."[87] Gavin repeated these claims when he formally left the army on 31 March 1958. Again citing his frustration with budgetary constraints and interservice rivalry, Gavin openly advocated an acceleration of missile development in order to close the missile gap.[88]

Less than five months later Gavin published *War and Peace in the Space Age*. Building on Ridgway's earlier assessment and on the events surrounding the launch of *Sputnik,* Gavin's book is a blunt and outspoken critique of the New Look. According to the dust jacket, Gavin shows why the United States "fell behind the Russians" and explains "how limited thinking crippled our ability to win limited wars and how poor decision making at the top and timid decision makers led us into our present grave position." According to the publishers, Gavin names names and fixes "responsibility in the highest places." Indeed, he does all of these things and more.[89] At the outset Gavin wrote openly of the missile lag. He predicted that during the years of the missile lag—"a period . . . that we are now entering"—the nation's "offensive and defensive missile capabilities will so lag behind those of the Soviets as to place us in a position of great peril."[90] The lag, in his view, was exacerbated, if not actually caused, by faulty decision making within the Pentagon that placed greater emphasis on the navy's satellite *Vanguard* than on the army's competing *Redstone* rocket program, which was under the direction of Wernher von Braun. But it was not too late. With concerted action, he stressed, the missile lag could be overcome. In many respects Gavin's work can be seen as a more critical iteration of Ridgway's previously stated concerns about the nature and direction of the nation's defense programs, particularly as they related to the balance of forces between the army, navy, and air force. His warnings were made all the more urgent by the events of the previous twelve months—especially the successful Soviet ICBM test and the launch of *Sputnik*—and therefore they had greater political resonance than Ridgway's earlier work had.

Gavin's book was immediately greeted by favorable reviews in a number of magazines and newspapers, including the *New York Times* and the *Chicago Tribune*.[91] In a mixed review of Gavin's work that appeared in the *New Republic* in September 1958, James E. King Jr. wrote that he sensed the influence of Henry Kissinger within Gavin's argument. Gavin, like Kissinger, doubted that the threat of massive retaliation would continue to deter limited wars. The United States had neglected to prepare itself for lesser threats, and Gavin therefore feared that the nation might be outmaneuvered during the Cold War in those crises that did not merit the use of nuclear weapons. King observed that Gavin also agreed with the Rockefeller and Gaither reports, which had called for more funding for defense, and that he had referred approvingly to those who argued that the nation could afford to spend much more on defense without harming the domestic economy.[92]

The Problem of National Security

In the summer of 1958, Eisenhower's New Look was also assailed by industry and business leaders in *The Problem of National Security: Some Economic and Administrative Aspects,* a report published by the Committee for Economic Development (CED). The CED was founded in 1942 by liberal-minded businesspeople and academicians who hoped to reconcile the competing interests of government and business.[93] The main purpose of *The Problem of National Security*, the authors explained, was to establish "the considerations upon which decisions with respect to the size of our defense program should . . . be based; and to clear away what we think are certain false ideas that have governed these decisions in the past." The most significant of these false ideas was that of the need for economies in defense. "We must not hobble ourselves," the authors maintained, "by the notion that there is some arbitrary limit on what we can spend for defense, now within reach, that we can exceed only with disastrous consequences to the economy."[94]

The CED report established certain assumptions about the hostile intent of Soviet leaders and also noted the recent technological gains achieved by the Soviets. The authors attributed these successes to two principal factors. First, the Soviets were able to extract more security from their military for less money by spending less on pay, comfort, and safety for their troops while dedicating their most productive resources to the manufacture of military goods. Second, the Soviets had made a conscious decision to dedicate their economy to the support of defense industries and economic growth "and not toward satisfying consumers' wants." As evidence of this the authors pointed out that "in a typical month of 1957 . . . the United States produced over 500,000 automobiles and 15 B-52s" and that "the ratio was vastly different in the Soviet Union." The authors contended that Soviet leaders had managed to achieve a rate of investment far greater than that in the United States precisely because they had managed to concentrate resources "on projects conducive to industrial and military development, whereas a large proportion of our best brains are engaged in designing and merchandising consumer goods and services."[95]

Eisenhower would likely have considered investment in consumer goods and services to be a sign of U.S. economic strength, not weakness. But the authors of the CED report and, one presumes, a majority of the members of the CED, did not agree with Eisenhower about the proper balance between military needs and consumer wants. The authors tacitly agreed with the president when they observed that "the strength of the United States rests overwhelmingly in the public and its resources, not in Washington." Then the authors directly contradicted the president: "The United States need not turn itself into a 'garrison state,' but it may have to divert to national security a larger proportion of its output . . . and forego standards and practices that impair the nation's strength but are not at all indispensable parts of our way of life."[96]

The report highlighted the need to develop a number of different weapon systems to ensure technological superiority given recent Soviet gains. Because the development of modern military forces takes years of advanced planning, the authors argued, "prudence requires that we insure against error, that we cover several bets on decisions involving high stakes." Elsewhere they wrote, "We cannot afford to gamble for the sake of the economy."[97] Again, this contradicted Eisenhower's view that the prudent course was to protect the domestic economy against wasteful and duplicative military spending.

The authors considered the economic parameters of the national security debate at some length. They began by discussing the relative burden of defense spending since the end of World War II, pointing especially to the years immediately before and after the Korean conflict. In 1948, when the secretary of defense and the service chiefs had called for a military budget of at least $18 billion, the president and the Bureau of the Budget had demanded that this figure be held to no more than $15 billion out of concern for harming the economy; but when defense spending after the outbreak of the Korean War rose to more than $50 billion, it had no appreciable negative impact upon the U.S. economy. The authors believed that in spite of this evidence from recent history, concerns about a "sound economy" continued to impede "rational" decision making by the nation's leaders. The strong belief in the "debilitating effects of large defense expenditures on the economy," the authors wrote, stood "in striking contrast to the paucity of our economic knowledge about such effects." Dismissing concerns about "the expenditures we can afford, the taxes we can stand or the debt we can bear" as largely irrelevant, they declared that faulty preconceptions about the limits of the U.S. economy "should not be allowed to interfere with informed and rational" efforts to enlarge the nation's security programs.[98]

Just as Keyserling, Tobin, and others had argued, the members of the CED foresaw that economic growth was a key element in the ability of the United States to provide for its security. The CED refused, however, to consider how high taxation might actually impede such growth. Specifically, the report rejected Eisenhower's fear that there was a "sharp breaking point" at which high levels of taxation would have a marked impact upon the economy. Rather, the authors were confident that inflation could be controlled "if the American public is willing to let itself be taxed sufficiently" and that "a somewhat larger burden" would be "fairly safe."[99]

Most important, the authors largely dismissed the possible detrimental economic effects of diverting skills, materials, and resources from civilian industries to defense. The authors conceded that "provision for national security is expensive" and that expenditures had already increased from a little over 1 percent of GNP in the 1930s to over 11 percent in recent years. But they declared that "even this huge amount may have been inadequate" to meet the Soviet threat. Then, in an argument that was repeated by observers—both liberal and conservative—in later years, the authors reiterated that fear "that a high defense burden will weaken the economy has been exaggerated." "The risk that defense spending of from 10 to 15 per cent of the gross national product, or if necessary even more, will ruin the American way of life is slight indeed," they said. "There is no factual basis for the notion that we are within reach of or exceeding some 'breaking point' beyond which tax-financed expenditures will critically impair economic growth." They concluded, with emphasis, *"We can afford what we have to afford."*[100]

Eisenhower expected criticism from disgruntled former officials of the Truman administration, he did not seek the approval of liberal academic economists, and he was disappointed, but not surprised, that army officers would question cuts in their service. The CED's findings and opinions were important, however, because they reflected the attitudes of the president's putative ideological allies in the business community, as well as a number of prominent individuals who served in his administration. Writing in 1962, liberal economist Seymour Harris specifically cited some of the CED's criticisms to support his contention that Eisenhower had "greatly overstressed" economic considerations in reducing conventional forces and in relying too heavily on nuclear deterrence as the foundation for his national security strategy.[101]

By the late summer of 1958, critics from all of these quarters had taken direct aim at many of Eisenhower's most closely held beliefs about national security and the economy. Military theorists such as Kissinger, Osgood, and Kaufmann had criticized the very foundation of the U.S. nuclear deterrent strategy. Senior army officers, including Ridgway and Gavin, had questioned the direction of the nation's military programs. Economists Tobin, Galbraith, Harris, and others had categorically rejected Eisenhower's contention that the burden of military spending would cause undue harm to the domestic economy and might lead to the creation of a garrison state. Even business leaders had called for more defense spending to meet the Soviet challenge. Armed with such information, journalists and politicians who had long questioned the wisdom of Eisenhower's entire defense program leveled a new round of charges centered around the missile gap.

Conclusion

The debate over the economics of national security in the nuclear era related directly to the balance between defense spending and development of the domestic economy. Truman was initially reluctant to embrace the enormous increases in defense spending called for in NSC 68, but by 1952, he was generally committed to spending more money on *both* nuclear and conventional forces. Conversely, the keys to Eisenhower's ability to hold down defense expenditures were his faith in the principle of nuclear deterrence; his willingness to cut military spending, particularly on conventional forces; and his commitment to strategic planning for the long haul. In spite of charges from his political adversaries that he was conceding the periphery to the communist advance, Eisenhower refused to become engaged in protracted conventional conflicts, and he generally refused to spend money on forces designed to fight such battles.

Critics of the New Look, then and since, questioned the utility of nuclear deterrence, particularly in the era of nuclear plenty when both the United States and the Soviet Union had acquired such a number of nuclear weapons that neither party could reasonably expect to achieve a strategic advantage. Such a condition of nuclear parity did not actually occur until the late 1960s, but in the mid-1950s strategists had already begun to prepare for such a contingency. They were particularly fearful that even the appearance of U.S. weakness might embolden the Soviets to engage in reckless behavior. Eisenhower himself was not particularly sanguine about the benefits of nuclear weapons, but he did believe that they were an effective deterrent. He was most concerned that even a minor military engagement between the superpowers was likely to escalate into a full-scale nuclear exchange, the prospect of which was too horrible to contemplate. Although his critics identified the many problems associated with nuclear deterrence and massive retaliation, they either downplayed or ignored concerns that limited wars were likely to escalate into total war.

Meanwhile, the economic theories underlying Eisenhower's national security strategy also aroused the scorn of his critics. They were particularly dismissive of Eisenhower's overarching belief that the nation's means were finite and that the public sector was generally not an efficient vehicle for allocating these scarce resources. These criticisms were grounded in an accurate sense of Eisenhower's general attitude toward government spending but often missed crucial nuances in his approach to the management of the economy. Eisenhower certainly resisted pressures to increase the defense budget; however, there was more to this resistance than a simple aversion to all forms of government spending. Eisenhower appears to have been most strenuously opposed to using defense dollars to boost the nation's economy. While he was not ignorant of the ramifications of his military decisions, the perceived need to maintain fiscal discipline remained paramount. A lack of appreciation for the limits of power occasionally led policy makers to pursue goals that placed an unacceptable burden on the U.S. economy during the Cold War. Eisenhower pursued an alternate strategy: he placed limits on the exercise of power, largely—although not exclusively, or even primarily—because he specifically did not wish to burden the U.S. economy.

Scholarly opinion on the wisdom or folly of Eisenhower's economic worldview varies. Most of the contemporary criticisms of the New Look implicitly rejected Eisenhower's view that the U.S. economy could not sustain the high level of expenditures necessary to support larger conventional forces. Many of the president's critics dismissed his economic beliefs as outdated at best and ignorant at worst. These criticisms were firmly grounded in the prevailing economic theory of the late 1950s and early 1960s.

By contrast, many modern observers have praised Eisenhower for his fiscal restraint, but these observations have been made with the benefit of hindsight. During the most dangerous days of the Cold War, when Eisenhower seemed to be surrounded by calls for a dramatically larger defense budget, his was a lonely voice, especially when he was publicly challenged by members of the military, by politicians of both parties, and even by individuals within his own administration.

The formulation of military strategy and national security policy is always susceptible to political influences, and the New Look was not immune to such pressures. The debate over the New Look had been building for several years, and the missile gap became the rallying cry for those who had previously been unable to dent Eisenhower's political armor. The rising controversy surrounding the New Look in the late 1950s, of which the missile gap critique was a crucial component, fundamentally altered the relationship between President Eisenhower, Congress, and the American people for the remainder of Eisenhower's presidency. An up-and-coming politician with his eyes on the White House would include the missile gap in his campaign to overturn Eisenhower's national security strategy while simultaneously boosting his own political fortunes.

CHAPTER TWO

A Senator Finds His Voice

"We are rapidly approaching that dangerous period which . . . others have called the 'gap' or the 'missile-lag period.'"

—Senator John F. Kennedy on the floor of the U.S. Senate in August 1958[1]

In the closing paragraph of his 1958 *Yale Review* essay, James Tobin argued that the American people might be willing to pay higher taxes and make other sacrifices if the nation's leaders accurately conveyed "the dangers the country and the world face." Recent Soviet success in space, he predicted, would "be well worth the blow it has dealt our national pride if it frees national policy from the shackles of fiscal orthodoxy." He further hoped that the Soviets' satellite program would "shake the American people from their complacency and cause them to demand the kind of leadership that elected democratic leaders are supposed to provide."[2]

At least one young politician aspiring for a position of national leadership took Tobin's arguments to heart. Although John F. Kennedy was not a Keynesian, he was not—in the words of James Tobin— "shackled" by fiscal orthodoxy. Kennedy had frequently supported additional spending for the nation's defense, and his critiques of the Eisenhower administration's defense policies during the late 1950s were grounded in a criticism of the president's economic philosophy.

Kennedy stepped confidently into the intellectual and political milieu of the late 1950s. In the years leading up to *Sputnik* and the missile gap, he had labored in relative political obscurity even while his personal charm had made him a favorite in the Washington social scene. His political fortunes began to improve following his surprise bid for the vice presidential nomination in 1956. Physically hampered for years by a weak back and an adrenal condition known as Addison's disease, Kennedy enjoyed improved health during the late 1950s. In 1957 the young, lanky senator who had once been bullied by more seasoned politicians, including Senate Majority Leader Lyndon Johnson, was handed a plum assignment on the Labor Committee, and by early 1958 he had submitted two major labor-reform initiatives that solidified his liberal credentials on the domestic front. With his service on the Senate Foreign Relations Committee, meanwhile, he established himself as a respectable liberal internationalist and was able to distance himself politically from his father, Joseph P. Kennedy, an outspoken isolationist prior to World War II.

John F. Kennedy had long been interested in foreign policy and national defense. During his undergraduate years at Harvard, Kennedy had majored in political science with a concentration in international relations. In his senior year he wrote a research paper examining England's lack of military preparedness prior to World War II. The paper was later published as a book with the assistance of ghostwriter Arthur Krock and with a foreword by Henry Luce. *Why England Slept* reportedly sold over eighty thousand copies.[3]

Kennedy believed that fear was a powerful motivator for democratic societies, which would otherwise be too slow to respond to genuine national security threats. In *Why England Slept* Kennedy blamed primarily the British public for failing to come to grips with the challenge posed by Adolf Hitler's Nazi Germany. The leaders in Great Britain in the 1930s were captives to public opinion, rather than shapers of it, he argued, and these leaders ultimately failed to convince their constituents of the need to rebuild the nation's defenses.[4]

Drawing on this and other lessons from history, Kennedy defined political courage as the ability of leaders to generate support for necessary programs. This point of view was celebrated in Kennedy's Pulitzer Prize–winning book *Profiles in Courage,* published in 1956. Very little of the book was actually written by Kennedy. Ted Sorensen, Kennedy's able and gifted assistant, later said that he, Sorensen, had "prepared the materials on which the book" was based.[5]

Regardless of who actually wrote *Profiles,* Kennedy was certainly very familiar with the book. He agreed with its precepts, and the ideas underlying the work reflected an image of leadership that Kennedy admired and wished to project. In practice, Kennedy showed the type of courage celebrated in *Profiles* when dealing with issues of great importance to him personally. On questions of national security and defense, he was eager to challenge prevailing popular opinion. Beyond this, however, Kennedy was a practical man. He valued similar qualities in his advisers.

While Kennedy was not above taking a stand on principle, his political senses became sharpened in the late 1950s. Early on, he realized the political importance of the missile gap. In contrast with the

British politicians in the 1930s who had become nearly paralyzed with fear of war with Germany, Kennedy used fear as a motivator to convince the American public of the need to support the national security programs necessary to close the missile gap.[6]

Congressional leaders had hammered away at Eisenhower's national security program during a series of hearings in the winter and early spring of 1958, but after firm assertions in April by both Defense Secretary Neil H. McElroy and Deputy Secretary of Defense Donald Quarles that there was no missile gap, the debate had briefly subsided.[7] Uncertainty within the intelligence community, however, allowed the missile gap debate to linger as a political issue.

Intelligence analysts harbored grave doubts about the Soviet Union's nuclear weapons capabilities, but they were unable to confirm the existence of a massive building program. Absent hard evidence, most of the estimates issued in the late 1950s were based on speculation about Soviet intentions. A number of individuals with access to the limited information that emerged from the secretive Soviet society were inclined to fear the worst-case scenario: that the Soviets were engaged in a crash program to build as many missiles as their capabilities would allow and were thereby threatening to overwhelm the U.S. deterrent. This point of view was particularly prevalent among air force analysts.[8] The worst-case scenario was only one of several estimates promulgated by the intelligence community during the missile gap years, but the most pessimistic interpretations were often picked up by intellectuals and journalists, and finally by politicians who had never been enthusiastic supporters the New Look. Inflated estimates of Soviet missile production were compared with too-conservative assessments of the progress and scale of U.S. missile programs to provide the basis for the alleged missile gap. And the gap, in time, became a vehicle for attacking Eisenhower's national security policies.

Senator Kennedy, Joseph Alsop, and the Missile Gap

In his campaign to stir his fellow Americans to action, Kennedy found a natural ally in syndicated columnist Joseph Alsop, the man who would later claim to have coined the term *missile gap*. Joseph and his brother Stewart formed one of the most successful journalistic teams in the 1950s. Born to a prominent family and with the Roosevelts among their forbears, the Alsops had cultivated their social standing with education at the finest eastern schools. Although many members of their family leaned toward the Republican Party, Joe was generally supportive of his distant relative Franklin Delano Roosevelt's domestic initiatives. Joe adopted a notably interventionist stance in the years leading up to World War II, and he developed a reputation as a hungry young journalist with a nose for a good story.[9] Stewart Alsop joined his brother in Washington, D.C., after World War II, and the two began to collaborate on a regular syndicated column for the *New York Herald Tribune*. Their "Matter of Fact" consistently conveyed the new internationalism of their generation, and the column circulated widely during the early Cold War period. By the mid-1950s the brothers had become particularly critical of Eisenhower's efforts to restrain defense spending, but Joe's increasing predilection for the Democratic Party troubled his longtime partner, and the siblings formally split in 1958. For the remainder of his career Joe would be the sole writer of "Matter of Fact," while Stewart continued on to a successful career with the *Saturday Evening Post* and, later, *Newsweek*.[10]

Soon after the breakup Joe resumed his attacks on the Eisenhower administration's national security strategy and on the related subject of the defense budget. The missile gap became his preferred rhetorical vehicle. An internal CIA history would later dub Joseph Alsop "the prophet of the missile gap."[11] Joe had long had a keen interest in the subject, and he and Stewart had been among the first to break the story of the Soviet intercontinental ballistic missile test in August 1957. But Joe's attacks on the popular Republican president became even more vitriolic in the spring and summer of 1958.

For example, Joe wrote an idiosyncratic piece in the May 1958 issue of the journal *Encounter* decrying the U.S. strategic disadvantage vis-à-vis the Soviets in light of the missile gap. He reiterated many of the concerns that had been voiced by New Look critics ever since John Foster Dulles had delivered his "massive retaliation" speech in January 1954, but Alsop added his own special flair. He declared that "the Dulles theory of American world strategy has become a phantasm. Massive retaliation is now massive nonsense." Arguing that the "Eisenhower administration's budget-firsters" had allowed the nation's "former great superiority in nuclear striking power to be lost to the Soviet Union," he conceded that neither side could expect to prevail in a nuclear exchange, even the nation that leveled the first blow.[12]

But Joe Alsop was less concerned about the threat of nuclear weapons than about the implications of the New Look for U.S. and Soviet policy in the Third World. "The great growth of the Soviet . . . nuclear striking power," Alsop wrote, has "given the Soviets a wholly new freedom" to "undertake almost any kind of local military adventure with conventional forces. *This is true because there is no real possibility of nuclear retaliation against non-nuclear action.*" He closed by appealing for "new American leaders who are capable of rallying the West" and who would reorient U.S. policy and spending priorities. "We need to make the taxing military-fiscal effort" to diversify the armed forces, Alsop contended. Such expenditures would "automatically discourage local military actions by the Soviets and their satellites."[13]

Then in early August Joe Alsop penned a harshly critical column titled "Our Government Untruths." In it, he accused the Eisenhower administration of a "gross untruth concerning the national defense of the United States," and he declared that Eisenhower himself either had been "consciously misleading" the American public or had been badly misinformed when he assured the nation that his defense program was adequate. Alsop claimed that only a "vastly greater national effort" could eliminate the "deadly danger" that the nation would face "during the period the Pentagon calls 'the gap'—the years between 1960 through 1963 or 1964."[14]

Alsop assumed that the Soviet Union would put its new long-range bomber into early production and that the U.S.-manned bomber force would be increasingly vulnerable. The greater disparity between the two countries, however, was in medium- and long-range missiles. Alsop declared that the Soviets would have between "1,000 and 2,000 ballistic missiles with suitable ranges to neutralize or destroy all overseas bases, on which the striking power of our manned bomber force heavily depends." The following table shows the missile "scorecard" he projected for the years from 1959 to 1963.

	U.S. ICBMs	*Soviet ICBMs*
1959	0	100
1960	30	500
1961	70	1,000
1962	130 (plus a few submarine-borne Polaris, perhaps)	1,500
1963	130 (plus more Polaris)	2,000

As for new weapons in development, Alsop accused the administration of "gambling the American future" on the Minuteman missile, which, he wrote, could not "possibly be ready for operational use before the end of 1963 or early 1964." A few more Polaris submarines would not appreciably alter the balance in U.S. favor, he contended.

Accordingly, he predicted that the United States would slip further and further behind the Soviet Union; the "indisputable" effect of the Eisenhower administration's defense policies would be to "allow the Soviets to gain an overwhelming superiority in over-all nuclear striking power." The United States was allowing the Soviets to gain this advantage, he concluded, while the "last chance to save ourselves is slipping through our hands."[15]

Although Alsop stated in his column that his missile scorecard was drawn from classified intelligence sources, his numbers were misleading. They did not match official opinion within the intelligence community as expressed in several national intelligence estimates (NIEs) prepared in late 1957 and early 1958. For example, whereas Alsop alleged that the Soviets would have five hundred ICBMs "in place" by the end of 1960, and as many as two thousand by the end of 1963, the most recent intelligence estimate (SNIE 11-10-57, issued in December 1957) suggested only that the Soviets could have five hundred ICBMs by the end of 1960 and made no predictions for subsequent years.[16]

John F. Kennedy would not have known about these disagreements within the intelligence community, however. He did not have access to classified information, and he did not realize that Soviet society in the late 1950s was a black box nearly impenetrable by Western intelligence. His belief in the missile gap came from public sources, including especially Joe Alsop's writings. As Kennedy could not know the extent to which news accounts had distorted and overstated the nature of the Soviet threat, he, like most Americans, believed that there was sufficient certainty about Soviet aims to warrant concern—and action. He was, therefore, receptive to Alsop's recommendation that he deliver a speech on the floor of the Senate on the subject of the missile gap.[17]

It was natural that Kennedy would learn about the missile gap from Joe Alsop. They were well acquainted with each other. Both lived in Washington's fashionable Georgetown neighborhood, and they appeared at many of the same social gatherings. The young senator respected Alsop's political judgments and valued the favorable publicity the columnist often steered his way. For his part, Alsop viewed Kennedy as a rising political star. Few pundits doubted that Kennedy's political ambitions extended beyond the Bay State, but Joe Alsop believed that he was the likely Democratic nominee for president in 1960. He also believed that the missile gap would be a major issue in that campaign. Alsop was happy to provide his friend with ammunition for the ensuing rhetorical battles.[18]

Kennedy had spoken of the missile gap on previous occasions. He was gearing up for his first Senate reelection campaign when *Sputnik* traced across the evening sky and into the morning headlines. In early November 1957 he charged that "the nation was losing the satellite-missile race with the Soviet Union because of . . . complacent miscalculations, penny-pinching, budget cutbacks, incredibly confused mismanagement, and wasteful rivalries and jealousies."[19] Then, in a speech in Chicago in early December 1957, Kennedy noted that the United States was "behind, possibly as much as several years, in the race for control of outer space and in the development, perfection, and stockpiling of intermediate-range ballistic missiles and long range ballistic missiles."[20]

Kennedy returned to these themes on the afternoon of 14 August 1958. Explicitly prompted by Joe Alsop and encouraged by favorable reviews of James Gavin's recent book, *War and Peace in the Space Age*, Kennedy delivered a major speech on the subject of the missile gap and the need for new measures to enhance U.S. security. The speech was replete with historical references, which had already become a Kennedy trademark. He began with dramatic comparisons to the 1558 British loss of Calais, which represented the last vestige of British power on the continent of Europe. "There is every indication," he declared, "that by 1960 the United States will have lost its Calais—its superiority in nuclear striking power." But Kennedy urged Americans not to despair. The British adjusted to their defeat at Calais with a new military strategy based on supremacy on the seas, and they secured for themselves "new power and new security." Kennedy was confident that the United States could do the same.[21]

Depending heavily upon the arguments of Joe Alsop, James Gavin, and Henry Kissinger, Kennedy eschewed the encouraging words that were typical of Eisenhower's statements about the gap. "We are rapidly approaching that dangerous period," Kennedy explained, "which General Gavin and others have called the 'gap' or the 'missile-lag period.'" Then, quoting directly from Gavin's book, Kennedy noted that during this period of the gap, the nation's "offensive and defensive capabilities will lag so far behind those of the Soviets as to place us in a position of great peril." Still later, Kennedy declared that "discussions of new armaments are not enough—and too late to halt the gap." He predicted that the gap would begin in 1960 and that the following several years would be a period in which "our threats of massive retaliation" and "our exercises in brink-of-war diplomacy will be infinitely less successful."[22]

Kennedy also dealt out his share of economic criticism. Calling Eisenhower's fiscal restraint a sign of complacency, Kennedy charged the president with placing "fiscal security ahead of national security." He then ridiculed Eisenhower for the "appealing shibboleths proclaimed to the nation each year" which held that military security could be obtained within the constraints of the budget. Kennedy argued that "during that period when emphasis was laid upon our economic strength instead of our military strength, we were losing the decisive lead against the Soviet Union in our missile capacity." He warned that the United States had "obtained economic security at the expense of military security" and that this policy would bring "great danger within the next few years."[23]

Averring that he had "never been persuaded" by Eisenhower's views with respect to the economy and defense spending, Kennedy contended that "to emphasize budgetary limitations without regard to our military position was to avoid an inconvenient effort by inviting the disaster that would destroy all budgets and conveniences." "Surely," he continued, "our nation's security overrides budgetary considerations." "Then why," he asked, "can we not realize that the coming years of the gap present us with a peril more deadly than any wartime danger we have ever known?" Kennedy found this all to be "tragically ironic" because "our nation could have afforded, and can afford now, the steps necessary to close the missile gap."[24]

Having placed the blame for the missile gap firmly at the feet of the president, Kennedy then described the steps that would need to be taken in order to reverse the dangerous decline in the nation's defenses. The initial focus, he said, should be on short-range steps to turn the tide immediately. Praising Senators Lyndon Johnson, Stuart Symington, and Henry M. "Scoop" Jackson for their "thoughtful addresses" and "committee actions" on the issues, Kennedy called for more "air tankers to refuel SAC bombers" and more air-to-ground missiles to defend bombers from Soviet interceptors. He urged an expedited program for developing longer-range ICBMs and intermediate-range ballistic missiles, including investment in solid fuels, and he specifically endorsed the Polaris and Minuteman programs. He also called for new continental defense measures, and he argued for the need to reverse what Gavin called the critical cut in military personnel that had begun in 1954.[25]

In the ensuing debate in the Senate, Kennedy's colleagues on the Democratic side of the aisle—including Senators Symington and Jackson—rose to praise his call for more spending on defense in order to close the missile gap. Earlier that day, Symington had aroused the ire of

Republicans when he had had inserted into the *Congressional Record* a series of published reports highly critical of the administration's response to the missile gap. When Kennedy rose later in the day to deliver his speech, he was confronted by an already hostile Republican minority. Several of the Republicans pressed him to define the precise size and scope of his proposed military buildup. For example, Homer Capehart of Indiana asked Kennedy if the nation should spend more for defense. Kennedy replied in the affirmative, but he refused to commit to defining a complete "military program." When Capehart then asked if enough money had been appropriated for defense, Kennedy replied that there had "been insufficient appropriations for the past 6 years, beginning in 1953."[26]

Capehart pressed again, asking Kennedy if defense appropriations should be increased from $40 billion to "perhaps $45 billion or $50 billion." Kennedy refused to discuss specific numbers. Noting that he was not a member of the Armed Services Committee and that he was "therefore not privy to confidential information" that was available to other senators, Kennedy referred instead to "a responsible column appearing in the *Washington Post* and elsewhere" that had predicted Soviet ICBM strength at 500 missiles in 1960; "something like" 1,000 by the end of 1961; and 1,500 in 1962. The article to which he was referring and the numbers he was citing were Joe Alsop's. Kennedy openly conceded that he did not know whether the numbers were true but said he believed that "the Soviet Union knows the answers" and that he thought "it would be well for the United States to know." "In any event," he continued, "we have not done enough."[27]

Republican senator Alexander Wiley of Wisconsin wanted to know how the military buildup would be funded, and he repeatedly asked Kennedy if taxes would have to be increased. Kennedy replied that he was "certain that the funds" could be raised "in order to do the things which must be done." He suggested that the difference could be funded either by tax increases or by deficit spending. Wiley continued his questioning. Concerned that the United States not "crack up our economy with a $12 billion deficit," he again asked if taxes should be increased. Kennedy again demurred, saying only, "I think the effort should be made to close the gap. Whether taxes should be increased now or whether deficit spending should be incurred now is uncertain. But I think the effort should be made to close the gap."[28]

Despite the loud protestations of Capehart and other Senate Republicans, who criticized Kennedy and the Democrats for demeaning the strength of the nation's military and "selling the United States short," Kennedy's speech might have escaped the attention of most observers had it not been for Joe Alsop.[29] In his nationally syndicated column published a few days later, Alsop called Kennedy's speech "one of the most remarkable. . . that this country has heard since the end of the last war," one that "every thoughtful American ought to read and ponder." He also asserted that because Kennedy was not "impeded by . . . access to classified information," he could speak frankly of the need to close the gap.[30] Then, on 18 August, Alsop followed up with his second column on the Kennedy speech in two days, claiming that Kennedy "had spoken no more than the truth . . . with no whit of exaggeration."[31]

In addition to filing these two columns praising Kennedy's courage and wisdom, Alsop went out of his way to bring Kennedy's speech to the attention of other journalists. He sent Richard Rovere, then of the *New Yorker* magazine and a prominent critic of the Eisenhower administration, a synopsis of the events surrounding Kennedy's speech, calling them "the most astonishing Senatorial debate I have ever heard."[32] Three weeks later Alsop tried to convince a skeptical Henry Luce, chairman and publisher of *Time* magazine and a longtime Republican insider, of the need for aggressive action to close the gap.[33] Luce had been introduced to John Kennedy's style of thinking years earlier. He had read the manuscript *Why England Slept,* the book derived from Kennedy's senior thesis at Harvard, after a personal entreaty by Joseph P. Kennedy. Luce had reluctantly acceded to the father's request, but the quality of the manuscript impressed him, and he penned an effusive foreword praising the young Kennedy for having written "such an *adult* book on such a vitally important subject." Since that time, Luce had followed Kennedy's rise to national prominence, a rise no doubt aided by the legitimacy that Luce's foreword had bestowed upon his first book.[34]

Alsop's kind words and deeds were not lost on the ambitious young senator. The missile gap speech, originally Alsop's idea, was a clear political winner, and Kennedy appreciated the wise and timely counsel. He personally thanked the prominent journalist "for your very fine columns and your original suggestion."[35]

The senator was not above self-promotion, however; he did his own part to ensure that his speech, and the subject of the missile gap, would figure prominently in that year's midterm elections. The Democratic National Committee asked Kennedy to distribute copies of the missile gap speech, called "United States Military and Diplomatic Policies—Preparing for the Gap," to all key Democrats, party leaders, and public officials. In a cover letter sent to Governor Abraham Ribicoff of Connecticut, Kennedy expressed his hope that the materials would help prepare Democrats on subjects that would "certainly figure in political debates across the nation." He characterized his speech on the missile gap as an attempt "to summarize the lag in our defense preparedness over the last six years of Republican rule, and the future implications this holds for our military and foreign policies." Although he conceded that some Republicans had objected "to such a warning's being sounded on the floor of the Senate," he was convinced that these were "facts the public needs to know."[36]

In September 1958, Kennedy called attention to his missile gap speech in the pages of *The Reporter* magazine. He explained that he had recently spoken "on the Senate floor about . . . closing the military 'gap,'" which he characterized as a "most pressing technological problem" facing the United States and which, he warned, seemed "certain to continue to grow during the next five years." Beyond the alleged disparity between U.S. and Soviet ICBM development, Kennedy also pointed out that "the other instruments of our military power, including our capacity to wage limited war" must not be overlooked. "Our ability to maintain a balanced ratio of nuclear deterrence and our ability to defy the non-nuclear threat of the Soviet Union and China, especially in the years of 1960–1964," he explained, "must be vigilantly analyzed and corrected in the next two years—not at some future date when the Soviet Union will have consolidated all the military advantages."[37]

At a Democratic National Committee regional conference in Atlantic City, New Jersey, on 10 September 1958, Kennedy focused on what he thought to be the Eisenhower administration's many failings, and he closed with yet another indictment of its military policies. The twin issues of economic decline and military inferiority were inextricably connected. "The Soviets' chief weapon is no longer military but economic—yet we have not revised our own arsenal of weapons accordingly," Kennedy alleged. Then, after repeating elements of his speech on the Senate floor and parts of the *Reporter* article almost verbatim, he confronted those who had accused him of selling the nation short: "I will tell you who is selling America short. It is the little men with little vision who say we cannot afford to build the world's greatest defense against aggression. . . . The men who lack confidence in America are the men who say our people are not up to facing the facts of our missile lag—who say they are not up to bearing the cost of survival."[38]

Kennedy returned to the theme of the missile gap in his Senate reelection campaign. During a speech in Massachusetts in late September 1958, he called for a "step up" in U.S. missile development that would address the danger posed by the "missile lag," which, Kennedy claimed, placed the nation "in a position of grave peril." The Soviets were continuing to increase their power relative to that of the United States, and this, he warned, might "open to them a new shortcut to world domination." Kennedy openly questioned why, in spite of these dangers, the United States was still emphasizing budgets over security.[39]

The missile gap combined with a deep recession in 1958 to deliver a punishing one-two punch against Republicans. The Federal Reserve's interest rate increase of 23 August 1957 failed to arrest rising prices. The Consumer Price Index rose by 2.1 percent during the economic downturn, also exacerbating unemployment, which rose to a high of 7.4 percent.

In mid-February 1958, Eisenhower announced several proposals to counteract the economic downturn. His federal spending initiatives included an increase in federal highway expenditures, an acceleration of defense spending, and modernization of post offices.[40] The actions were not sufficient, however, to turn around the faltering economy before it became a problem for the GOP. Kennedy and his fellow Democrats fixed upon the issue, and it resonated with the electorate. The Democratic Party also capitalized on the public's rising anxiety associated with the Soviet threat, which was made all the more tangible by the presumed missile gap. The depths of popular disenchantment with the president's party were revealed in the midterm elections of 1958, which delivered a stunning victory for the Democrats, who increased their majority in the House by nearly fifty seats and added another sixteen members in the Senate. When the dust had settled, the Democrats held a majority of 292 to 153 in the House, and they outnumbered Republicans by a margin of 65 to 35 in the Senate.[41]

Results in other major elections were no more encouraging for the president's party. Although relative newcomer Nelson Rockefeller was elected governor of New York and a rising star from Arizona named Barry Goldwater was reelected to his second term in the Senate, the GOP lost in other major statewide races, including the gubernatorial race in California, where Edmund G. "Pat" Brown soundly defeated Republican William F. Knowland. Local issues and local candidates certainly affected the Republicans' fortunes. Individual candidates, including Knowland and John Bricker of Ohio, had run on right-to-work platforms that roused organized labor in a concerted effort to defeat them. The GOP was also hurt in farm states by Secretary of Agriculture Ezra Taft Benson's effort to reduce government supports for agriculture.[42] As a national issue, however, the missile gap won the day because it tapped into deeply felt anxieties about both national security and the economy.

Eisenhower had not taken a very active role during the campaign, having bestowed this thankless task on Vice President Nixon. Nevertheless, he was the nominal party leader, and the results of the 1958 elections shook his confidence and made his dealings with Congress even more difficult during the final two years of his presidency.[43] The groundwork for this defeat had been laid in the weeks and months after *Sputnik*. The missile gap was a political winner, and John F. Kennedy, who easily won reelection to the Senate, knew this as well as anyone. He was poised to continue to use the issue in 1959 and beyond.

Prelude to a Presidential Election
—The White House versus Congress

With the Democratic Party more firmly in control of Congress than at any time during Eisenhower's presidency, the debate surrounding the missile gap continued to center on whether it was wise or foolish to dedicate a larger share of the nation's resources to military spending. On 22 November 1958, only a few weeks after the Democrats' sweeping victories, Representative George Mahon, a Democrat from Texas and chair of the House Military Appropriations Subcommittee, blasted the administration for proposing cuts in the army and marine corps despite a congressional mandate that had called for maintaining the number of military personnel at then-current levels. Although the administration was struggling to close an expected $12 billion budget shortfall, Mahon countered that recent Soviet moves made it unsafe for the United States to cut defense spending.[44]

Rowland Evans, who had penned a story on Mahon's opposition for the *New York Herald Tribune,* agreed. Repeating many of Mahon's arguments in an opinion column, Evans claimed that Eisenhower's most recent economy drive seemed almost designed to "install the Democrats in the White House in 1960" because Vice President Richard Nixon would be forced to defend his role within a "do-nothing" executive branch. Evans reported that the economy measures were "stirring up some sharp discord on the Eisenhower team," with one unnamed cabinet member reportedly telling the president that "fiscal retrenchment will have drastic political repercussions in 1960." The "secret debate in the Cabinet," Evans predicted, might "spill out into the open in an embarrassing way before it ends."[45] The internal debate over Eisenhower's spending priorities had indeed spilled out many times, but in the years after *Sputnik,* the missile gap was a useful subtext to this internal battle over the budget that emboldened the president's critics.

Yet throughout 1959 Eisenhower continued in his struggle to contain government spending, just as he had in his earlier years in office. His political opponents fought him every step of the way. For FY 1959 government outlays exceeded projections, and Eisenhower faced a $12.4 billion deficit. In this case the Department of Defense was not the chief culprit in the cost overruns. Although defense spending had exceeded targets by $1.4 billion, this paled in comparison to the cost of civil benefits, which exceeded projections by over 28 percent, and agricultural spending, which came in 41 percent over budget. Eisenhower was determined to balance the final budget of his administration, for FY 1960. In the end he got his way. He bequeathed to his successor a budget with a $1 billion surplus, and *Time* magazine praised him for achieving the "political miracle" of "making economy popular."[46]

This miracle seems all the more remarkable in retrospect given that Eisenhower faced many other challenges in his final two years in office. As difficult as his many tasks would have been in their own right, Eisenhower had to accomplish them with a badly disorganized and inexperienced administration operating amidst the growing turmoil and distraction of an approaching presidential election. The president had lost some of his most trusted and able lieutenants during the first two years of his second term. Secretary of the Treasury George Humphrey, one of Eisenhower's closest advisers, resigned from his post in July 1957. Charles E. Wilson, a politically unpopular but managerially savvy secretary of defense, also departed of his own volition several months later, in October 1957. Then, in October 1958, White House Chief of Staff Sherman Adams resigned from his post after members of Congress and the media raised questions about his past business dealings.[47]

The biggest blow, however, came in early 1959, when Secretary of State John Foster Dulles resigned from his post, only months before losing a battle with lung cancer. This strong-willed and highly intelligent member of the eastern establishment was a perfect number two for a plainspoken Midwesterner like Dwight David Eisenhower. They were a team in many respects, but Dulles never lost sight of his supporting role. In spite of their differences, and there were many, Dulles consistently supported the president in public. In 1956 and 1957, Dulles and Eisenhower repeatedly clashed over questions of national security and foreign policy,[48] but in every instance, Eisenhower's view prevailed, and Dulles's disagreements with the president were carefully concealed from the public and the media.

Although the nature of the Eisenhower-Dulles relationship has become more clear in retrospect, it was lost on many contemporaries. One exception was nationally syndicated columnist Arthur Krock. In

July 1959, Krock recorded that "it was quite a break when John Foster Dulles died," given that "no subordinate was ever more assiduous" in establishing the president's authority. In a meeting with Krock and several other journalists, Eisenhower himself said that Dulles "used to give me little lectures" on the importance of administration officials supporting the president and his policies.[49]

When Eisenhower appointed Christian Herter, a loyal Republican who had been serving as undersecretary of state for two years, to complete Dulles's term, both Dulles and Eisenhower recognized that the president would assume greater responsibility for articulating the administration's position on foreign policy issues. Meanwhile, key State Department deputies whose concerns about the New Look had been voiced in National Security Council (NSC) debates by Dulles but had not surfaced in public knew they would find a receptive audience for their concerns about strategic and military insecurity in the inexperienced and ill-informed Herter.

The difficulty of maintaining a consistent administration message was manifest soon after Dulles's death, in July 1959. One particularly troublesome miscommunication prompted an exasperated Eisenhower to lecture his subordinates on "the need for proper measures, such as John Foster Dulles had consistently employed, to insure [sic] that State Department action and my own thinking were exactly in step." Eisenhower blamed himself in part for the problem, but the message was clear: Dulles had helped to ensure that the State Department's work reflected the president's wishes, and Ike would now have to do that himself.[50] Within this environment of major change at the top of the administration and growing dissatisfaction within the midlevel bureaucracy, Eisenhower would spend as much time trying to convince his own cabinet of the wisdom of his decision to hold down defense expenditures as he did trying to convince a skeptical nation.

Speculative and Misleading Intelligence Estimates

Disagreements within the administration spilled over into the public realm. Eisenhower's critics eagerly seized upon the confusing and contradictory statements made by administration officials to question the adequacy of the nation's defenses. In 1959 and into 1960, concerns over U.S. national security policy were grounded in uncertainty about the Soviet threat.

The missile gap served as rhetorical shorthand for all of these concerns, but there was far more to the debate than a simple disagreement over the number of missiles on both sides. At the same time Secretary of Defense McElroy admitted to the possibility of a gap in ICBMs, he pointed out that there was no, and would be no, deterrent gap. McElroy's statement would have been far more accurate if he had argued that there *was* a deterrent gap—in the U.S.'s favor. The United States possessed a vast array of platforms capable of delivering nuclear warheads to the Soviet Union. These included bombers launched from bases in Europe and Asia and would eventually include shorter-range IRBMs as well. By contrast, the Soviets, who lacked any forward bases in the Western Hemisphere, could reach the United States only with ICBMs or possibly with bombers flying one-way suicide missions.

An overly narrow focus on the number of missiles on each side also understated the qualitative difference between delivery platforms. Here again the United States possessed a tremendous advantage over the Soviets. Bombers were far more reliable than missiles in the late 1950s. The first-generation ICBMs developed by both nations—the U.S. Atlas and the Soviet SS-6 respectively—used highly volatile liquid fuel for propulsion. The earliest models had to be stored above ground and had to be fueled before launch. This made them particularly vulnerable to preemptive attack. By contrast, aircraft armed with nuclear weapons could remain in the air for long periods of time and could even be recalled after an attack order was issued. The forward placement of the American nuclear deterrent was a further qualitative advantage for the United States. American attacking forces launching from overseas bases would have far less distance to travel and were therefore more likely to reach their final destination, and they would do so far more quickly than a comparable attack launched against the United States by the Soviets. Furthermore, with less warning time the Soviets would have fewer opportunities for implementing countermeasures against an incoming attack. Nonetheless, few contemporary observers took heed of the these obvious quantitative and qualitative advantages over the Soviet Union.

Members of the Eisenhower administration repeatedly asserted that there was no deterrent gap in the Soviets' favor, but their arguments were insufficiently compelling to change their critics' conviction that far more was needed in the field of defense and national security. Many commentators focused on the speculative estimates of Soviet ICBM strength issued during the late 1950s and early 1960s to argue that concern over a potential missile gap was warranted in the absence of definitive and conclusive information about the nature of the Soviet ICBM programs.[51]

Conclusive information was sorely lacking while the public assertions about the extent of the missile gap ranged from the fantastic to the hysterical. The official intelligence estimates of 1958 and

1959 are most notable for their cautious tone and their explicit uncertainty. The disparity between the official classified estimates and the unofficial public projections further confused the national security debate. For example, in a long feature article that appeared in *The Reporter* magazine in early January 1959, retired army general Thomas R. Phillips quoted alleged intelligence reports as saying that the Soviets had manufactured about twenty thousand ballistic missiles and had fired more than a thousand of them.[52] Later, when Secretary of Defense McElroy declared that the United States had "no positive evidence" that Russia was ahead in the development of ICBMs, Phillips countered that there was no such thing as "positive evidence" in intelligence reports. Given the confusion surrounding the missile gap, Phillips predicted that senators and representatives were now ready to challenge the man "whom former Secretary of Defense Charles E. Wilson called 'the greatest military expert in the world,' in his own field."[53]

In truth, critics had been challenging Eisenhower for years. The criticisms did intensify, however, in 1959. Senator Symington flatly rejected the administration's claims that the United States was leading the Russians in the development of missiles. On the same day that Eisenhower cast doubts on the existence of a missile gap, Symington countered that the Soviets would lead the United States by a margin of four missiles to one.[54] Dr. Wernher von Braun said during an appearance before the Senate Joint Hearings on Missile and Space Activities that it would take five years, "even with the utmost effort," to catch up with the Soviets. "We are behind them," he continued, "and we have to drive faster than they if we are to catch up with them."[55]

Informed sources disputed these pessimistic figures. For example, in late November 1958, air force general Bernard Schriever, a leading force behind the development of the Atlas, the nation's first operational ICBM, defended Eisenhower's national security program. He declared that the United States had made important gains and that the number of its operational ICBMs might be equivalent to that of the Soviets.[56]

Either way, the exact source of the myriad official and unofficial Soviet missile numbers remains a mystery; hard evidence of Soviet successes or failures was limited. Still, the national intelligence estimate that formed the foundation for the administration's congressional testimony in early 1959, NIE 11-5-58, did report that the Soviets had tested at least four, and perhaps as many as six, missiles with a range of approximately 3,500 nautical miles. On the basis of this data the intelligence community predicted that the Soviets might have as many as 10 "prototype" ICBMs in 1959, or perhaps even in late 1958.[57] While the report projected that there would be between one hundred and five hundred ICBMs in the Soviet arsenal in the coming years, depending upon whether the Soviets chose to embark on a "crash program" to build up their missile strength, the authors hastened to add in a footnote that their numbers were "selected arbitrarily in order to provide some measure of the Soviet capacity to produce and deploy ICBMs." The numbers "do *not*," the authors emphasized, "represent an estimate of probable Soviet requirements or stockpiles."[58] Administration officials returned to this theme time and time again. If nothing else, the widely disparate estimates of Soviet missile strength in 1959 point to the confusion and uncertainty inherent in the intelligence of that era.

Agreement within the intelligence community alone, however, would not have been sufficient to calm the troubled political waters because the controversy remained, at its core, a dispute over spending priorities. The administration chose not to spend money on a crash program to close a presumed gap that was based on presumed Soviet capabilities. What the Soviets *could* do, the administration consistently pointed out, was not the same as what they *would* do. Given the uncertainty, Eisenhower reasoned, the wiser course was that of moderation.

The president's most fervent critics believed exactly the opposite, repeatedly accusing him of deliberately neglecting the nation's defenses. Consider the line of questioning used by Senator Symington during McElroy's testimony before the Joint Committee on Missile and Space Activities in late January 1959. When the secretary of defense admitted that the Soviets would likely do more than the United States in the field of ICBM development, Symington pounced. Paraphrasing McElroy's statement for effect, the senator asked whether the Eisenhower administration was "voluntarily passing over to the Russians production superiority in the ICBM missile field because we believe that our capacity to retaliate with other weapons is sufficient to permit them that advantage despite the great damage that we know we would suffer if they instigated an attack." McElroy replied by admitting that his own words would not be "very much different from what" Symington had said, although he weakly noted that he would "modify the expression a little bit."[59]

Other key members of the administration attempted to make the case for restraining defense spending given the uncertain nature of the Soviet threat, and they repeatedly were caught in rhetorical traps.

For example, before the House Defense Appropriations Subcommittee on 23 January 1959, General Nathan Twining, the chairman of the Joint Chiefs of Staff, admitted that "according to our intelligence now, if they do what we think they can do, they will have more than we have for a while. There is no question about it."[60]

Then, on 4 February 1959, McElroy explained that the Soviets would have more ICBMs than the United States if the Russians used their full production capabilities. The secretary stressed that the administration did not know whether the Soviets would exercise these capabilities, but, he continued, "we are assuming that they probably will."[61] McElroy reiterated this view two days later. Congressman Samuel Stratton of New York asked McElroy if it would be accurate to say that the Soviets would have more ICBMs than the United States and that this was "the result of a deliberate decision on our part not to utilize our full ICBM capacity." In his reply, McElroy agreed that there was a conscious decision on the part of the United States not to build more ICBMs, but he disagreed with Stratton's contention that the Soviets would have more ICBMs than the United States: "We do not say that they will have this. We say they can have this."[62] McElroy later reiterated that the administration did not intend "to match, missile for missile, in the ICBM category, the Russian capability in the next couple of years."[63]

Although some members of Congress were impressed by the administration's forthright testimony, Senator Kennedy locked horns with Joint Chiefs of Staff chair Twining during his appearance before the Committee on Foreign Relations in late January 1959. A few weeks earlier, W. Barton Leach, a professor from Harvard Law School who advised the air force chief of staff and who had previously worked in the Truman administration, had counseled Kennedy to keep hammering away at the administration in an effort to discredit Eisenhower's concern with limiting defense expenditures. When Kennedy questioned the validity of the administration's predictions about the missile gap, an exasperated Twining again explained the importance of the range of weapons available in the U.S. arsenal. Kennedy was not convinced. After the hearing, he and other Democrats complained that the Eisenhower administration did not comprehend the gravity of the Soviet threat.[64]

The intelligence community was unable to reach consensus on the nature and extent of the Soviet missile program; projections about Soviet future missile strength were speculative, at best. But officials within the Eisenhower administration were equally tentative in their statements about the number of missiles in the *U.S. arsenal*. On 26

January 1959, McElroy told Representative Mahon of Texas that the United States was "about even with the Soviet Union in our ability to produce ICBMs."[65] Just over a week later, however, McElroy admitted in testimony before the House Armed Services Committee that the nation did not, at that time, possess any ICBMs. His subsequent assertions—that there would be "a few" ICBMs in the U.S. arsenal by July of that year, and "a few more" by December 1959—did little to calm skeptics' fears.[66]

When congressional leaders called on the administration to match the Soviets missile for missile, Deputy Secretary of Defense James Douglas complained that it seemed as though Congress was "providing for a wholly unnecessary overkill" by focusing on the number of missiles that the Soviets were expected to have without due consideration of the breadth and depth of the U.S. strategic arsenal.[67] Two days later, when pressed by Congressman Mahon, Douglas conceded that the Soviets would be ahead of the United States in ICBM production and that this lead might be considerable. Yet he stressed that he did not think that this lead would be important. When Mahon asked Douglas, "If you had the money and the ability to do so, would you close the ICBM gap between the United States and the Soviet Union now?" Douglas answered that although he believed it important to close the missile gap at some point, he "would not try to do it in the 1960 period with the 1960 budget." Air Force Chief of Staff Thomas D. White seconded this view. The crucial point throughout this testimony, driven home by Michigan congressman Gerald R. Ford, was that of timing: it was important to close the gap, but it did not have to be done all at once.[68]

The Media Weighs In

Prominent media outlets varied in their assessments. Editors at the *Boston Herald* surveyed the administration's arguments and the claims of the critics, then declared on 6 February 1959 that the United States had surrendered to the Soviets.[69] The day before, editors at the *New York Herald Tribune* had expressed a very different conclusion, praising the administration for its "balanced program which can maintain sufficient deterrence without going hog-wild" on missile production.[70] The staff at *U.S. News and World Report* appeared to agree. In bold headlines it dismissed the "big fuss about missiles," and in a two-page spread complete with pictures of the array of weapons in the American arsenal, it outlined "why the U.S. still holds the edge over Soviet Russia."[71] But a *Washington Post* editorial published that same day expressed worry that "some new budget drive" might cut into U.S. efforts to "regain parity" with the Soviets in ICBMs. The *Washington Post* editors argued that they were not alone and pointed to the "many members of Congress, including some of the Administration's stanchest [*sic*] Republican supporters," who were "seriously worried by the missile numbers game."[72]

The debate continued to rage in early 1959, with knowledgeable outsiders, such as Lyndon Johnson, Symington, and von Braun, arguing that there was a missile gap,[73] while knowledgeable insiders, including Twining, McElroy, and the president himself, countered either that there was no gap or that the gap was not militarily significant.[74] Some objective observers attempted to draw a balanced picture by laying out both arguments.[75] Others recognized the deeper economic issues associated with the debate.[76] Many people believed that there was, in a narrow sense, a missile gap between the United States and the Soviet Union—that the Soviets did have more ICBMs than the United States—but there were competing interpretations about whether that gap threatened U.S. security interests.

The doubts lingered, grounded especially in the Democrats' suspicion that the Republican president was deliberately downplaying the nature of the Soviet threat to deflect criticism of his defense budget. One skeptical observer questioned how "it happened that the White House revised its estimates of Soviet missile capabilities downward just as it was submitting its balanced budget to the Congress." Although McElroy had flatly denied that politics had anything to do with the revision of the estimates, Symington and others thought this coincidence to be too neat.[77]

McElroy was not alone in arguing that the missile gap had been overstated. Other experts stepped forward to make the administration's case. In September 1959 Herbert York, the Defense Department's director of research and engineering, said in an interview with *U.S. News and World Report* that while the Russians "were very much ahead of the United States at one time," he hoped and he believed that the United States was closing the gap. While York refused to predict when the gap would ultimately be closed, he did explain that the United States had surpassed the Soviets in guidance and accuracy. He also pointed out that the United States was "probably . . . somewhat better off" with respect to the number of warheads in its nuclear arsenal.[78] York repeated these claims less than a month later, conceding that the Soviets led the United States in space research, but arguing that the two nations were "roughly equal in the development" of ICBMs.[79]

Joseph Alsop disagreed. In his interpretation of York's statement about the nature of the strategic balance, he alleged that the United States continued to lag well behind the Soviets. When York had claimed that the U.S. and Soviet ICBM development programs were "essentially in the same position," Alsop called York's statement an "offense against human decency." To back up his claims, Alsop published what he said was "the best official forecast" of U.S. and Soviet missile development:

1960	U.S. 30 ICBMs	versus	U.S.S.R. 100 ICBMs	
1961	U.S. 70 ICBMs	versus	U.S.S.R. 500 ICBMs	
1962	U.S. 130 ICBMs	versus	U.S.S.R. 1,000 ICBMs	
1963	U.S. 130 ICBMs	versus	U.S.S.R. 1,500 ICBMs[80]	

But just as Alsop's missile scorecard of August 1958 grossly overstated the gap, his numbers in this column of October 1959 failed to match the intelligence community's best estimates. The official national intelligence estimate still in force (NIE 11-5-58, dated 19 August 1958) had estimated that the Soviets could have as many as one hundred ICBMs in 1960 on the basis of the conclusion that they would achieve their first operational capability "some time during calendar year 1959" or perhaps in "the latter part of 1958." On the basis of these speculative estimates, the analysts projected that the Soviets would have perhaps as many as five hundred ICBMs "some time in 1961, or at the latest 1962."[81]

Since that time, however, intelligence analysts had found no evidence of a Soviet crash building program, and they were therefore in the process of downgrading their earlier estimates. The draft national intelligence estimate that would be published less than a month after Alsop's column (NIE 11-5-59, dated 3 November 1959), projected that the first Soviet ICBMs would be operational by 1 January 1960.[82] Subsequent estimates published in late 1959 and early 1960 would further lower projections of the number of Soviet missiles. Perhaps anticipating criticism from those with deeper knowledge, Alsop dismissed the accuracy of the official estimates with a rhetorical wave of the hand. Calling it "self-deluding" to "use the national intelligence estimates as . . . absolute measures of Soviet performance," Alsop worried that the intelligence services' susceptibility to a "Soviet deception plan" would lead the United States to "underrate Russian ICBM power until a grand surprise can be sprung and a brutal ultimatum can be sent."[83]

As often as not, the participants in the missile gap debate of 1959 simply talked past one another. To those who charged that the United States was risking a missile gap and must spend more, others replied that the total package of defense spending was more than sufficient to deter the Soviet Union and that it would be risky to spend too much on defense. As the controversy raged in Congress and in warring headlines, the public was generally not convinced that it was a major issue, but several prominent politicians with aspirations for higher office—including Lyndon Johnson, Stuart Symington, and John F. Kennedy—intended to ride the missile gap to victory.

The New Look under Assault

The debate over the missile gap was not confined to Washington, D.C. Leading intellectuals continued to question Ike's strategic judgment, and their doubts often centered on the gap. One such critic was Rand analyst and noted expert on nuclear strategy Bernard Brodie. In his book *Strategy in the Missile Age,* published in 1959, Brodie advocated continued commitment to nuclear deterrence, with particular emphasis on the survivability of a nuclear second strike. Brodie made a comprehensive military and strategic argument for vigorous nuclear deterrence, but he disputed the Eisenhower administration's contention that such a strategy made economic sense. He argued that the nation must also develop and maintain its ability to fight and win nonnuclear, limited wars. Brodie conceded that this would require "quite considerable funds beyond those already provided," and he explicitly rejected the notion that the economy could not support considerably more defense spending, as, in his words, "persons who have no competence for making such a judgment" had argued.

"Very few if any economists," Brodie asserted, "would support the proposition that the United States could not safely spend more than 10 per cent of its gross national product on defense." Later he wrote, "Military spending would have a serious adverse effect on the economy only if it seriously cut into investment for the civilian economy or caused an inflation rapid enough to have self-intensifying effects."[84] In the late 1950s Brodie's arguments accorded both with the dominant economic theory and with many of the political critiques of Eisenhower's New Look strategy, and they found favor with those hoping to blow the lid off of Eisenhower's defense budget.

Another Rand analyst, Albert Wohlstetter, eschewed explicitly economic arguments, but his policy prescriptions would have had the same budgetary consequences as Brodie's because he also called for increasing both nuclear and nonnuclear forces. In his classic essay "The Delicate Balance of Terror," published in the January 1959 issue of the journal *Foreign Affairs,* Wohlstetter stressed that nuclear deterrence was neither automatic nor easy. It was, however, essential to American security. He urged that in order to retain a viable second-strike capability, which was the very essence of deterrence, the United States must provide greater protection for its nuclear forces and must expand the missile and bomber programs to foster greater diversity among delivery systems. He expressed concern about the vulnerability of U.S. forward bases, noting their broader geopolitical importance.

While Wohlstetter stressed the importance of deterrence, he also rejected the view that deterrence was "in itself an adequate strategy," and he called for greater measures to "meet limited aggression, especially with more advanced conventional weapons."[85] Wohlstetter's article presented to the public the same arguments he had been making in confidential circles for years. Kennedy had an advance copy of the piece when he delivered his missile gap speech in August 1958, and he explicitly referred to the "balance of terror" when making his case for a substantial increase in military spending.

Another prominent critic of the New Look, retired army general Maxwell Taylor, joined Brodie, Wohlstetter, and others in late 1959 with the publication of his book *The Uncertain Trumpet,* a critique of U.S. national security policy that includes specific references to the missile gap. A West Point graduate who had served with the 82nd Airborne Division and had later led the 101st Airborne during World War II, Taylor had succeeded Matthew Ridgway as army chief of staff in 1955. Taylor was one of the most celebrated military leaders of his time and was well-connected politically, but these factors notwithstanding, he repeatedly clashed with the commander in chief. His outspoken criticisms of the New Look became increasingly vocal in the wake of the launch of *Sputnik,* and he resigned his post in the spring of 1959. He continued to criticize Eisenhower's defense program after his retirement.

Taylor later became one of the most important military advisers in the Kennedy administration, and he is often credited with coining the phrase *flexible response,* which later became synonymous with that administration's defense program, but he was not an avid Kennedy supporter in the years leading up to the election of 1960. The views he expressed in *The Uncertain Trumpet* were exclusively his own, and he presented them to the nation as a guide for the next presidential administration—whether it be Republican or Democratic.[86]

In *The Uncertain Trumpet,* Taylor echoed the sentiments of Ridgway and Gavin that the army had unfairly borne the brunt of defense budget cuts and that a more diversified capability to fight limited wars was needed. While all three men criticized Eisenhower's insistence on holding down defense expenditures, Taylor went one step further by charging that determination of U.S. national security strategy had become no more than an "incidental by-product of the administrative processes of the defense budget." Taylor called instead for "a scientific budget formulation directed at supporting requirements with all of the resources available for national defense." Taylor recognized that such a shift in policy would require a considerable realignment of national resources. Thus when he urged a 20 percent increase in total military spending, he conceded that the increase would require sacrifices by all Americans, including the payment of higher taxes, in order to enable the nation to "get over this dangerous period."[87]

A number of prominent magazines and journals reviewed Taylor's book. The *Christian Science Monitor* declared that "of all the voices raising questions recently about the wisdom of the Eisenhower administration's defense policies, General Taylor's most deserves a hearing."[88] The British journal *The Spectator* noted that Taylor spoke with the "authority of a recent Chief of Staff of the U.S. Army, and without the limitations which law and convention would impose upon a British retired soldier in a similar position." The article praised Taylor for his "important contribution to a debate which, for all its horrific implications, should be the concern of all serious citizens on both sides of the Atlantic."[89] Another leading expert on military matters, Jack Raymond of the *New York Times,* noted that the publication of Taylor's book was timed to coincide with the opening of Congress "in the hope that it might trip off a great debate on national security in the final year of the Eisenhower Administration." As Douglas Kinnard observed years later, "it did that and more."[90]

Eisenhower versus the Military

Besieged by his critics and increasingly isolated even within his own administration, Eisenhower hoped that the active-duty military leaders would speak to him of their concerns frankly and privately, rather than waiting to air their complaints publicly. He knew that these men would be called before Congress and asked for their personal views about the defense budget. Legislators would ask them about their original budget requests in the hopes of exposing the White House's penchant for cutting military expenses. In an attempt to forestall such criticisms, Eisenhower urged the chiefs to come see him whenever they wanted to in order that they might "find a program in which all would believe." Then they could appear before Congress and the American people with unity.[91]

Ike had been concerned about the public airing of disagreements within his administration for years. He had suffered through Matthew Ridgway's criticisms largely in silence, but when the chief of staff crossed the line in 1955, the president pointed out to congressional leaders that Ridgway was presenting an overly parochial point of view.[92] Ridgway had still been in uniform when he first went public with his dissent, but Eisenhower believed that an officer's duty to support the civilian chain of command did not stop after retirement. Maxwell Taylor, who as chief of staff had been even more outspoken than Ridgway in his criticisms of the New Look, did not share Eisenhower's point of view. As a private citizen, he felt no obligation to support the president. The publication of *The Uncertain Trumpet*, therefore, posed a special challenge for Eisenhower.

But retired officers were not Eisenhower's only problem; he still had to contend with those still in uniform. The military's persistent criticisms of the budgetary limitations of the New Look grew even more strident. When Secretary of Defense McElroy met with the president in November 1959, he expressed his worry about holding the defense budget to $41 billion as Eisenhower had specified. McElroy's concerns did not fall on deaf ears, but the president remained convinced that his proposed defense budget was sufficient. The president told McElroy that the correct balance could be found "only if the Congressional committees want to do what is right, rather than make political attacks."[93]

Two guiding principles continued to govern Eisenhower's actions and words during these tumultuous months in late 1959 and early 1960. First, in spite of what his critics argued, Eisenhower still believed that deficit spending was a sign of weakness, and he did not think the public would support military programs if the tax burden needed to support higher defense spending became too onerous. More important, even as Eisenhower became increasingly concerned about the devastating effects of a global nuclear war, he believed that the likelihood of such a war occurring was becoming more and more remote, and he was determined to ensure that it remained so. According to Campbell Craig, "the avoidance of a thermonuclear war with the Soviet Union" had become the primary objective of Eisenhower's presidency as early as 1956. Robert Bowie and Richard Immerman argue that this had been Eisenhower's primary objective dating back to 1953.[94]

Eisenhower had taken Nikita Khrushchev at his word when the Soviet leader told him, "We are coming to the time where neither side can afford to declare or initiate missile warfare." The president simply did not "believe that when the Soviets got all their missiles ready, they would turn them loose against us." Eisenhower related to the NSC that Khrushchev had told him, "We know you won't start a war," and that Khrushchev had been emphatic about "stopping Russian plant production."[95] Accordingly, the president continued to stress nuclear deterrence. "We must keep certain missiles so that neither side can bluff the other," he told McElroy in November 1959. "Beyond that the need on both sides is to disarm."[96] As far as Eisenhower was concerned, the stability and survivability of the nation's nuclear deterrent was already assured.

The president stressed these themes when he called the chiefs of the military services together at Augusta, Georgia, in late 1959. He was seeking still more reductions in defense spending. The Joint Chiefs of Staff chairman, air force general Nathan Twining, volunteered that costs were increasing faster than anticipated, making continued cuts even harder to accomplish. Eisenhower was unmoved. He turned to Chief of Naval Operations Arleigh Burke and to Army Chief of Staff Lyman L. Lemnitzer and urged them to proceed with further force reductions by focusing on "things that have become simply a matter of habit."[97]

The nation's economy was threatened by burdensome defense spending, Eisenhower explained. He knew that everyone was concerned about the nation's security and safety, but he appealed for everyone to look at the defense establishment afresh, since changes in technology had changed defense needs. For Eisenhower the issue revolved around "putting too much money in certain things," and he urged the service chiefs to approach the question of what "needs to be done within a pattern that will keep our economy healthy and expanding."[98]

One specific difference of opinion within the administration revolved around the B-70, the next-generation bomber. The B-70 was the darling of air force generals. In the November meeting, Air Force Chief of Staff General Thomas D. White offered a spirited defense of the bomber. Missiles, he said, could not be relied on in every respect because they had not yet been tested with nuclear warheads. Further, White explained, missiles could not be recalled once launched.

The president was not persuaded by such arguments. The B-70 left Eisenhower "cold in terms of making military sense." He doubted that the plane could be put into production in less than eight years—"too far into a period in which the major destruction would come from missiles." Eisenhower was "convinced that the age of aircraft . . . is fast coming to a close," and he saw the fight over the B-70 as yet another instance of people trying to hang onto "the old forms of warfare too long." He argued that "talk of bombers in the missile age" was akin to talk "about bows and arrows at the time of gunpowder."

When White countered that the continuation of the bomber program would be worthwhile because the nation would gain from having different systems for attack, Eisenhower retorted that in ten years each nation's missile capacity alone would be sufficient to destroy both countries "many times over," and he despaired over the chiefs' apparent willingness to go "overboard in different ways to do the same thing." The duplication inherent in the B-70 program, he said, was the very kind of opportunity for savings that he had hoped the chiefs would find. His arguments failed to convince the assembled brass: when he informally polled the group, only Admiral Burke opposed extended funding for the bomber project.[99]

Eisenhower found that the chiefs' civilian bosses—the secretaries of the army, navy, and air force—were equally committed to duplication and redundancy within the nation's weapon systems. So too were many of the president's other advisers. For example, Herbert York, speaking on behalf of science adviser George Kistiakowsky, urged the president to go forward with the B-70 "even if there is no good military reason" because it was technically sound. A frustrated Eisenhower replied that he was not interested in building an aircraft for civilian uses. For him, the only meaningful issue was the strength of the nation's deterrent force. Accordingly, he said, "If the Soviets think the B-70 is more effective than missiles, then it has value. If they do not, it is valueless."[100]

As troubling as such internal squabbles were for Eisenhower, he was most concerned about "undercover sniping" at the defense program. He explicitly directed the service secretaries to back a uniform program that everyone could support. When Eisenhower informed Army Secretary Wilbur Brucker in November 1959 that he intended to stick to his plan for reducing the number of personnel in the National Guard and Reserves, Brucker responded that some members of Congress intended to fight him on that issue. The president did not back down. Conceding that the question revolved around "how much to fight for what is . . . right, or how much to bow to expediency," Eisenhower intended to "stick to what he thought was right" even as he realized that he would probably be defeated. He complained that "Congress would take things out of the program that he wanted and put things in that he did not want."[101]

A New Secretary of Defense and a New Intelligence Estimate

Assailed by his critics in Congress and the media, an exasperated Eisenhower sought out new civilian leadership for the Pentagon. He hoped to find someone who could more effectively communicate the administration's position on defense and national security. It was the third such change at the top in three years. On 2 December 1959, Thomas S. Gates was appointed to replace Neil McElroy as secretary of defense. One of Gates's first tasks was to convince the president of the need for more ICBMs for the U.S. arsenal. In December 1958 Eisenhower had approved a substantial increase in the number of ICBM squadrons from the planned thirteen (nine Atlas and four Titan) to a total of twenty (nine Atlas and eleven Titan) and an increase in the Polaris program from six to nine submarines. One year later the Department of Defense was requesting still further increases in all three programs. When Gates appeared before a meeting of the NSC in January 1960, the Pentagon was calling for twenty-seven ICBM squadrons—for a total of 270 operational missiles—and an additional three Polaris missile submarines, bringing the total complement to twelve.[102] Eisenhower deemed these increases to be reasonable and responsible and accepted Gates's recommendations without objection.[103]

The next item on the NSC's agenda raised new questions about the need for more nuclear weapons. Throughout the missile gap controversy, Eisenhower had asserted that existing nuclear weapons programs constituted a sufficient deterrent force. The president believed that Soviet leaders would never risk a first strike against the United States knowing that such an attack would likely result in their own annihilation. Eisenhower had also always doubted pessimistic intelligence reports that the Soviets were engaged in a crash program to build nuclear missiles at a time when a more promising solid-fuel-powered alternative would soon render such first-generation weapons obsolete. A similar belief that the Soviets were engaged in a crash weapons building program, he frequently pointed out, had created the illusory bomber gap in 1955.[104] Further, during face-to-face meetings with Eisenhower in September 1959, Soviet premier Nikita Khrushchev had explained why the Soviets would not agree to an arms control pact at that time: the United States possessed an overwhelming strategic advantage over the Soviets, and he would not agree to anything that would effectively freeze this American superiority into place.[105]

Eisenhower's confidence about the true nature of the Soviet buildup was bolstered yet again by classified intelligence—including photos from the U-2 surveillance aircraft. The U-2 program had failed to locate missile construction or testing sites in large numbers. While some within the intelligence community were reluctant to give much weight to so-called negative intelligence (that is, the intelligence agencies' *inability* to find ICBMs in great numbers), the absence of hard evidence of Soviet ICBM deployments aligned with Eisenhower's own beliefs about the limited nature of the Soviets' missile buildup. These findings were reflected in the new intelligence estimates prepared in the autumn of 1959, in which projections of Soviet ICBM strength were revised substantially downward from those in previous reports.[106] CIA Director Allen Dulles presented drafts of these soon-to-be-released national intelligence estimates (NIE 11-4-59 and 11-8-59) to the National Security Council for the first time on 7 January 1960.

The past intelligence estimates, which had been based on what the Soviets were capable of doing rather than on what they would probably do, had speculated that the Soviets had one hundred ICBMs in their current inventory and that they would have as many as five hundred by mid-1961.[107] Those estimates had formed the basis for McElroy's claim in early 1959 that the Soviets could achieve a three-to-one advantage in ICBMs over the United States in the coming years. Although McElroy had hastened to add that he did not believe the Soviets *would* have such an advantage, the administration's critics claimed that McElroy had projected a substantial missile gap.

Since that time, however, intelligence analysts had found no hard evidence that the Soviets had built as many missiles as their capabilities would allow. The new estimates reflected these findings and concluded that there was "virtually . . . no missile gap." Gates recognized that the United States had "a very strong deterrent force" if the estimates were correct. Although this was good news, the newly appointed secretary of defense realized that the administration "was in a difficult position" with regard to its upcoming testimony before Congress because many members of Congress would question the sudden change. CIA Director Dulles agreed, predicting that the new estimates would evoke many questions in the upcoming session of Congress.[108]

The president favored a direct approach. He believed that in its testimony before Congress the administration should stress that there was no evidence that the Soviets had launched a crash program for the development of missiles. Vice President Nixon continued that thought. The missile gap in the earlier intelligence estimate, Nixon observed, had "resulted from an assumption that the Soviets would do all they were capable of doing and would make no mistakes . . . and from the further assumption that we would not do all we were capable of doing and would make a number of mistakes." Such assumptions were flawed, and the new intelligence estimates reflected a clearer understanding of the actual scope of the Soviets' ICBM program.[109] While the president believed that the strength and credibility of the U.S. deterrent force was far more important than the new estimates of Soviet missile numbers, he would need the new NIE numbers to back up his defense budget before Congress. However, as the NSC soon learned, these intelligence numbers reflected a jumble of competing interpretations, differing assumptions, and, in Allen Dulles's own words, "guesswork," particularly for the period after 1961.[110] The consensus opinion of the United States Intelligence Board, as expressed in the new national intelligence estimate, predicted Soviet ICBM strength at 50 in mid-1960 and as high as 560 by 1963. Substantial disagreement, however, was revealed in a series of dissenting footnotes contributed by Major General James H. Walsh, the air force's assistant chief of staff for intelligence. Whereas a majority of the members of the board predicted that the Soviets would have between 450 and 560 ICBMs in their inventory, and between 350 and 450 on launchers by mid-1963, the air force predicted that the Soviets would have 800 missiles and 640 on launchers in the same period.[111]

The air force estimate was predicated on a substantially different reading of Soviet intentions from that of a majority of the board, a panel that included representatives from the army, the navy, and the air force. In spite of the persistent efforts of General Walsh and his staff to convince them otherwise, the majority had expressed their own opinion in the text of NIE 11-8-59, concluding that the Soviets' primary goal in attaining "a substantial ICBM capability at an early date" was "to provide a substantial deterrent and pre-emptive attack capability." This interpretation was consistent, the report continued, "with the present deliberate and orderly tempo of the Soviet ICBM test-firing program, with current Soviet military doctrine," and with the Soviets' "observed policy" of maintaining balance "between the several branches of their military."[112] In other words, the majority of the members on the USIB concluded, as Eisenhower had consistently maintained, there was—and there had been—no crash program to build ICBMs within the Soviet Union.

Contrast this assessment with the air force's dissenting views. The same assumptions that had governed the U.S. estimates of Soviet intentions since the end of World War II resonated in Walsh's lengthy dissent. He did not believe that Soviet behavior warranted "the judgment that their objectives would be satisfied by attainment of only substantial deterrence and pre-emptive attack capability." Rather, "the Soviet rulers are endeavoring to attain . . . a military superiority over the United States" so as to "enable them either to force their will on the United States through threat of destruction" or launch an attack so "the United States as a world power would cease to exist." "Conceptual levels of deterrence" would be insufficient if, as Walsh believed, "the Soviet leaders intended . . . to exploit their capabilities in political offensives."[113]

Because the majority opinion of the national intelligence estimate echoed Eisenhower's own beliefs, the president rejected the air force's pessimistic claims. He could not, however, keep a lid on their dissent: the assumptions underlying the air force estimate had already been circulated widely. Within weeks, their opposing point of view would move from the footnotes of classified government reports to the front pages and headlines of the nation's leading newspapers.

The president had always been concerned about leaks, and the arrival of the new year—an election year—gave him reason to be more concerned. Political adversaries could easily use perceived failures in any weapons program, no matter how small, against the administration. Such concerns filtered down through all layers of the administration. Even Eisenhower's politically insulated science adviser George Kistiakowsky fretted over a particularly critical General Accounting Office study of the Nike-Zeus antiballistic missile program because he feared that if the report were made public it would "provide ammunition to those who choose to attack your Administration irresponsibly."[114]

Eisenhower was most concerned, however, about the distortions inherent in the selective reading—and the selective leaking—of highly classified intelligence reports and of the proceedings of National Security Council meetings. It was here that the air force's spirited dissent posed the greatest threat to the White House's efforts to set the record straight on the missile gap.

For example, a front-page story in the *Washington Post* published only days after the NSC meeting of 7 January 1960 correctly reported that the president had chosen to expand U.S. missile programs "by about a third," but the same article cited inflated estimates of presumed Soviet missile strength that were based largely on the previous flawed assessments. *Post* reporter John G. Norris wrote that "some estimates" showed the Soviets with "well over 1000 ICBMs by 1963," but even the air force's most pessimistic estimates in the new NIE, reported only in the footnotes, had predicted Soviet missile strength at only eight hundred by 1963.[115] Less than a month later, the *New York Times* reported that there was "clear evidence that the Russians have superiority in intercontinental ballistic missiles," but the most current intelligence estimates stated that there was "no direct evidence" of Soviet ICBM deployment.[116]

The press also focused on military spending, and here again the distortions and oversimplifications posed problems for the White House. In his 13 January article for the *Post,* Norris claimed that the Eisenhower administration's proposed missile increases were to be paid for through reductions in the B-70 and navy construction programs, even though such issues had not been discussed during the NSC meeting. An Associated Press article that appeared alongside Norris's missile article provided only circumstantial evidence for such a claim when it reported that the navy had postponed construction on five warships "because of lack of funds." Both articles lent considerable weight to the arguments of those who had said for years that Eisenhower's budgetary restrictions were forcing painful trade-offs in the development of the nation's weapon systems. Implied, but left unsaid, was that such trade-offs weakened the nation's overall defense posture.[117]

The unhappy task of informing the commander in chief of the Norris story fell to presidential aide Gordon Gray. When Gray told Eisenhower the news, the president responded, in Gray's words, with the "most vigorous irritation." Gray then suggested that the cabinet receive a missile briefing similar to that presented to the NSC so all parties within the administration could speak "from the same set of facts and conclusions." Gray was certain that the leak had not come from the NSC, and given that Norris, who covered defense matters for the *Post,* had broken the story, he was "pretty sure" that the leak had come from the Pentagon. Eisenhower asked his assistant to convey his "deep concern" to Secretary of Defense Gates.[118]

Gates already had more than enough to worry about. He expected a tough line of questioning when he appeared before a series of congressional panels to present the administration's defense budget for FY 1961, which was supported by the new intelligence estimates. He got something worse than that. Just as Eisenhower, Nixon, and Allen Dulles had predicted during the NSC meeting on 7 January, Congress and the media greeted the new estimates with great skepticism, prompting yet another round of missile gap charges and countercharges.

The Beginning of the 1960 Presidential Campaign

These controversies within the administration developed amidst a presidential campaign that had begun years earlier but became official in January 1960. Using his victory in the senatorial election of 1958, one of the most lopsided in Massachusetts history, as a springboard for his presidential ambitions, John F. Kennedy had begun planning for a presidential run in early 1959. By the turn of the new decade Gallup polls showed Kennedy leading the Democrats; he was ahead of runner-up Adlai Stevenson, the party's nominee in the past two elections, by twelve percentage points.[119] Few insiders were surprised when Kennedy came forward to announce his candidacy for the presidency before a crowd of supporters on 2 January 1960 in Washington, D.C.

Kennedy's campaign announcement stressed many of the same themes that he had been speaking of for years. The presidency, "the most powerful office in the Free World," he said, held the key for a "more vital life for our people" and a "more secure life" around the globe. The most crucial decisions of this century—"how to end the burdensome arms race, where Soviet gains already threaten our very existence . . . and how to give direction to our traditional moral purpose, awakening every American to the dangers and opportunities that confront us"—would have to be made in the next four years. He closed with a prediction that the American people would help the nation to fulfill "a noble and historic role as the defender of freedom in a time of maximum peril."[120]

Kennedy was not the first presidential hopeful to declare his candidacy, and he was not the only Democrat actively engaged in a presidential campaign. Other likely candidates, including Lyndon Johnson and Stuart Symington, were staging stealth campaigns aimed at securing delegates for the Democratic convention without having to slug it out in the primaries. But Kennedy had one important challenger. Minnesotan Hubert Humphrey had announced his intention to run for president a week before Kennedy. Humphrey was a tireless campaigner and an eloquent orator. His bread-and-butter issues pertained to the economy, civil rights, and federal aid for education and urban areas. He enjoyed the support of northern liberals, a core Democratic constituency in several primary states.

Kennedy planned to counter Humphrey's strategy with a better funded, better organized campaign. On the issues he deliberately downplayed his differences with Humphrey by saying he and his opponent were both liberal democrats. Kennedy's message and his emphasis, however, were different. Running slightly to the right of Humphrey, Kennedy hoped to gain the support of at least some conservative southern Democrats by emphasizing foreign policy and defense issues and by downplaying talk of civil rights during his campaign.[121]

Kennedy's strategy was immediately apparent. A front-page article in the *Washington Post* by reporter Chalmers Roberts highlighted Kennedy's views on the budget and defense. Kennedy's prepared remarks stressed the arms race and the rebuilding of the country's stature in science and education. Roberts also noted that in the question-and-answer session following the announcement of his candidacy, the senator had declared that relations with Russia and Red China would be "the top campaign issue." In response to another question Kennedy proclaimed that the lame duck administration's proposed new military budget was too low by "a substantial margin." Regarding the missile gap, Kennedy added that Russia would have an important and significant "missile lead," but he expressed hope that this would not be decisive.[122] The following day, on the NBC television program *Meet the Press,* Kennedy repeated this theme, arguing that the United States was "going to be faced with a missile gap which will make the difficulties of negotiating with the Soviet Union and the Chinese in the 1960s extremely difficult."[123]

Foreign policy and defense, then, would be two of the main issues for the leading Democratic candidate for the presidency. Kennedy was expected to hammer away at the administration for its perceived complacency in the face of the missile gap, and he would criticize Eisenhower and the rest of his administration—including vice president and likely Republican nominee Richard Nixon—for allowing American prestige to wane.

On the day Kennedy announced his candidacy, Gates was preparing to sell the administration's defense program for FY 1961 to a skeptical Congress. The man most responsible for responding to Kennedy's charges had been in his position for exactly one month, and he had yet to be confirmed by the Senate. It was a recipe for disaster. That Gates and the rest of the administration would struggle was almost a foregone conclusion, but Gates's task was certainly complicated by his own inexperience. The wrangling and infighting within the Eisenhower administration made Gates's mission all the more difficult.

Gates's first responsibility was to refute McElroy's erroneous assertion of the previous year that the Soviets could outproduce the United States to the extent that they would gain a three-to-one advantage in nuclear missiles. Before the Senate Armed Services Committee, Gates informed the senators that McElroy had been mistaken: new intelligence data showed that the Soviet Union had far fewer missiles than had been earlier estimated. The Soviets, therefore, lacked "sufficient power to justify a 'rational decision' to attack this country." While Gates's claims encouraged some Democrats, including committee chairman Richard Russell of Georgia, the secretary found himself in the crossfire of an increasingly contentious political fight between two powerful Democratic senators, Lyndon B. Johnson and Stuart Symington, as they angled for a good shot at the Eisenhower administration in the hopes of boosting their own chances for the nomination. Symington in particular asserted that Eisenhower's proposal to hold defense spending below $41 billion would lead to the United States becoming "a second-rate power."[124]

Gates must have felt like he had a bull's-eye painted on his chest. His efforts to portray accurately the nation's strategic posture grew more difficult as other administration officials, senior military officers, and members of Congress openly challenged his statements. What began as a concerted effort to clarify the administration's position ended as a hopeless muddle of confusion and contradiction.

Only hours after Gates's appearance before the Senate Armed Services Committee on 19 January, the commander of the Strategic Air Command, General Thomas S. Power, raised new questions about the latest intelligence estimate because he appeared to be giving official credence to Khrushchev's inflated and unsubstantiated claim that a single Soviet factory was "turning out some 250 missiles a year." In remarks before the New York Economic Club, Power declared that the one hundred U.S. facilities from which nuclear weapons could be launched were "soft targets" that as few as three hundred Soviet missiles could "virtually wipe out."[125]

Power's true motives will never be known. Some individuals with knowledge of the intelligence gathering and assessment process of the late 1950s suggest that he and other senior air force officers were exaggerating the Soviet threat. By interpreting fuzzy images in aerial photographs as missile sites when they could have been housing sites, the air force boosted their claims that a substantial increase in U.S. missile and bomber programs was still needed.[126] But while Power's motives are obscure, the result of his statements is clear: whereas the air force and General Walsh were practically alone within the intelligence community in arguing that Soviet missile production was progressing rapidly, Power's well-publicized remarks were afforded instant legitimacy in the public realm. Within days the administration's critics stepped up their attacks. The juxtaposition of Gates's claims with those of other "informed" sources within his own department left the impression that Gates was misinformed, at best, or giving false testimony before Congress, at worst.

Amid this confusion over the latest intelligence estimates, the missile gap debate intensified. Take, for example, an article that appeared in the partisan magazine *Missiles and Rockets*. Published less than a week after Gates's first appearance before the Senate Armed Services Committee, the article proclaimed in its headline, "Gates Sees Narrower 'Gap,'" but the lead paragraph of the same article declared that the "Nation's view of the size of the Missile Gap remained cloudy." Gates's "rosier" new estimates, the magazine reported, had been "retouched in more somber tones" by congressmen, including Symington, and by military leaders, such as Power. The magazine quoted from Symington's speech on the floor of the Senate and repeated Power's claim that the "Russians could almost wipe out all U.S. retaliatory power in 30 minutes with . . . 300 ICBMs and IRBMs."[127]

These numbers, of three hundred Soviet missiles destroying the U.S. arsenal in thirty minutes, were central to Power's charge that the Soviets would soon have enough missiles to incapacitate the U.S. deterrent force. Disproving these numbers, or at least calling them into question, was equally important for the administration's claim that the Soviet Union lacked "sufficient power to justify a 'rational decision' to attack this country." Both assertions were founded upon highly speculative assessments of what number of nuclear weapons constituted an effective first-strike force. For example, when Air Force Chief of Staff White asked for supporting data to assist him in replying to questions about Power's speech, White was told that as few as 100 or as many as 430 enemy missiles might be needed to deliver a knockout blow to the U.S. retaliatory capability.[128] Given this uncertainty, Gates ultimately tried to divert attention away from Power's numbers and toward the more important point that there was no "deterrence gap"—which was essentially the same argument that McElroy had made a year earlier. Gates also explicitly denied that politics had prompted the recalculation of the intelligence numbers

Reporters and politicians were skeptical, however. In a 21 January 1960 front-page story in the *Washington Post*, John Norris compared the new "system" of estimating Soviet missile strength on the basis of intentions rather than capabilities to one of the most serious intelligence failures in the nation's history: the failure to anticipate the Japanese attack on Pearl Harbor in 1941.[129] Meanwhile, Lyndon Johnson charged Gates with adopting a "dangerous new method for estimating Soviet" missile strength and criticized the administration's emphasis on Soviet intentions. "The missile gap cannot be eliminated with the stroke of a pen," Johnson said, and he blasted the administration for staking the lives of "175 million Americans on the ability . . . to read Nikita Khrushchev's mind."[130]

All indications pointed to continued disagreement punctuated by partisan wrangling, and the media showed no signs of wanting the conflict to subside. On 23 January former president Truman and Washington senator Henry M. Jackson also stepped forward to criticize the Eisenhower administration's response to the missile gap.[131] Even more ominous for the administration, however, was the report that General Maxwell Taylor would testify before Johnson's Preparedness Committee in the coming week. In a remarkable display of parochialism, Army Secretary Brucker was looking forward to Taylor's testimony, believing that the Congressional wind was blowing in the army's favor.[132]

Notwithstanding the bureaucratic pressure within his administration, Eisenhower considered options for suppressing Taylor's criticisms, at one point directing the judge advocate general of the army to brief him on "what 'strings' there were on retired officers in such situations as that of Max Taylor and whether any action could be taken" to restrict his testimony. Eisenhower recalled that "retired Army officers had been dealt with for being critical of the administration in power."[133]

Eisenhower also contemplated ways to control the testimony of the active duty chiefs. In a White House meeting on 25 January with Joint Chiefs of Staff chair Twining and his staff secretary, army colonel Andrew Goodpaster, Eisenhower listened as Twining tried to put the best possible spin on the past week's activities. Ultimately, however, General Twining admitted that he too had become tangled up in the "argument over intelligence based on intentions v. capabilities." A week earlier Twining had sharply criticized those "writers and commentators" who were "inclined to degrade the capabilities of the American people" while at the same time reporting Soviet achievements in "glowing terms."[134]

In anticipation of the coming week, Twining was troubled by Lyndon Johnson's Preparedness Committee's practice of requiring the members of the Joint Chiefs of Staff to testify under oath. Committee staffers, he explained, had been "talking to military and civilian personnel up and down the line in the Pentagon and gathering all kinds of material, much of it non-authoritative," in a deliberate effort to set them up for contradicting the administration. The president had a simple solution for such situations: "any military man who appears before the group and is required to take an oath," he said, "should refuse to give opinion and judgment and limit his testimony strictly to facts."[135]

But such measures, even if legal, would not have stopped the momentum of the growing controversy because the many different interpretations of the facts within the administration could not be confined to hearings before Congress. On the same day that Eisenhower and his lieutenants pondered new ways to frame the missile gap debate, Joseph Alsop launched into yet another bitter critique of Eisenhower's defense policies. In the first of a six-part series, Alsop highlighted the differences within the administration by presenting information from Gates's and Twining's recent testimony alongside excerpts from Power's speech. Presenting Power as the man most willing to take on the responsibility of "bridging the missile gap," Alsop declared Power's speech to be "the first authoritative statement" on the danger.[136]

Alsop's criticism revolved around the folly of "gambling" the nation's future on new estimates of questionable accuracy. His 25 January 1960 front-page article in the *New York Herald Tribune* appeared directly below another article in which Air Force Secretary Dudley Sharp proclaimed that there was no deterrent gap. Sharp stressed that this was true "even if the Soviet Union now has more ICBMs than the United States."[137] *Tribune* readers would have to decide whom to believe, the civilian secretary of the air force (and, by extension, the entire chain of command—the secretary of defense, the chairman of the Joint Chiefs, and the president) or a single subordinate commander.

Alsop had chosen to believe the latter. He led the next day's column with a direct quote from Power's speech, and he compared the statements of the commander of the Strategic Air Command (SAC) with those of his putative superiors, Twining and Gates. With the nation's survival hanging in the balance, Alsop argued, Gates had placed far too much confidence in the latest "official guess" at Soviet military capabilities.[138] The stage was easily set for the third article in the series, in which Alsop declared that the Eisenhower administration was "gambling the national future" on flawed assumptions and a flawed intelligence estimate that was yet another in a long and "consistent series of gross . . . underestimates of Soviet weapons achievements" dating back to 1946.[139]

Readers again had a choice of whom to believe, for even as Alsop blasted Eisenhower, the commander in chief's response was printed inches above Alsop's column on the *New York Herald Tribune*'s front page. During his weekly press conference, Eisenhower defended the new intelligence estimates and argued against engaging in a debate over intentions and capabilities. Reporters were not convinced. Warren Rogers of the *New York Herald Tribune* opined that Ike had "tossed . . .

an election year hot potato back" to his secretary of defense when he had failed to end the confusion surrounding the new estimates.[140] When reporters repeated Gates's statement from the previous week that the new estimates were based on what the Soviets would do, as opposed to what they could do, Eisenhower demurred, contending that Gates had been misunderstood. Reminding reporters again of the mythical bomber gap of the mid-1950s that had arisen on the basis of inaccurate intelligence estimates, the president argued that both intentions and capabilities were important in formulating intelligence projections; the new estimates, he said, were simply more accurate than past estimates.

Ultimately the commander in chief lost the battle over the missile gap. The statements Eisenhower made during his many press conferences did not change the minds of skeptical reporters and editors, largely because the evidence on which he based his assertions was inconclusive. It was also confusing and, at times, contradictory. Interested parties, including both Democratic and Republican political critics and members of the military seeking ways to increase their share of a finite defense pie, circulated within the public domain the estimates that supported their claim that there was a missile gap. The president's words of encouragement competed with these more pessimistic estimates, allowing doubters and skeptics to pick and choose from the available data. Although Eisenhower dismissed his critics as alarmists, they chose to continue believing that there was a missile gap.

Consider, for example, the way Eisenhower's reassuring statements were crowded out on the front page of the *Baltimore Sun*. The headline over the press conference story "Intelligence on Russia Improves" was contradicted by the subhead "U.S.-Soviet Missile 'Gap' Seen Likely to Get Worse"—a reference to comments made by Senator Richard Russell of Georgia—and an additional front-page article that criticized the Pentagon for its "inept handling" of the new intelligence estimates.[141] Senator Symington, meanwhile, refused to ascribe the confusion to "inept handling"; instead, he charged that the administration was deliberately manipulating the intelligence estimate to mislead the public. The missile gap, he said, was greater than three-to-one in favor of the Soviets and growing. "The intelligence books have been juggled," Symington concluded in a written statement, "so the budget books may be balanced."[142]

In yet another attempt to get everyone in his administration talking from the same script, Eisenhower planned a full-scale information blitz of his own. For the president the real danger came not from Soviet missiles but "from the possible failure of understanding on the part of our people of what the situation really is." Given that he had "long felt that communication . . . was important," Eisenhower said that he would approve a plan to bring "responsible people in positions of leadership to Washington" for briefings on national security, provided that the discussions did not become "absorbed with considerations of numbers" of missiles and bombs.[143]

Such an effort was already taking place. Gates and Air Force Chief of Staff White deliberately avoided talk of numbers during presentations before television audiences, again stating explicitly only that the United States was strong enough to deter the Soviets from starting World War III on the basis of the overall balance of the deterrent forces.[144] And yet it was nearly impossible for the administration to make its case clearly. When Gates rejected Power's contention that a mere three hundred missiles could wipe out the nation's deterrent force, Symington and other skeptics on the Senate Defense Appropriations Subcommittee confronted him. Under questioning, Gates conceded that the Soviets would continue to outproduce the United States in missiles over the next three years, but argued this advantage was "more than offset by U.S. preponderance in air and sea strength."[145] But the administration had been making this case unsuccessfully for years. Most observers misunderstood or ignored the strategic significance of overall U.S. superiority and focused instead on the presumed threat from ICBMs.

Eisenhower's most carefully orchestrated efforts at spin control were thus thwarted. Consider again the case of the controversial B-70 bomber. The air force continued to push the program in spite of Eisenhower's misgivings, which were clearly stated behind the scenes. When questioned about the B-70 program during Congressional testimony, Twining reluctantly testified under oath that he differed with the administration's official position and was opposed to halting the program. But some generals only feigned reluctance. On 11 January SAC commander Power had advised Air Force Chief of Staff White of the advantages of the B-70s.[146] Armed with this information, General White openly pushed for continued spending on the B-70 on two separate occasions in testimony before Congress during the next two weeks. When asked explicitly during a television interview if "he thought it necessary for a general who disagrees to get out of the service before speaking his mind," White replied that he "had absolutely no fear" about speaking out, even when his opinions conflicted with those of the administration.[147]

Retired general Taylor, a former member of the Joint Chiefs of Staff, also had no fear about speaking out. When he testified before Congress on 4 February 1960, he repeated many of his themes from *The Uncertain Trumpet*. Taylor's son and biographer notes that when he was "out of uniform his testimony was far more blunt than it had been as chief of staff." As he had in his best-selling book, Taylor called for "heroic measures" to build up the nation's defenses. He predicted that "from about 1961 on the tide will run against us" and that it would require "men, money and sacrifice" to change the current trend toward "military inferiority." If the nation did not make the necessary sacrifices, he warned, then this inferiority would threaten the nation's very survival: "There is no living long with communism as an inferior." Under questioning, Taylor quantified what sacrifices would be necessary, suggesting, as he had written in *The Uncertain Trumpet*, that the defense budget should grow to roughly $50–55 billion per year, more than 20 percent greater than the Eisenhower administration's proposed budget of $41 billion for FY 1961.[148]

In spite of the testimony of these outspoken critics, the media began to speak of a conspiracy within the Eisenhower administration to muzzle those with dissenting points of view. Joseph Alsop charged that a "uniformity of viewpoint" had been enforced by the administration, and he claimed that the White House had condemned those who disagreed with the president's position as "non-team players."[149] On the same day, columnist George Dixon postulated that some military leaders might "take the fifth" rather than openly criticize the administration before Congress. In a caustic article that ridiculed Eisenhower for supposing that he was better informed than most for judging the nation's military needs, Dixon suggested that senior military officers should be assigned to read a manual on how to testify before Congress rather than receiving a rebuke from the president. The latest object of the commander in chief's displeasure, according to Dixon, was SAC commander General Power.[150]

By the second week in February, the president had grown decidedly pessimistic about his ability to frame the national security debate. Fear of security leaks from Congress came to dominate consideration of almost every issue relating to the nuclear deterrent force. Meanwhile the behind-the-scenes interservice battle within the administration raged on. Ike was troubled when Admiral Burke used his appearance before Congress to push for yet another Polaris submarine.[151] The air force was also concerned about Burke's independent effort, albeit for different reasons. Anxious to retain control over the nation's nuclear deterrent, the air force had pushed on several occasions for Polaris missiles to be placed under a single unified command, preferably SAC. In a series of memoranda in early February, prominent New Look critic William W. Kaufmann presented General White with ammunition that could be used against the Polaris program in his testimony before Congress.[152] It was clear that if Burke and the navy went around the president again with a direct appeal for more Polaris submarines, the air force had a ready reply.

The administration's efforts to present a united front on questions of weapons and intelligence estimates came crashing down once and for all when General Walsh made public his dissent from the official intelligence estimate. In testimony before Lyndon Johnson's committee, alongside his fellow air force generals White and Power, Walsh stated unequivocally that the Soviet Union had considerably more ballistic missiles than was previously reported. Then, just for good measure, White pressed again for continued development of the B-70.[153]

These military men were motivated by a genuine desire to protect the nation's security, but there was an element of parochialism in their approach to national security. Their differing interpretations of what was required to defend U.S. interests reflected their own diverse backgrounds and experiences. The proper functioning of the Joint Chiefs of Staff—or of any other consultative body—depends upon the presence of differing points of view. It is not at all surprising that Generals Power and White believed that the Strategic Air Command was the best vehicle for ensuring the nation's survival and that the B-70 was the best weapon. Likewise, it is not surprising that Admiral Burke favored the Polaris submarine; or that Generals Ridgway and Taylor believed in the need for a larger conventional army. For any one of these men to have argued that his own service was not prepared to defend the interests of the nation would have been tantamount to surrender.

There is no evidence to suggest that these men deliberately mistook the true nature of the Soviet arms buildup, or that they mischaracterized their individual services' ability to fulfill their mission as specified by the commander in chief. Nonetheless, lacking a complete picture of the Soviet threat, these military leaders bought into the Soviets' missile gap deception. To be sure, there was also an element of self-deception in the military's view of the Soviet threat. Air force personnel were especially focused on the ICBM threat partly because their service had primary responsibility for targeting Soviet ICBM sites.

Looking back on the period, former secretary of defense Robert McNamara said that he believed air force leaders were looking through "air force tinted glasses" when they reviewed aerial photographs of suspected Soviet ICBM sites, but that he did not believe their flawed interpretations of the raw intelligence data arose from an intent to mislead.[154] Raymond Garthoff, who was working in the Office of National Estimates in the late 1950s, agreed that the air force had not fabricated evidence, but he did believe that there was a certain readiness on the part of air force officers to see certain types of evidence and to argue that the possibility of a Soviet ICBM threat could not be excluded. Parochial concerns were not limited to the air force, however. Garthoff noted that the army and navy tended to downplay certain aspects of the ICBM threat in ways that might have translated into gains for their respective services.[155]

Ultimately, the generals were wrong and Eisenhower was right—there was no missile gap. The president had access to more and better information about the true nature of the strategic balance, including what he learned from one-on-one conversations with Soviet leader Nikita Khrushchev. The service chiefs erred further by making their private concerns public, effectively circumventing the chain of command. The national security bureaucracy, in other words, inadvertently contributed to the confusion associated with the missile gap. By calling into question the soundness of the official intelligence estimates and by criticizing the direction of the nation's security policies, military leaders undermined the confidence of the American people, and simultaneously eroded the faith of U.S. allies.

Senator Kennedy and Joseph Alsop, Redux

The nation's military leaders were not alone in their criticisms of Eisenhower's New Look; they were joined by politicians and journalists who were equally concerned about the direction of U.S. national security policy. Joseph Alsop had rejoined the chorus of criticism with his six-part series on the missile gap that was published in late January 1960, the first installment appearing only days after Power's speech.

John F. Kennedy, on the other hand, was not actively engaged in the missile gap debate in January and early February of 1960. Publicity surrounding Maxwell Taylor's book may have encouraged Kennedy to revisit the subject, however. Kennedy's friend Joe Alsop also appears to have piqued the senator's interest in the topic, prompting Kennedy to deliver yet another major missile gap speech on the floor of the Senate in late February.

Alsop had gone to extraordinary lengths to promulgate his ideas among Washington's elite, hoping to influence that year's debate over military spending as well as the presidential race. When Alsop assembled his most recent missile gap articles into a specially prepared pamphlet and distributed them to every member of the Senate, as well as to the members of the House committees on appropriations and armed services, he received a tepid response. The one exception was John Kennedy. Alsop's files contain numerous form letters perfunctorily acknowledging receipt of the pamphlet, so a personal, handwritten note from John Kennedy stands out. On 27 February 1960 Kennedy wrote, "Thank you for sending me your series of articles on The Missile Gap. I have read these as published, but will read them again with great interest. You have done a great thing for the country and I hope we may see results. Sincerely, John."[156]

Further evidence that Alsop's arguments had resonated in Kennedy's mind was dramatically displayed only two days later when Kennedy delivered a scathing critique of Eisenhower's military budget. The speech echoed many of the concerns expressed in the Alsop series. Kennedy began by referring to Winston Churchill's argument that it was necessary to arm for war in order to deter war. Kennedy agreed: "We depend on the strength of armaments, to enable us to bargain for disarmament." He alluded to a speech that he intended to deliver later in the week on the subject of disarmament, but now he highlighted the state of the nation's current and future defense needs. Kennedy called for a diversification of the nation's defenses, focusing especially on closing the missile gap. He tacitly agreed with Eisenhower's contention that the current mix of forces was "undoubtedly" far superior to that of the Soviets. Still, there were other areas where the United States was deficient. In particular, the senator-turned–presidential candidate was concerned about the nation's shortcomings in the field of ballistic missiles, which were "likely to take on critical dimensions in the near future."[157]

Kennedy admitted that "we cannot be certain that the Soviets will have . . . the tremendous lead in missile striking power which they give every evidence of building—and we cannot be certain that they will use that lead to threaten or launch an attack upon the United States." Nevertheless, he disagreed mightily with those who argued that such uncertainties provided justification for holding defense spending below a certain level. Counting himself among those who called "for a higher defense budget" and who were accused of "taking a chance on spending money unnecessarily," Kennedy turned this criticism around. "Those who oppose these expenditures," he said, "are taking a chance on our very survival as a nation."[158]

Kennedy noted the irony that the electorate would never have a chance to determine who was right. "For if we are successful in boosting our defenses," Kennedy explained, "and no Soviet attack is ever launched or threatened, then we shall never know with certainty whether our improved forces deterred that attack, or whether the Soviets would never have attacked us anyway." "But, on the other hand," the candidate continued, "if the deterrent gap continues to go against us and invites a Soviet strike sometime after the maximum danger period begins, a large part of our population will have less than 24 hours of life in which to reflect that the critics of this administration were right all along."[159]

For Kennedy, the only real question was over which gamble the nation should take. While it would be easier to gamble with survival because it saved money now and balanced the budget now, Kennedy proposed an alternate course. "I would prefer," he said, "that we gamble with our money—that we increase our defense budget this year— even though we have no absolute knowledge that we shall ever need it—and even though we would prefer to spend the money on other critical needs in more constructive ways." Although agreeing that there were other uses for this money—including "schools, hospitals, parks and dams"—he predicted that the total needed to close the gap would be less than one percent of gross national product, less than the total of the projected budget surplus. It would be "an investment in peace that we can afford—and cannot avoid."[160]

Among these investments were increased funding for a number of missile programs including Polaris, Minuteman, and "long-range air-to-ground missiles" that would close the gap when completed. In the meantime, Kennedy urged a step up in the production of the Atlas missile in order to "cover the current gap as best we can." Finally, he called for rebuilding and modernizing our "Army and Marine Corps conventional forces, to prevent brush-fire wars that our capacity for nuclear retaliation is unable to deter."[161]

Kennedy's subsequent comments further indicate his prevailing misconceptions about the missile gap: "Whether the missile gap—that everyone agrees now exists—will become critical in 1961, 1962, or 1963 . . . whether the gap can be brought to a close . . . in 1964 or in 1965 or ever—on all these questions experts may sincerely differ. . . . The point is that we are facing a gap on which we are gambling with our survival."[162]

Kennedy traced the genesis of the gap by comparing the histories of the defense programs in the United States and in the Soviet Union in the 1950s. In the years since 1953—a crucial year in which the H-bomb transformed the military situation—the Soviets had "made a clear-cut decision to plunge their resources into ballistic missiles." In that same year the United States had "embarked on a policy of emphasizing budgetary considerations in the formulation of defense goals."[163] The result of these policies, Kennedy asserted, was a steady decline in the relative missile strength of the United States vis-à-vis the Soviet Union.

Kennedy perceived a similar decline in U.S. conventional forces relative to those of the Soviets. Mistakenly asserting that the Soviets had expanded and modernized their ground forces under the guidance of Khrushchev and Marshal Georgi Konstantinovich Zhukov, Kennedy pointed out that the New Look had held sway in the United States.[164] General Ridgway had lost the funding battle that Zhukov had won. In the United States conventional ground forces, especially those of the army and the marines, were consistently being cut. According to Kennedy, the nation had also failed to modernize the remaining forces and had failed to provide the necessary airlift and sealift capacity to provide these forces with the mobility they would need to protect U.S. interests around the globe.

Much of Kennedy's speech reflected his misunderstanding of the strategic balance. Because he lacked access to classified intelligence information, Kennedy's belief in the missile gap was exacerbated by his reliance on flawed public data, often fed to him by Joseph Alsop. But Kennedy's greatest error was his assertion that everyone believed in the existence of a missile gap. Even those senators who had been briefed on the intelligence estimates could not have known the degree of uncertainty and doubt among many analysts who, having yet to find a single deployed ICBM, were increasingly skeptical about the gap.[165]

Despite these misunderstandings, Kennedy had correctly identified the core elements of the debate over the New Look that extended back to the mid-1950s, long before the missile gap had surfaced as a public issue. Kennedy argued that events since 1953 had shown that nuclear power alone was not sufficient to deter those forms of communist aggression which were "too limited to justify atomic war." Nuclear weapons would not prevent the Soviets and their allies from using "local or guerilla forces" to take power in "uncommitted nations." Nuclear weapons could not be used in "so-called brush-fire peripheral wars." Alone, therefore, nuclear weapons could not "prevent the Communists from gradually nibbling at the fringe of the free world's territory and strength, until our security had been steadily eroded in piecemeal fashion—each Red advance being too small to justify massive retaliation, with all its risks." "In short," Kennedy concluded, "we need forces of an entirely different kind to keep the peace against limited aggression, and to fight it, if deterrence fails, without raising the conflict to a disastrous pitch."[166]

These were the facts, Kennedy explained. Eisenhower had argued the week before that "knowledgeable and unbiased observers" respected the nation's strength, but Kennedy disagreed. Although the range of opinions made public during the past few months suggested, at best, disagreement and confusion over the true nature of the missile gap, Kennedy saw only one message emerging. "Every objective committee of knowledgeable and unbiased observers," including the Killian, Gaither, and Rockefeller committees; "every private or public study; every objective inquiry by independent military analysts; every statement by Generals Gavin, Ridgway, Taylor, Power, . . . and others; every book and article by scholars in the field," he said, all, "regardless of party, have stated candidly and bluntly that our defense budget is not adequate to give us the protection for our security or the support for our diplomatic objectives." Every study, he said, agreed with the Rockefeller Brothers Report from 1958, which concluded: "All is not well with present U.S. security policies and operations. . . . Corrective steps must be taken now. We believe that the security of the United States transcends normal budgetary considerations and that the national economy can afford the necessary measures."[167]

Kennedy stressed that time was short. Yet he was confident that the situation, which "should never have been permitted to arise," could be resolved if the nation took immediate action. He implored his fellow senators and the nation, "If we move now, if we are willing to gamble with our money instead of our survival, we have, I am sure, the wit and resource to maintain the minimum conditions for our survival, for our alliances, and for the active pursuit of peace." He stressed that his was not "a call for despair." It was a call for action, "a call based upon the belief that at this moment in history our security transcends normal budgetary considerations."[168]

Kennedy closed by reaffirming his faith that these measures would ultimately enable the nation to turn toward disarmament, to put "an end to war" and to put "an end to these vast military departments and expenditures." "We are taking a gamble with our money," Kennedy reaffirmed, "but the alternative is to gamble with our lives."[169]

Conclusion

Who had the final word on the missile gap during the first two months of 1960? Ironically, it was the man who had had little to say about the gap during the first eight weeks of his presidential campaign but who would derive the most benefit from it in the final eight weeks—John F. Kennedy. Kennedy's views on foreign policy and defense were well-publicized long before he secured his party's nomination at the time of the Democratic convention in July 1960, and he would continue to emphasize these themes throughout the fall campaign.

Kennedy's motivations for using the themes of foreign policy and defense were varied. He genuinely believed, as did Joseph Alsop and other prominent critics of the New Look, that Eisenhower's national security strategy took unnecessary risks in the name of protecting the nation's economy. Kennedy and his fellow Democrats believed that the federal government should spend more money, including more money for defense. John Kennedy had long believed that political leaders must exhort their citizens to do more for their own defense. He was also motivated, however, by his political ambition. The missile gap was a salient political issue. Charges that the nation had fallen behind the Soviet Union resonated with voters.

In the final analysis, Eisenhower had failed. Although the president was confident that the latest intelligence estimates had accurately captured the true character of the Soviet missile program, the evidence remained too uncertain to convince the skeptics who feared that the Soviets had been particularly adept at concealing their missiles from the prying eyes and ears of American intelligence.

But confusion over the interpretation of inconclusive intelligence data was only part of the problem. Most of the missile gap debate revolved around Eisenhower's attitudes toward defense spending. He had tried to convince Americans that it was unwise to spend more money on defense when the nature of the threat was unclear. He had hoped his administration could present a united front to the American people, but he and other senior officials had failed to redirect attention to the deterrent value of the nation's defenses, including the broad range of assets in the American arsenal, rather than to a presumed gap in the number of Soviet and American ICBMs. Eisenhower was unable to resolve disagreement among the members of the Joint Chiefs of Staff over the military budget and over major weapon systems, such as the B-70. And even his persistent, perhaps even unconstitutional, attempts to keep such disagreements out of the headlines had failed, or even backfired. In the end, John Kennedy and Eisenhower's harshest critics had the final word on national security strategy and the missile gap. The critics had the most to say, and they had the loudest voices. Although Kennedy did not lead in framing the debate in early 1960, he operated within the boundaries established in the post-*Sputnik* years and would continue to do so in the coming months as his campaign for the presidency gained momentum.

As for Eisenhower, perhaps the president can be faulted for his naïveté. The career military officer did not believe it proper for officers to publicly question the decisions of the chain of command. While writing his memoirs in 1962, Eisenhower deleted a passage referring to the growing conflict in Indochina that might have been deemed critical of Kennedy's policies. Writing of this incident in 1992, Fred Greenstein and Richard Immerman observed: "It seems likely that the former president, who reverted to the lifetime rank of general of the army after leaving office, would have felt obligated to back the incumbent."[170] Perhaps. But Eisenhower might also have wanted no part in a repeat of the "Revolt of the Generals"—Ridgway, Gavin, Taylor, Power, White, and Walsh—that had caused him so much anguish in the closing days of his White House career. For whatever reason, the ex-president refrained from publicly criticizing his successors, Kennedy and later Lyndon Johnson, the two politicians who had derived political benefit from the generals' revolt, even as their misjudgments dragged the nation into a deepening quagmire in Southeast Asia.

CHAPTER THREE

The Presidential Election of 1960 and the Politics of National Security

"Just as long as Kennedy can keep Nixon at least neutralized on foreign affairs, he can club him to death with domestic issues. However, foreign and domestic issues must constantly be related to each other by the point that we cannot be strong abroad if we are not strong at home."

—Pollster Louis Harris to John F. Kennedy, October 1960[1]

For years scholars have downplayed the significance of policy issues in the presidential election of 1960. Most observers have attributed Kennedy's ultimate success in this pivotal historical event to factors unrelated to his stance on issues. Some focus on Kennedy's success in a series of televised debates, while others emphasize Kennedy's religion as a factor working either in Kennedy's favor or to his detriment. Some emphasize Kennedy's call for Americans to embark on a national crusade toward a "New Frontier," while still others credit John Kennedy's personality and a superior campaign organization for his success in the election.[2]

With the notable exception of Robert Divine, few historians have examined the relative significance of foreign policy and national defense issues in the campaign. Divine's *Foreign Policy and U.S. Presidential Elections*, vol. 2: *1952–1960*, devotes over one hundred pages exclusively to foreign policy issues in the 1960 campaign, from the primaries through the general election. Divine notes that Kennedy believed as early as December 1959 that foreign policy would be the paramount issue of the campaign.[3]

Divine concludes that foreign policy cost Kennedy votes and that the differences between Nixon and Kennedy on foreign policy were remarkably small, Kennedy's rhetoric notwithstanding. A more nuanced view suggests that while the two candidates agreed on the underlying goals of American foreign policy, they differed over the appropriate means for achieving those common goals. The divergence between the two political parties was more pronounced. In exploring these differences in this chapter, Kennedy's references in his campaign speeches to the missile gap and to declining American prestige are given particular attention.

Kennedy's message about the need to get the country moving again addressed both foreign and domestic concerns. The external threat of communism enabled Kennedy to ask more from his audiences. He called on voters to make sacrifices in their personal lives in order to serve the needs of their fellow Americans. By raising living standards across the board at home, he contended, the nation would send a strong message to those living abroad who looked to the United States for guidance and inspiration in their struggle against communism. In this way, Kennedy combined his discussion of foreign policy with references to domestic economic policy. This combined message was a persistent theme throughout Kennedy's campaign.

To the Nomination

Religion, not foreign policy or economic matters, dominated the early intraparty contest between John F. Kennedy and Senator Hubert Humphrey of Minnesota, Kennedy's only major rival in the primaries. Kennedy's first major victory over Humphrey, in Wisconsin in early April, was inconclusive. Critics attributed Kennedy's success to the disproportionate number of Catholics in the state. The true test came in West Virginia, an overwhelmingly Protestant state, which held its primary on 10 May. Kennedy confronted the religious issue head-on by suggesting on numerous occasions that a vote against him was a vote for bigotry. He won 61 percent of the votes cast in that state, and detractors who argued that no Catholic could ever be elected president were quieted. Soon thereafter prominent Democrats, including Chicago mayor Richard Daley and Ohio governor Michael DiSalle, endorsed Kennedy.[4]

Although other issues crowded out foreign policy concerns during Kennedy's run-up to the nominating convention, the missile gap remained a crucial element of his overarching theme that the nation must accelerate its efforts on a broad front. In an article for the magazine *Ground Support Equipment,* Kennedy explained that the Soviet Union possessed "rocket engines of far greater thrust" than any in the U.S. arsenal. "This lead," he declared, accounted "for Soviet superiority in the field of ICBMs." He feared that new developments in space technology would lead "almost inevitably . . . to scientific break-throughs of military importance." "The Russians," the candidate warned, "must not be first with these breakthroughs."[5]

After securing a string of primary victories, culminating in his win in Oregon in May, Kennedy raised the issue of the missile gap and the nation's military deficiencies in another speech on the floor of the Senate in late June. The nation's task, Kennedy began, was to rebuild its strength "to prove to the Soviets that time and the course of history are not on their side, that the balance of world power is not shifting their way." "The hour is late," Kennedy said, "but the agenda is long."

The items on that agenda included many of the same reforms Kennedy had been advocating for years. First, the nation must move to "make invulnerable a nuclear retaliatory power second to none . . . by stepping up our development and production of the ultimate missiles" including Polaris, Minuteman, and long-range air-to-ground missiles. Such measures, Kennedy argued, would "close the gap" and ensure that the nuclear deterrent force would not "be wiped out in a surprise attack." In the meantime he urged an increase in the production of Atlas missiles, better defenses for nuclear weapons bases, and improvements to the nation's "continental defense and warning systems."[6]

Beyond missile development, Kennedy articulated a broad-based program for regaining the initiative in the Cold War. The nation, he said, must be able "to intervene effectively and swiftly in any limited war anywhere in the world," and this necessitated increasing the "mobility and versatility" of conventional forces. Kennedy also called for "more flexible and realistic tools for use in Eastern Europe" and a reassessment of the nation's policy toward China. Finally, he argued that the nation "must begin to develop new, workable programs for peace and the control of arms." In closing, Kennedy reiterated his long-standing belief that national security was tied to the nation's economic security. "We must work," he declared, "to build the stronger America on which our ultimate ability to defend the free world depends." Specifically, Kennedy sought "to create an America with an expanding economy, where growth is not dissipated in inflation, and consumer luxuries are not confused with national strength."[7]

Concerns about the missile gap continued to influence President Eisenhower's behavior in the spring of 1960. In May a planned summit meeting between Eisenhower and Nikita Khrushchev collapsed after an American U-2 reconnaissance plane was shot down over Russia. Photographs from the highly successful U-2 program had reinforced Eisenhower's suspicions that there was no missile gap. The Soviets had been aware of these flights and had tracked the aircraft passing at high altitudes over their otherwise secluded country, but before Francis Gary Powers's fateful flight on 1 May, they had been unable to bring down the high-flying spy planes.

Eisenhower had approved the flight only a few weeks before the planned summit between the two superpowers. Although the Soviets considered the flights to be a serious provocation and were humiliated by their inability to defend their airspace, Eisenhower's primary concern was with determining the nature and extent of the Soviet arms buildup. Evidence from the U-2 mission might have further dispelled any notion that the Soviet Union was leading the United States in missile development, and this information could have been used against the president's political opponents, including John F. Kennedy, who continued to speak of the missile gap.

When the spy plane failed to land at the appointed time, the administration issued a statement saying that the United States had lost an aircraft conducting weather research. Confident that the pilot would never be taken alive, Eisenhower believed that he could maintain the secrecy of the entire U-2 program. Within days, however, the Soviet media was airing images of the captured pilot for the world to see. Eisenhower traveled to Paris for the planned summit on 14 May, but when he rebuffed Khrushchev's demand for an apology, the Soviet premier left the summit before it could begin.[8]

Contemporary observers bemoaned the failure of the summit and criticized the president for conducting the overflight so close to the date of the meeting. They also used the occasion to blast Eisenhower's defense program. The Democratic Advisory Council criticized the "Eisenhower-Nixon Administration," saying that it had "floundered in a series of contradictory statements." The U-2 incident and the collapse of the Paris summit had "made it clear that the inadequacies of the United States in building economic growth . . . and in strengthening its defenses" were threatening the prospects for world peace. The council recommended a program to restore the country's standing, calling for an expansion of the nation's economic growth and security and the development of stronger tactical forces for the army and navy, including modernization of the marine corps and its restoration to full power, in order to "deter local aggression aimed at limited objectives, and to defend our interests when this local deterrence fails." Although John Kennedy had recommended similar changes to the nation's military, he was less willing to criticize Eisenhower so harshly. Backing off from the tone of the council's statement, Kennedy conceded that Eisenhower "could not have avoided . . . attending the conference without harm to the prestige of the United States."[9]

But Kennedy could not distance himself so easily from the platform of the Democratic Party on which he ran, nor did he wish to. Abram Chayes, a Harvard University law professor and Kennedy adviser, was staff director for the Democratic Platform Committee. Chayes took a leading role in ensuring that the issues of primary concern to Kennedy were accorded a prominent place in the document that would guide the party's efforts in the coming months.[10] Reflecting the importance of foreign policy and national security in Kennedy's campaign, the platform led off with an outspoken attack upon the Eisenhower administration's military policies, stating, in part, that the United States had lost its "position of pre-eminence" relative to the Russians, the Chinese, and their satellites. The platform stressed that these criticisms were not "a partisan election-year charge," because "high officials of the Republican Administration" had said in testimony before congressional committees "that the Communists will have a dangerous lead in intercontinental missiles through 1963—and that the Republican Administration has no plans to catch up." These same officials had allegedly admitted that the nation's conventional forces had been "dangerously slashed for reasons of 'economy.'" "As a result," the platform claimed, "our military position today is measured in terms of gaps—missile gap, space gap, limited-war gap." The Democrats pledged to close these gaps.[11]

The platform also addressed the subject of economic growth. The Democrats believed that the economy could achieve an annual level of growth of at least 5 percent without the risk of inflation. They called for an end to "tight money," they reaffirmed their commitment to full employment as a "paramount objective of national policy," and they called for "action to create new industry in America's depressed areas of chronic unemployment."[12]

John F. Kennedy would repeat many of these themes over and over again on the campaign trail. He did so for the first time as the Democratic Party's official nominee in his acceptance speech on 15 July 1960. Although he made no mention of the missile gap in his address, his discussion of domestic problems was framed within the context of the global challenges confronting the United States. "Abroad, the balance of power is shifting," Kennedy warned. "Communist influence has penetrated further into Asia, stood astride the Middle East and now festers some ninety miles off the coast of Florida." These threats called for bold actions. "We stand today on the edge of a New Frontier," Kennedy declared, "the frontier of the 1960s—a frontier of unknown opportunities and perils—a frontier of unfulfilled hopes and threats," and he pledged to lead the nation into this New Frontier.[13]

Further Confusion

The Democratic platform alleged that officials within the Eisenhower administration had implied, deliberately or otherwise, that more could be done to protect national security. Such comments bolstered the Democrats' case against Eisenhower's defense program. Then in late July 1960 Vice President Richard Nixon met with New York governor Nelson A. Rockefeller in a secret meeting at Rockefeller's home in New York City. The erstwhile rivals for the Republican presidential nomination reached agreement on a number of foreign policy and defense issues. The so-called Fifth Avenue Compact declared that new efforts were necessary in national defense because of "the swiftness of the technological revolution—and the warning signs of Soviet aggressiveness."[14]

"The two imperatives of national security in the 1960s" the statement read, were, first, a nuclear retaliatory force "capable of surviving surprise attack to inflict devastating punishment on any aggressor," and second, a "modern, flexible and balanced military establishment with forces capable of deterring or meeting any local aggression." According to the statement, these security imperatives required "more and improved bombers, airborne alert, speeded production of missiles and Polaris submarines, accelerated dispersal and hardening of bases, full modernization of the equipment of our ground forces, and an intensified program for civil defense."[15]

The statement by these two leading Republicans was widely interpreted as a slap at President Eisenhower's defense program. Joseph Alsop reported years later that Eisenhower was planning a last-minute push to increase military spending by as much as $4 billion in late July 1960. The president allegedly changed his mind, however, after the release of the Nixon-Rockefeller agreement. According to Alsop, Eisenhower concluded that a decision to increase defense spending at such a late stage in his administration would have given the appearance of "admitting the validity of the criticism" included within the Nixon-Rockefeller statement.[16]

Rockefeller and other liberal Republicans posed major problems for the Eisenhower administration. The Fifth Avenue Compact demonstrated Nixon's concern over persistent criticisms of Eisenhower's defense program. Nixon harbored doubts about Eisenhower's economy measures, and he—like Kennedy—was genuinely committed to expanding the nation's defenses. The vice president, however, had been reluctant to criticize his most important political asset—a still-popular president. Despite the Democrats' successes in eroding Eisenhower's credibility on questions of national defense, the president enjoyed broad public support. Even in the years after *Sputnik,* Americans approved of the president's record in office by a two to one margin.[17] John F. Kennedy skillfully exploited Nixon's quandary, in part by citing Rockefeller's criticisms in order to highlight the bipartisan nature of the missile gap critique. Believing that Eisenhower's defense program was Nixon's primary political liability, Joseph Alsop told an interviewer that given the "approach that Kennedy took, the character of Nixon's campaign, including the defensiveness which resulted from the fact that . . . Nixon, genuinely believed that the Defense effort was inadequate," if Eisenhower had decided to increase defense spending in the summer of 1960, "it would have changed political history."[18]

Alsop's speculation notwithstanding, however, the defense budget did not receive a last minute boost. Kennedy continued to press for more defense spending, and he remained concerned about and continued to speak of the missile gap. He did not close the door on competing points of view, however. He was willing, indeed anxious, to gain a deeper understanding of the nature of the Soviet threat, and he actively sought out information from classified sources. The Eisenhower administration granted his request for special intelligence briefings on several occasions after Kennedy secured the Democratic Party's presidential nomination.

Ultimately, however, Kennedy's concerns were not dispelled by these sessions. He would receive a total of three such briefings by the CIA prior to the election, between July and November. A fourth meeting was held on 18 November, shortly after the election. The Defense Department briefed Kennedy in early September. The content of these briefings has become the subject of intense historical speculation, with most of the focus on whether Kennedy was informed of the Eisenhower administration's plans with regard to Cuba.[19] Many scholars simply assume that Kennedy was informed of the specifics of the Soviet missile program and that he continued to speak of a missile gap in spite of having received this information.[20]

One may surmise that any information about the true nature of the Soviet missile buildup did not differ substantially from that which the administration had already presented, privately and publicly, during the preceding two years. Kennedy and his fellow senators had been told in 1959 that there might be a missile gap, but that it was militarily insignificant. Then in January and February 1960 the Eisenhower administration had presented information from a new set of intelligence estimates, raising further doubts about the existence of a gap. Kennedy and the president's other critics, however, were skeptical of the administration's method for determining the size and scope of the Soviet forces, so they had rejected the new intelligence estimates and had continued to speak of a missile gap. By late July 1960, at the time of the first intelligence briefings, Kennedy and the rest of the country also knew about the U-2 program, and accordingly they had greater reason to accept Eisenhower's judgment. Nonetheless, Kennedy and others continued to question the president's repeated assertions that there was no missile gap.

The first CIA briefing took place on 23 July 1960 at the Kennedy family's estate in Hyannisport, Massachusetts. Although CIA Director Allen Dulles left no detailed record of what was said, any attempt to draw on the latest intelligence estimate would have revealed the deep divisions within the intelligence community over the question of the missile gap. NIE 11-8-60, officially issued on 1 August 1960, reflected even greater uncertainty than the February estimate (NIE 11-8-59) had, noting, for example, that the intelligence community had found "no direct evidence of the present or planned future rate of production" of ICBMs. Likewise, the authors revealed that they had not observed any "ICBM-related troop training activities" and that they could not identify even a single operational ICBM launching site.[21] If the February estimate had been correct, the Soviets would have had some thirty-five missiles on launchers by mid-1960. As a formerly classified study of the missile gap conceded, "With this much deployment," it should have been "possible to find some confirming evidence." But the U-2 program, abruptly halted after the ill-fated flight of Francis Gary Powers, never photographed even a single deployed ICBM. Other attempts to gather hard evidence of Soviet missile development, including information from human sources and communications intercepts, also failed to confirm the existence of a single operational Soviet ICBM.[22]

In a confidential memorandum to Eisenhower written shortly after the Hyannisport meeting, Allen Dulles revealed that Kennedy had a particular interest in information on the missile gap. Continuing his long-standing practice of not attempting to resolve the question of the gap, Dulles explained that he had focused solely on estimates of Soviet missile production. He had informed Kennedy that "the Defense Department was the competent authority" on the question of the gap.[23] But in early September, when army general Earle Wheeler gave Kennedy an intelligence briefing on behalf of the Defense Department, he allegedly told Kennedy that there was no missile gap and that the source of the inflated estimates of Soviet missile production was the CIA, not the Pentagon.[24]

It is understandable, therefore, if Kennedy was frustrated by the confusing signals emanating from the Eisenhower administration. The classified intelligence briefings failed to alter the candidate's public position on the missile gap, and there is no evidence that they caused him to give any greater credence to Eisenhower's assertions that there was none. Instead, Kennedy continued to refer to the missile gap, and the related prestige gap, until the very last days of the campaign.

The Kennedy Campaign—The Best and the Brightest

Kennedy's team of defense and foreign policy advisers included some of the most vocal critics of the Eisenhower administration. A handful of these experts, including Roswell Gilpatric, Adam Yarmolinsky, and Arthur M. Schlesinger Jr., had worked for Kennedy's Democratic rivals and joined the Kennedy campaign after JFK secured the Democratic nomination in July. The core Kennedy group, however, remained unchanged. Kennedy's most important political adviser was his brother Robert, or "Bobby," who had observed Adlai Stevenson's failed presidential campaign of 1956 at close range.[25] Speech writing, meanwhile, was dominated by Theodore "Ted" Sorensen and Richard Goodwin. Sorensen had joined Kennedy's senatorial staff in 1953, and by 1960 he had become one of Kennedy's most influential advisers.[26] Goodwin had clerked for Supreme Court Justice Felix Frankfurter and then worked on the House Subcommittee on Legislative Oversight, investigating, among other things, the television quiz show scandals. He officially joined the campaign in late 1959.[27] Harris Wofford had been assisting Kennedy from time to time since early 1959 and was responsible for crafting some of his early foreign policy speeches.[28] Finally, pollster Louis Harris was also an influential adviser. Harris was one of only nine people—including the candidate's brother Bobby; his father, Joseph Sr.; and his brother-in-law Steve Smith—who attended the first organized meeting of the campaign in April 1959.[29] Harris's confidential polling reports for the campaign specifically documented the relative significance of various issues on a state-by-state basis.

Kennedy and his staff devised a strategy for addressing the candidate's known weaknesses. First and foremost, millions of Americans were expected to vote against Kennedy, a Roman Catholic, on religious grounds. But Kennedy's staff had postulated in 1956, when the senator sought the vice presidential nomination, that his Catholicism might work to the Democrats' advantage.[30] Kennedy's staff also believed that their candidate's youth and inexperience might be used against him, particularly on foreign policy issues, and the campaign developed a series of counterattacks or responses for this as well. For example, the campaign pointed out that Kennedy and Nixon had been elected to Congress in the same year and that Nixon had served in the Senate for only two years before becoming vice president, while Kennedy, first elected to the Senate in 1952, had served in that body for nearly eight years. On foreign policy specifically, Kennedy stressed his service on the influential Senate Foreign Relations Committee, where he chaired the subcommittee on Africa.[31]

Another part of Kennedy's strategy for overtaking Nixon on foreign policy was to draw attention to the Republican Party's foreign policy failures of the past eight years. Several of Kennedy's campaign advisers urged him to conduct an aggressive campaign focused on foreign policy and national security, but the candidate likely did not need much prompting.[32] Kennedy had explained to Harris Wofford in the spring of 1959 that he wanted to craft a new foreign policy that would "break out of the confines of the cold war."[33] His interest in foreign affairs and national security transcended politics and traced back to his undergraduate years at Harvard. Kennedy was particularly concerned about democratic nations' inability or unwillingness to confront foreign threats, a lesson he had learned from his firsthand observations in pre–World War II England and had articulated in his senior paper at Harvard that became the book *Why England Slept*. As a journalist for the Hearst newspapers immediately after World War II, Kennedy had covered several major foreign policy events, including the first meeting of the United Nations. During his first campaign for Congress in 1946, Kennedy was concerned about the threat of international communism even though his working-class constituents had little interest in the subject.[34]

Kennedy's more liberal advisers tried to pull him in a different direction, recommending instead that the candidate emphasize traditional domestic themes, with defense and foreign policy far down the list.[35] Meanwhile, several other advisers urged Kennedy to be cautious with his talk of arms control and peace, particularly because defense spending was related to employment. Although many vital-center liberals favored arms control and nuclear disarmament in principle, Democrats remained wary of being perceived as soft on communism. The concerns of defense workers further mitigated Democrats' zeal for scaling back the arms race. Before Kennedy embarked on a grand new initiative to replace persistent Cold War conflict with cooperation and coexistence, the candidate was told, "the hundreds of thousands of people who are employed in defense industry are entitled to know that some thought is being given to their place in a peaceful world."[36]

On the subject of military policy and strategy, Kennedy promised to strengthen the nation's defenses in order to close the missile gap. He proposed expanding the production of several specific weapon systems including the B-70 bomber, the Atlas and Minuteman missiles, and the Polaris submarine. More generally, he advocated the development of a stronger conventional force bolstered by expanded airlift capabilities to enable the United States to fight limited, nonnuclear conflicts. Kennedy also favored extending the draft. He had spoken to all of these issues at various times during his political career, and they blended naturally into his stump speeches. At a later stage of the campaign, Kennedy further tied defense spending to economic issues by pledging his support for Defense Manpower Policy Number 4, a procurement regulation first promulgated during the Korean War that called for the awarding of defense contracts to areas with high unemployment. On a related note, Kennedy also proposed to reform federal procurement policies to enable small firms to compete with large ones for defense contracts.[37]

Each of these issues appeared sporadically in Kennedy's stump speeches. By contrast, the nation's sagging prestige was a constant, and it reflected deficiencies in both foreign and domestic affairs.[38] Kennedy pledged to restore the nation's prestige by means of a combination of progressive reforms to be employed both at home and abroad. By combining his critique of Republican ineptitude and apathy in managing the domestic economy with frequent observations about Soviet successes, Kennedy succeeded in killing two birds with one rhetorical stone.

Foreign policy and national security were tied to domestic concerns in other ways as well. In criticizing the Eisenhower administration's defense policies, Kennedy and his fellow Democrats also assaulted the GOP's economic philosophy, which, they said, harkened back to the failed policies of Herbert Hoover in the early 1930s. But a new voice and a new assessment emerged in 1960, when Walt Whitman Rostow, a professor of economic history at the Massachusetts Institute of Technology, published *The Stages of Economic Growth: A Non-Communist Manifesto*.[39]

The Stages of Economic Growth was a formal rebuke of Marx's dialectical materialism. Rostow's assessment of the U.S.-Soviet military confrontation reinforced some of the most enduring myths of the Cold War years. Rostow distinguished himself from many other prominent cold warriors, however, by combining virulent anticommunism with a plausible and cogent argument against the Marxist-Leninist paradigm that saw imperialism as a natural and necessary by-product of capitalism. The work is indeed a noncommunist manifesto: Rostow's explicit goal was to formulate a theory to refute communist dogma. He did this, in part, by crafting arguments that were not narrowly deterministic, offering instead a decidedly noneconomic explanation for imperialism in recent history.[40]

The Soviets, Rostow argued, had accumulated a relative military advantage by deliberately controlling domestic consumption. Therefore, the Soviet economy, including its system of resource allocation, was of direct concern to the United States. Rostow appealed to the West and to newly independent countries throughout the world to recognize that economic growth was essential if the superiority of capitalism was to be demonstrated. As a leader of the West, the United States had an obligation to lead this effort, and therefore it should perceive the Soviet Union as a business rival as well as a strategic threat. It was bad enough that a weak U.S. economy meant that millions of Americans were unemployed or underemployed. It was worse, however, that this weakness sent a message abroad. The strength of the U.S. economy relative to that of the Soviet Union thus had profound ramifications in Rostow's—and ultimately John F. Kennedy's—worldview.

As Rostow told an interviewer in 1981, he played only a minor role in the Kennedy campaign. When the two men first met in February 1958, Kennedy was interested in Rostow's views on economic development. Rostow impressed upon the senator the need to "get the country moving again." Kennedy first used this phrase while campaigning in Oregon in May 1960 prior to the Democratic primary in that state, and it became one of his most persistent campaign slogans.[41] The notion of doing more in the domestic economy in order to win the Cold War was also a popular theme within the coterie of Keynesian economists who advised Kennedy, including James Tobin, Walter Heller, Paul Samuelson, and John Kenneth Galbraith, all of whom had criticized the policies of the Eisenhower administration in the late 1950s. These men helped to shape Kennedy's complex and at times contradictory economic philosophy, which called for Americans to sacrifice in order to turn the tide in the Cold War while also calling on government to do more to help citizens who were in need.

Kennedy's Vision for National Security

Throughout his political career, Michael Meagher notes, Kennedy considered the call to arms to be one of the most noble expressions of political leadership.[42] Kennedy's vision of leadership was popularized in his best-selling *Profiles in Courage,* published in 1956; his broad national security vision was further sharpened after the launch of *Sputnik;* and his views on foreign policy and defense during the missile gap period were summarized in a collection of his speeches titled *The Strategy of Peace,* published in early 1960.[43]

Kennedy's authorship of these and other works has long been a subject of scholarly debate. Harris Wofford collected the senator's speeches in *Strategy of Peace.*[44] Ted Sorensen drafted many of the other essays and articles that were eventually published under Kennedy's name.[45] But while Kennedy may not have written all the entries published in *Strategy of Peace,* the articles and speeches do reflect his point of view. For example, one item published under Kennedy's byline in the national weekly *Saturday Review* provided a succinct and revealing glimpse into Kennedy's strategic vision for the future. The occasion was a review of British military critic B. H. Liddell Hart's *Deterrent or Defense.* Kennedy neatly summarized the arguments in Liddell Hart's book under a single grand theme—"The West must be prepared to face down Communist aggression, short of nuclear war, by conventional forces."[46]

Kennedy repeated the British military critic's call for military reforms, which, like James Gavin's and Maxwell Taylor's before, included increased mobility for conventional forces and an expansion of forces under NATO command. In pushing this structure, Kennedy explicitly endorsed Liddell Hart's underlying strategic vision, behind which was the judgment, Kennedy wrote, "that responsible leaders in the West will not and should not deal with limited aggression by unlimited weapons whose use could only be mutually suicidal." Kennedy then seized the opportunity to pitch his own national security agenda to a wide audience by warning that the U.S. nuclear deterrent was vulnerable to a sudden attack, and he concluded by again calling for an acceleration of the production of "the new generation of mobile missiles, notably Polaris and Minuteman" as he had done in the Senate and on numerous occasions during the campaign.[47]

During the late stages of his campaign Kennedy was also interested in the writings of American general John B. Medaris. Formerly head of the army's ordnance missile command, Medaris had retired from the service in January 1960 to write *Countdown for Decision,* yet another in a long line of books by former military officers who were frustrated by what they perceived as the failures of the nation's defenses. Although the book appears to have been overshadowed by the heated presidential campaign and was not as widely reviewed as Taylor's and Gavin's earlier works, Kennedy specifically asked CIA Director Allen Dulles for his opinion of it when they met for an intelligence briefing at Kennedy's home in mid-September, and he mentioned Medaris in his February 1960 speech on the missile gap.[48]

Kennedy's interest in Medaris's book suggests a continuing desire on his part to deepen his understanding of military strategy and national defense issues. In substance, Medaris's critique of the military services and of the Eisenhower administration did not differ substantially from those of Ridgway, Gavin, and Taylor. Though his criticisms were not entirely parochial—for example, he called the navy's Polaris missile program "the best bet for retaliatory striking power" in the coming years[49]—Medaris was particularly critical of the air force. He argued that the army and the air force should again be merged, and he questioned the duplication inherent in the Atlas, Titan, and Minuteman ICBM programs.

Elements of the broad foreign policy and national security themes that Kennedy had spoken of for years—the need to spend more on missile programs to close the missile gap, the benefits of diversifying the nation's defenses with strong and flexible conventional forces, and the importance of winning the fight with the Soviets not just for the United States but for the entire free world—are discernible within one of Kennedy's most important speeches of the campaign. When Kennedy spoke to the American Legion meeting in Miami Beach, Florida, on 18 October 1960, he came before the group as a fellow legionnaire. He stressed the common heritage that all veterans share, and he underscored the need for the nation to sacrifice for the good of the world, as all had done in World War II.

Calling "the steady erosion of American power relative to that of the Communists" the "fundamental problem of our time," Kennedy harshly attacked the Republican administration. "No amount of oratory," he said, "can hide the harsh facts behind the rhetoric [and] the soothing words that our prestige has never been higher and that of the Communists never lower. They cannot hide the basic facts that American strength . . . has been slipping, and communism has been steadily advancing."[50]

The key to the "Communist drive for power," according to Kennedy, was their military power. "It is here that the Communist advance and relative American decline can be most sharply seen, and it is here that the danger to our survival is the greatest." Citing a host of bipartisan critics, including H. Rowan Gaither, Nelson Rockefeller, and again Generals Gavin and Taylor, who had all argued that the United States was "slipping . . . into a period of danger," Kennedy called for an aggressive new program to rebuild the nation's defenses, including a "crash program" to build the Polaris submarine and the Minuteman missile, "which will," he said, "eventually close the missile gap."[51]

Arguing that the Soviets questioned whether Americans had the will and determination "for a long, long hard fight," Kennedy challenged the assembled legionnaires to do more, then he concluded on an aggressive but chilling note:

> I want to make it very clear to Mr. Khrushchev and to anyone else who wonders, I will not cut our present commitments to the cause of freedom. . . . I don't want to be the President of a nation perishing under a mushroom cloud of a nuclear warhead. . . . But neither do I wish to be the President of a nation which is being driven back, which is on the defensive, because of its unwillingness to face the facts of our national existence, . . . to bear the burdens which freedom demands.[52]

This speech by Kennedy and a similar address by Nixon, who spoke to the convention on the same day, were afforded extensive coverage by the national news media, including side-by-side stories on the front page of the *New York Times*.[53] But while the two candidates had figuratively faced off on the front pages of major newspapers, the literal face-off that took place during a series of televised debates had a far greater impact on the presidential election of 1960.

The General Election

The Debates

The Kennedy-Nixon debates are often cited as the most important event of the 1960 presidential campaign.[54] In the course of these four verbal confrontations, Kennedy never once spoke explicitly of a missile gap; however, the underlying themes of his campaign—that the country's prestige had fallen and that bold new action was needed to recover the initiative in the global competition with the Soviet Union—came across clearly each time.

Kennedy's broader strategy of tying foreign policy to domestic matters also came across clearly. In the first of the four televised debates, held on 26 September, Kennedy repeatedly invoked the threat to national security to justify his domestic agenda even though moderator Howard K. Smith explained that this first debate, per the candidates' own rules, was to be "restricted to internal or domestic American matters." "We discuss tonight domestic issues," Kennedy said in his opening statement, "but I would not want that [to imply] that this does not involve directly our struggle with Mr. Khrushchev for survival."

The stakes were particularly high because it seemed that the burden of the world rested on the shoulders of the citizens of the United States. In a statement repeated many times during his stump speeches around the country, Kennedy explained, "If we do well here, if we meet our obligations, if we are moving ahead, then I think freedom will be secure around the world. If we fail, then freedom fails." Kennedy explained the significance of the lagging U.S. growth rate in the context of the international competition, again tying economic issues to foreign policy. He doubted that the nation would "be able to reduce the Federal debt very much in 1961, 2, or 3" because of the "heavy obligations which affect our security which we're going to have to meet." In a similar vein, Kennedy explained that while he believed "in the balanced budget," he "would unbalance the budget . . . if there was a grave national emergency or a serious recession."

The broader debate revolved around where the nation's resources were concentrated—in the public sector or the private sector. Nixon claimed that the Eisenhower administration had had monies for schools, hospitals, and highways because it had "encouraged individual enterprise." The result had been "the greatest expansion of the private sector of the economy" in the nation's history. Kennedy disagreed. Although the United States was a rich and powerful country, he contended, this was not enough. The president and the nation's political leaders must "set before our country exactly what we must do in the next decade . . . so that by the year 1970 the United States is ahead" of the Soviet Union.

Nixon, who had passed up several opportunities to attack Kennedy's positions during the debate, now challenged Kennedy's central contention that the Soviet Union was going to surpass the United States. While it was technically accurate to say that Soviet growth had exceeded that of the United States, Nixon pointed out that the Soviets remained far behind the United States in total economic output. But then, reflecting his own ambivalence about the wisdom of Eisenhower's policies, Nixon weakened his argument. The relative economic strength of the United States, he said, should not be a cause for complacency. The Soviet leaders "are determined men, they are fanatical men, and we have to get the very most out of our economy. I agree with Senator Kennedy completely on that score. Where we disagree," he said, "is in the means that we would use to get the most out of our economy."

In his closing comments, Kennedy agreed with Nixon: the goals for all Americans, as they looked at their own country and at the world around them, were the same. The people, like the candidates, however, disagreed on the means to achieve those goals. In this context the choice was clear, he said to the seventy million television viewers and to the millions more listening on the radio. "If you feel that the relative power and prestige and strength of the United States is increasing in relation to that of the Communists, that we are gaining more security, . . . then I . . . think you should vote for Mr. Nixon."

Then Kennedy appealed to those who believed otherwise, those who yearned for a president who would "set before the people the unfinished business of our society." The question before the nation, he said, was this: "Can freedom in the next generation conquer, or are the Communists going to be successful?" The stakes were high. If the nation met its responsibilities, then freedom would conquer, but, Kennedy warned, "if we fail to move ahead, if we fail to develop sufficient military and economic and social strength here in this country, then I think that the tide could begin to run against us, and I don't want historians" to say that "these were the years when the tide ran out for the United States."[55]

The first of the four debates captured the largest audience of prospective voters and is therefore seen as a key turning point in the campaign. After the first debate Kennedy's poll numbers improved, and the size and intensity of the crowds that came to hear him speak notably increased.[56] In the context of Kennedy's broader strategy of tying domestic to foreign policy, the first debate is doubly significant because it was ostensibly focused only on domestic issues.

In the subsequent three debates Kennedy returned to the themes from the first, and Nixon, caught between defending the Eisenhower administration's record and setting out a bold policy agenda of his own, failed in many instances to differentiate his views from those of his Democratic challenger. In the second debate, held on 7 October, when Kennedy was asked about the sacrifices he might ask of his fellow citizens, he said, "These are going to be very difficult times in the 1960s and . . . we're going to have to meet our responsibility as citizens. . . . I'm talking about our willingness to bear any burdens in order to maintain our own freedom" and to extend freedom abroad. Nixon essentially agreed with Kennedy, contending that spending for defense would increase in the coming years, prompting a need to "economize elsewhere."

Nixon was caught in another potential contradiction of the Eisenhower administration when Edward Morgan of ABC asked him to explain how well the country was doing in the Cold War. In his past statements, the vice president had said that the nation was "doing basically well." But how, Morgan asked, did this "square" with the "considerable mass of bipartisan reports and studies, including one prominently participated in by Governor Rockefeller," that had concluded "almost unanimously" that the nation was not reaching its full potential? In his response, Nixon was unable to set his position apart from that of his Democratic opponent. He complained of the "distortions" about the nation's prestige that had been put forward by Kennedy and others, but he concluded by saying that he, too, was "not satisfied with what we're doing in the cold war."

Kennedy returned to Morgan's original question, stressing the bipartisan nature of the criticisms leveled against the Eisenhower administration. "Governor Rockefeller," he noted, "has been far more critical . . . of our position in the world than I have been." But many others had also criticized the administration, Kennedy argued, lending credibility to his position that America was in a period of relative decline. As he had in February on the floor of the Senate, Kennedy noted:

> The Rockefeller brothers report, General Ridgway, General Gavin, the Gaither Report, various reports of congressional committees, all indicate that the relative strength of the United States both militarily, politically, psychologically, and scientifically, and industrially, . . . compared to that of the Soviet Union and the Chinese Communists together, has deteriorated in the last 8 years.

Alvin Spivak of United Press International then asked Kennedy how he would "go about increasing the prestige you say we're losing," and further, whether this could be done "without absolutely wrecking our economy." Kennedy responded to the latter question in the affirmative. Not only did he think that "the United States can afford to do these things" he further stated that "we could not afford not to do these things."

The need for action was so critical because the world depended on the United States to lead the cause of freedom. Alluding to the arguments of Walt Rostow and others, Kennedy claimed that "in the next 10 years the balance of power is going to begin to move . . . towards us or towards the Communists and unless we begin to identify ourselves not only with the anti-Communist fight, but also with the fight against poverty and hunger," then the people of the world would "begin to turn to the Communists as an example." Such measures would not, as Spivak suggested, "wreck the economy." On the contrary, Kennedy said, "if we build our economy the way we should," then the nation can and must "afford to do these things."

As he had done in the first debate—and as Nixon had also done from time to time—Kennedy repeatedly tied domestic economic conditions to the Cold War and to the competition with the Soviet Union and global communism. He reiterated that the nation's "power relative to that of the Communists" had declined and that as a result the nation was "facing a very hazardous time" in the 1960s. Both the debate and the election, Kennedy said, should focus on what would be done in the coming years to reverse this decline, which had been exacerbated, if not precipitated, by an administration that had not "met its responsibilities in the last 8 years."[57]

In the third debate, held on 13 October, Kennedy was asked about his plans to build up the nation's military strength before entering into another summit conference with the Soviets. Douglas Cater of the *Reporter* magazine asked how long it would be before there could be progress on arms control and nuclear disarmament, given that weapon systems took "quite a long time to build." "It may be a long time," Kennedy conceded, "but we must get started immediately." Specifically, he called for an immediate increase in conventional forces and a greater airlift capability for these forces. He also advocated a "full time" effort on missile production, particularly of the Minuteman and Polaris missiles.

Later the discussion turned to the price tag for Kennedy's various proposals. Nixon had claimed that they would cost at least an additional $10 billion each year, an estimate that conformed to what Maxwell Taylor and others had recommended earlier in the year. Cater asked the Democrat to supply his own figures, but Kennedy evaded the question. Instead, he reiterated his support for a balanced budget, noting that he had expressed that support in both of the previous debates and during his years in Congress. "The only two times when an unbalanced budget is warranted," he continued, "would be during a serious recession" or during "a national emergency where there should be large expenditures for national defense." He closed by stressing that the costs of his proposals could be alleviated by a change in monetary policy.

Nixon immediately attacked Kennedy's call for a looser monetary policy, charging that such a move would politicize the Federal Reserve and generate inflationary pressure, but the vice president was hardly off the hook on questions of economic growth and government spending. Roscoe Drummond of the *New York Herald Tribune* noted that Nixon and Governor Rockefeller had both said "that the Nation's economic growth ought to be accelerated." Drummond further pointed out that the Republican platform called for the nation "to quicken the pace of economic growth." "Is it fair," the journalist asked, "to conclude that you feel that there has been insufficient economic growth during the past 8 years; and if so, what would you do beyond present administration policies to step it up?" Nixon was again caught between defending Eisenhower's policies of the past eight years and acquiescing to Rockefeller's—and Kennedy's—complete rejection of those policies. Although Nixon bristled at Kennedy's repeated criticism that the nation had been standing still under President Eisenhower, he believed that "we can and must move faster, and that's why I stand so strongly," he said, "for programs that will move America forward in the sixties." In the end, in his prescriptions for greater economic growth, Nixon seemed to be articulating half-hearted imitations of Kennedy's proposals.

The broader issue separating the two men revolved around achievable and acceptable levels of growth; these issues had been at the center of the debate between the two political parties for many years. Nixon claimed that the nation had not been standing still, and Kennedy disputed that claim, contending that the United States had "had the lowest rate of economic growth . . . of any major industrialized society in the world in 1959." During the past eight years, growth had averaged only 2.5 percent annually, and the nation had failed to achieve full employment, whereas the appropriate level of economic growth, as called for by both Governor Rockefeller and the Democratic platform, was 5 percent.

The candidates also differed over the nation's prestige. Drummond asked Kennedy to "spell out . . . more fully" how the nation "should measure American prestige, to determine whether it is rising or whether it is falling." The issue was critical because the United States was "so identified with the cause of freedom," Kennedy agreed. "If our prestige is spreading," he explained, then those who were standing "on the razor edge of decision, . . . wondering whether they should use the system of freedom to develop their countries or the system of communism," would be "persuaded to follow our example." Kennedy noted that he was not the only person to have claimed that prestige was declining. George Allen, head of the U.S. Information Agency (USIA), had said that the nation's failure to be first in space had caused a decline in American prestige. Beyond this, the Soviet Union's economic growth was as much as two to three times greater than that of the United States; that also contributed to the view, Kennedy said, that "our prestige is not so high."[58]

In the fourth and final debate Nixon argued that the economy had grown over the past seven years and that he believed it could and would grow even more in the next four years. This growth was critical, Nixon said, "because we're in a race for survival; a race in which it isn't enough to be ahead. . . . We have to move ahead in order to stay ahead." For these reasons, Nixon explained, he had made policy recommendations that he believed would "move the American economy ahead, . . . so that there will never be a time when the Soviet Union will be able to challenge our superiority in this field."

Kennedy's prepared remarks focused on a series of central questions: "Are we moving in the direction of peace and security? Is our relative strength growing? Is—as Mr. Nixon says—our prestige at an alltime high . . . and that of the Communists at an alltime low?" Kennedy answered no. While Kennedy agreed with Nixon that the United States was the "strongest country in the world," he also believed that the nation had been "far stronger relative to the Communists five years ago." "The balance of power," Kennedy warned, was "in danger of moving with them."

This change in the relative strength of the two nations, Kennedy argued, was evident in missile technology. Although he made no explicit reference to the missile gap during any of the debates, Kennedy came closest in this fourth and final contest. The Soviets, Kennedy alleged, had "made a breakthrough in missiles," and he predicted that "by 1961, '2, and '3, they will be outnumbering us in missiles." Accordingly, he was not as confident as the vice president that the United States would "be the strongest military power by 1963."

America's relative decline vis-à-vis the Soviets was also evident in the economy, and this had wide-ranging ramifications. Kennedy ended his opening statement with a refrain that had become familiar: "when we are strong and when we are first," he said, "then freedom gains. Then the prospects for peace increase. Then the prospects for our society gain."

During his opening remarks Kennedy also explained that the nation's declining prestige was so dramatic that the State Department was unwilling to release the results of recent polls conducted by the U.S. Information Agency. In response to a question from Walter Cronkite of CBS, Nixon admitted that he was aware of the report, but he charged that Kennedy had contributed to the decline in the nation's prestige. While his opponent had "a responsibility to criticize those things that are wrong," Nixon proclaimed, he also had "a responsibility to be right in his criticisms."

Kennedy bristled at the charges. He emphasized that he had denigrated the leadership the country was getting, not the country itself. Kennedy believed that the Soviet Union was first in space in part because of displaced priorities in the United States. These differing priorities were highlighted in Nixon's famous "kitchen debate" with Khrushchev, in which the vice president had said to the Soviet leader, "You may be ahead of us in rocket thrust but we're ahead of you in color television." Color televisions were not as important as rocket thrust, Kennedy said. Nixon's comments to Khrushchev spoke directly to the Democrats' broader critique that the United States had squandered its lead over the Soviet Union by focusing too much on consumer goods.

Questions about an impending summit also surfaced in this final debate, as they had in the second and third debates. Kennedy stayed on message, arguing that the nation "should not go to the summit until there is some reason to believe that a meeting of minds can be obtained." Before this could happen, the nation needed to build up its strength. Kennedy believed that a summit could not be successful "until we're strong here, until we're moving here." Therefore, Kennedy argued, "the next President should go to work in building the strength of the United States," because the "Soviet Union does understand strength."

In his closing remarks, Kennedy reiterated his reasons for seeking the presidency. "I run," he said "because I believe this year the United States has a great opportunity to make a move forward, to make a determination here at home and around the world, that it's going to reestablish itself as a vigorous society." If the nation could get new leadership, Kennedy said, from a party "which believes in movement, which believes in going ahead," then he was confident that the nation could reestablish its position in the world. This preeminent position would be characterized by a strong defense and strong economic growth.

While Kennedy targeted his comments for a domestic audience, he had a message for foreign observers as well: "I want Mr. Khrushchev to know that a new generation of Americans who fought in Europe and Italy and the Pacific for freedom in World War II have now taken over in the United States, and that they're going to put this country back to work again." The possibilities for the nation were limitless. "I don't believe that there is anything this country cannot do," Kennedy said, "I don't believe there's any burden, or any responsibility, that any American would not assume to protect his country, to protect our security, to advance the cause of freedom."[59]

The Campaign in the States

The broad themes of the Kennedy campaign were clear. Kennedy proclaimed to a national audience—during the debates, in print, and in major addresses covered by the national media—that the nation's prestige was falling and that more must be done to get the country moving again. The missile gap was one indication of this relative decline. Other signs of regression were the nation's sluggish growth rate overall and the particular economic hardships felt by key industries and regions around the country. In accord with this overarching theme, Kennedy devised separate strategies for delivering his message in different states.

The changes of message and tone discernible within Kennedy's stump speeches, juxtaposed with internal campaign documents, show that Kennedy altered his references to foreign policy and national security issues according to the perceived interests of voters in particular areas. He was aided by fellow Democratic officeholders as he made his way across the country. He campaigned with them on the stump and solicited their advice on particular issues. On several occasions he incorporated this advice directly into his campaign speeches. These practices are customary.

In Pennsylvania, New York, Michigan, and California, Kennedy spoke on the broad themes that had served him so well in the run-up to the nomination and had succeeded in the televised debates. In addition to tailoring the themes for local audiences, he further modified his message as the campaign drew to a conclusion. In Pennsylvania, New York, and Michigan, Kennedy won ninety-seven electoral votes on the day of the general election, over one-third of the total needed to win. Kennedy ultimately failed to carry Nixon's home state of California, but he waged a spirited campaign there.

Although the newspapers routinely noted the size and enthusiasm of the crowds that greeted Kennedy, in truth only a handful of voters actually saw him in person. For the millions of others who did not, Kennedy depended upon newspaper reporters to repeat his locally tailored messages for him. At times his message that the nation must do more and that foreign policy was related to domestic policy did not come through clearly in the stories filed by local print journalists.

Pennsylvania—Philadelphia, the Key to the Keystone State—With thirty-two electoral votes, Pennsylvania was tied with California as the second-largest prize in the election of 1960. The state had voted for Democrats in the past—including the current governor, David Lawrence, a Catholic and a Kennedy ally—but it had cast 57 percent of its vote for the Republican Eisenhower in 1956 and had not voted for a Democrat for president in twenty years. A large plurality in the state's urban areas—particularly Philadelphia, Pittsburgh, and Erie—would be the key to a Kennedy victory statewide.

A survey of voter sentiments taken in early September by Kennedy pollster Louis Harris showed the Democratic nominee holding a slight lead in the Keystone State with 44 percent to Nixon's 42, with the remainder undecided. On specific issues the same poll found that voters were less concerned about "war and peace" than about "economic bite" and "taxes and waste in government." Nixon, the poll showed, had the advantage on foreign policy, as well as on rebuilding American prestige and "doing something about Cuba," issues that had worked for Kennedy elsewhere.[60]

Harris argued that the voters of the state needed "to be awakened on the fundamental issues of the loss of U.S. prestige and the need to rebuild our strength throughout the world. As long as they sleep, they will contentedly believe that all has been rosy under the Eisenhower administration." But while the prestige issue, per se, did not yet work to the Democrat's advantage, voters did think that Kennedy was strong on defense. In this apparent paradox, Harris saw both a dilemma and an opportunity. Harris recognized that by urging Kennedy to "work hard on foreign policy," he was asking him to tackle issues that were not currently working for him. Nevertheless, he advised, "the issue must be met—and turned." This would "require alerting the voters—at least of Pennsylvania—to the *need* for solutions."[61]

Kennedy set out immediately to implement this strategy by tying foreign policy themes to domestic concerns. During a brief swing through central and southeastern Pennsylvania in mid-September, Kennedy called his campaign "an effort to mobilize the great strength which is in . . . the great American Republic . . . for the great struggle." Stressing that "the United States cannot be strong in its foreign policy unless it is also strong domestically," he called for a "liberal foreign policy marked by . . . a domestic policy here in the State of Pennsylvania and around the country that moves." He warned: "We will not win the greatest contest in our history if our economy limps along at the lowest rate of growth of any major industrialized society in the world. . . . The resources that we need . . . are lost . . . when men are out of work and cannot find work, and when we have a lack of economic growth."[62]

On the following day Kennedy drew attention to Pennsylvania's unused resources and again related this to the global struggle. "When half of the steel mill capacity in this State is unused and, therefore, half of the steel-workers in this State do not find a good job," he told a crowd in Lebanon, "then you know that a basic asset which distinguishes us from our adversaries, the productive capacity of the United States, is not being used."[63]

However, Kennedy's references to the need for developing unused resources were not sufficiently explicit to satisfy some of his listeners. A leading newspaper in the state, the *Philadelphia Inquirer,* criticized the senator for not explicitly promising to provide jobs in depressed areas. Kennedy "spoke of the reduced operation of the State's steel mills, which he said resulted in unemployment," the *Inquirer* story read, "but he did not take advantage of the opportunity to make an all-out pledge of job development." This was of particular concern in Reading, "where several thousand unemployed workers jammed Market Square hoping to hear him discuss plans to provide work."[64]

The *Inquirer's* criticisms notwithstanding, Harris's second poll in the state showed that Kennedy had widened his lead over the vice president by hammering away on economic issues, but that foreign policy continued to work for Nixon in the state. Harris predicted confidently that if Kennedy deliberately avoided the foreign policy issues that would serve him well in other states, he could score an upset victory by focusing on the industrial centers of the state and by discussing solutions "to the economic problems besetting the people."[65]

Harris placed particular emphasis on the importance of Philadelphia.[66] Seeking as much as 60 percent of the popular vote in the greater Philadelphia area, Kennedy returned to the City of Brotherly Love in the waning days of the campaign. He carried his message of sacrifice to suburban voters as well as to the strong Democratic base within the city. Images of declining prestige and the nation's lackluster performance vis-à-vis the Soviet Union continued to pay dividends here for Kennedy. He also mixed in some humor. Kennedy poked fun at his rival's boast to Khrushchev during their famed "kitchen debate" in 1959 that the United States had built the biggest shopping center. Kennedy countered that the Soviets had built "the largest dam, the largest missile, the largest army." And while, in Kennedy's words, Nixon had "put his finger in Mr. Khrushchev's nose, and said, 'You may be ahead of us in rockets, but we are ahead of you in color television,'" Kennedy declared, "I would rather take my television black and white and have the largest rockets in the world."[67]

Kennedy also criticized Nixon for his inconsistent statements about the nation's standing in the world. At one point during the campaign Nixon had said that the nation was still "first in space and the strongest power militarily in the world." According to Kennedy, however, "the vice president's own written statement on space had said 'The space gap is not yet closed.'" Kennedy's caustic observation that "we would really have an interesting discussion . . . if Mr. Nixon and Mr. Nixon would debate" drew laughter and applause from the assembled crowd.[68] These comments were not lost on John S. McCullough, who was covering Kennedy's visit for the *Philadelphia Evening Bulletin.* Noting that the crowds that greeted Kennedy were larger and more enthusiastic than those that had gathered to hear the vice president speak during the preceding week, the reporter highlighted Kennedy's repeated charges about declining American prestige worldwide.[69]

But while Philadelphia was a crucial area for Kennedy, he did not ignore the concerns of voters in the heart of the anthracite coal communities to the north and west of the state's largest city. In Pottsville on 28 October he explicitly raised the issue of high unemployment. Perhaps having learned from the criticisms he had received in nearby Reading the month before, that he should promise to do more to provide jobs for the unemployed, Kennedy proposed channeling defense contracts to areas of high unemployment by reinstating Defense Manpower Policy Number 4, which had been repealed, as he told his audience, in 1953 by a Republican Congress.[70]

Harris's third and final poll found that Kennedy had a "decisive" lead in the state, with respondents supporting him by a margin of 48.1 percent to Nixon's 40.4. Harris predicted that Kennedy would win easily if the undecided vote held, but an "all-out effort" was called for, particularly in Philadelphia.[71] Harris's prediction proved prophetic. When the final vote was counted, Kennedy had won Pennsylvania with 51.1 percent of the popular vote. A majority of those who had been undecided had cast their votes for Nixon, and Philadelphia proved to be the key to Kennedy's victory. With a fervor that left veteran politicians "glassy-eyed and speechless," according to the *Evening Bulletin,* 88 percent of registered voters in Philadelphia turned out on election day, and they voted for the Democrat by a decisive two-to-one margin.[72]

Although Kennedy believed that more must be done to build the nation's defenses and to regain the initiative in the Cold War, Harris had urged Kennedy to downplay foreign policy and defense in his campaign speeches in Pennsylvania. Neither of these issues was a major factor in Kennedy's victory in the state. He would tailor his message in other states as well.

New York—One State, Worlds Apart—John F. Kennedy had reason to worry about his prospects for victory in New York. With the exception of native New Yorkers Franklin Roosevelt and Al Smith, no Democrat had carried the state since Woodrow Wilson in 1912, and the state's electoral votes had been counted in the Republican column since 1948. But there was some evidence that Kennedy's message would resonate.

In 1958, New Yorkers had elected as governor Nelson Rockefeller, a liberal Republican who had been harshly critical of Eisenhower's spending priorities. Kennedy had spoken favorably of Rockefeller and had used the governor's own statements to attack Nixon's positions on defense, national security, and domestic affairs.

Kennedy knew that success in the state depended upon big pluralities in New York City. Nevertheless, the senator also directed attention to the string of industrial towns along the shores of Lakes Erie and Ontario, far removed from Gotham in both spirit and outlook. His messages to voters in New York City and upstate are notable for their differences.

After two brief visits to the state in August, Kennedy returned for a day of campaigning in New York City in mid-September. During this stop, Kennedy laid heavy emphasis on domestic and economic issues, including the problem of joblessness, and he tied these themes to broader international issues. Speaking at a Citizens for Kennedy rally, the candidate said that the nation could not "possibly separate our domestic policy from our foreign policy as the Republicans seek to do."[73] That evening, in a speech at the New York Liberal Party Convention, Kennedy declared that "The cause of liberalism . . . cannot content itself with carrying on the fight for human justice and economic liberalism here at home. For here and around the world the fear of war hangs over us every morning and every night." The situation called for actions, not words. The nation could not banish this fear of war, he continued, "by repeating that we are economically first or that we are militarily first, for saying so doesn't make it so."[74]

After these few brief visits, a new Harris poll taken in mid-September found Kennedy with a slight lead of 43 to 40 percent over Nixon in the state, with the remainder undecided. In contrast to polls in neighboring Pennsylvania, where economic issues were of primary concern, this poll of New York voters found "war and peace" to be the leading issue (55 percent) with "taxes and spending" second (40 percent). Harris determined that "the roster of issues . . . in New York" worked for Kennedy, and he predicted that this could "provide an enormous momentum in this state."[75]

Harris observed that the relative importance of foreign policy did not automatically favor Nixon in New York. "The issue of rebuilding this nation's prestige" was a leading issue, and it worked for Kennedy. Harris therefore recommended a continued emphasis on the need for action. There were some indications, Harris wrote, that "the Kennedy theme" of "promising action and motion that can propel America from the 'stalled on a dime,' 'standstill' sorry lot we have now fallen into" was just beginning to penetrate. "However, as with all massive concepts," Harris urged, it would require "constant reiteration."[76]

Although foreign policy worked for Kennedy, Harris found that the defense issue and "getting tough with the Russians" continued to work to Nixon's advantage. The pollster concluded, therefore, that Kennedy had not yet made his case for a stronger national defense. Harris cautioned, however, that while the issue of the nation's declining defenses "must be pinpointed," it should not be done "to the point of conjuring up an image of sword-rattling," which would open up the candidate to the "charge that . . . the Democrats are the party of war."[77]

Kennedy was mindful of these concerns, but he was genuinely committed to spending more on the nation's defenses. He also recognized the political value of stressing this theme at particular times and in particular places. Two weeks after Harris's study was written, Kennedy eschewed caution in a bold-faced appeal for the votes of defense industry workers who had been displaced by changing defense priorities. After a stop in Erie, Pennsylvania, Kennedy traveled less than one hundred miles east to speak at the Bell Aircraft factory in Niagara Falls, New York. The factory that had employed 10,000 during the Korean War had seen its number of jobs cut to a mere 1,800 in recent years.[78] In a speech before nine hundred of these workers, Kennedy began by asserting that the "Democratic Party stands for a stronger America; not strong if, but, when or something, but strong this year, now, period." The next president, he said, should "send a message to Congress in the first 3 months of his office which will request appropriations which" would place the United States "in a position to stand up to the Soviet Union or the Chinese Communists. or anyone else who wishes to threaten our security."[79]

From there Kennedy moved immediately to the issue of full employment. Deploring the underutilization of factories and resources in the United States, Kennedy reaffirmed his belief that defense spending and employment went hand in hand. "If this country is moving ahead," he said, "if we have fiscal and monetary policies which stimulate employment, if we have a defense policy which provides not only protection for the United States but strength for our economy," then this would "provide security for our people" and "security for freedom."[80]

Then, no doubt mindful of criticisms lodged against him in Reading, Pennsylvania, two weeks earlier, Kennedy called for governmental action to solve the problem of unemployment. When asked during the ensuing question-and-answer session, "Why are all the defense contracts going to California, to the west coast?" Kennedy made clear his views about the relationship between the defense industry and regional economic development:

> I represent a section of the United States, New England, which has had the same problem that upper New York has had, defense contracts leaving, industries laying off, and we have begun to bring them back. . . . I think defense contracts should be fairly distributed across the Nation. I also support the reestablishment of the Defense Manpower Policy No. 4, which was thrown out in 1952, which provided that . . . defense contracts would go to those areas which were able to meet the competitive price and had over 8 percent unemployment.[81]

"I think we can use defense contracts to strengthen the economy as well as strengthen the country," he said, and he pledged, if elected, to "try to distribute defense contracts fairly so that it protects the United States and protects the economy."[82]

Comments such as these played well in the upstate cities of Buffalo, Rochester, and Niagara Falls. One front-page account in the *New York Times* observed that the Democratic nominee's emphasis on three big themes, including the "contention that Republicans were committed to limitations on the nation's productive capacity," were popular "in areas where incomes have been hit by curtailed steel production and lay-offs in airplane and electrochemical plants."[83]

Kennedy then shifted his New York message once again. When he returned to the state in mid-October, he concentrated his efforts within New York City, and he downplayed the use of defense spending to boost employment. He did not, however, tone down his criticism of what he considered to be the inadequacies of the Eisenhower administration's defense program. In a speech before the Democratic national and state committees, Kennedy questioned Nixon's zeal for action against China "at a time when we have been steadily reducing our conventional forces and inviting a lag in missile power."[84] Then, during a series of appearances the following day, Kennedy declared that he and the Democratic Party stood for making the nation stronger "here at home . . . so that people around the world who wish to be free" would "identify themselves with us" and follow U.S. leadership.[85] Kennedy also emphasized that the welfare of union workers and the security of the country were inextricably connected, and he declared that "the labor movement and all Americans" had "an obligation to participate in strengthening our country, making it work, making our system move."[86]

By all media estimates, Kennedy's visit was a stunning success. Still, his message relating foreign policy to domestic concerns was often drowned out in the print media by other considerations. News coverage focused primarily on the size of the crowds that greeted Kennedy—estimated to be in excess of one million people, the largest in the city since Charles Lindbergh's triumphant return.[87] Domestic policy was the only substantive issue addressed by the major papers, and it was relegated to page twenty-six within the massive Sunday edition of the *New York Times*.[88]

That same page of the *Times* contained some good news for the Kennedy campaign: the results of a *Daily News* poll showed the Democrat with a slight lead in the state. Kennedy's own poll, taken during the second week of October, also found him holding a slight lead, but Harris had warned that the "Catholic vote is far from satisfactory." Moreover, he viewed Kennedy's weakness on foreign policy as a concern that must be "frontally assaulted."[89]

When Kennedy returned to New York a few days later, he did just that. Before the Trade Union Council of the Liberal Party, Kennedy lamented the nation's declining prestige.[90] Later, in Queens, Kennedy charged that the country was "not moving ahead like it is going to have to move ahead if we are going to meet our responsibilities to ourselves, to those who come after us, to those who look to us around the world for leadership."[91]

These last-minute efforts seemed to have paid off. The third and final Harris poll in the state, taken during the last week of October, found Kennedy pulling away from Nixon. Harris noted that "war and peace" had "soared in importance and now works for Nixon to a slight degree," but hastened to add that "this does not mean the Senator should not talk about foreign policy." Instead, Harris urged, Kennedy "should tie in his foreign policy recommendations with the domestic issues as he so often has during the campaign saying that in order to rebuilt [*sic*] prestige throughout the world we must also move here at home."[92]

In the end, Kennedy carried New York with a comfortable 52.5 percent of the popular vote, bettering Stevenson's 1956 vote total by more than 1.1 million. Although his plurality in New York City was a crucial factor in Kennedy's win, his appearances in upstate New York, where jobs were so closely tied to the defense industry, appear to have been particularly effective. In Erie County, Kennedy won a sizable 56.6 percent of the popular vote, a significant improvement over Stevenson's showing in 1952 and 1956. Kennedy won a narrow victory in Niagara County, home to the Bell Aircraft factory in Niagara Falls. Although he failed to carry Monroe County, his 48.8 percent of the popular vote there represented a significant increase over Stevenson's 33.2 percent in 1956.

Michigan—The Motor City and Macomb County—Michigan's twenty electoral votes were crucial for the Kennedy campaign. Once again Kennedy was depending upon big pluralities in urban areas, in this case Detroit. Unlike in New York and Pennsylvania, however, Kennedy had important allies in Michigan, including outgoing governor G. Mennen Williams, United Auto Workers chief Walter Reuther, and state party chairman Neil Staebler. These men and the other members of the state Democratic machine intended to help Kennedy become the first Democrat to carry the state since 1944.[93]

From August to November, Kennedy campaigned in Michigan no fewer than five days. His first visit to the state, however, had little to do with local concerns. In late August, Kennedy appeared before the Veterans of Foreign Wars (VFW) convention in Detroit and used the occasion to emphasize his own wartime service and to praise the VFW for taking a firm stand for a stronger defense.

In his speech Kennedy blasted Republicans for offering "rosy reassurances" that all would be well in the future. Asserting that national prestige was at an all-time low, that enemies were treating the United States with disrespect, and that the nation's friends were doubting U.S. resolve, Kennedy laid out the "facts": "Our security and leadership are both slipping away from us . . . the balance of world power is slowly shifting to the Soviet–Red Chinese bloc," and "our own shores are for the first time since 1812, imperiled by chinks in our defensive armor." Although Kennedy argued that the United States was still the "greatest Nation on earth," he questioned whether the same would be said five or ten years hence. The candidate was doubtful, and he used the missile lag to press home his point: "The facts of the matter are that we are falling behind. . . . The missile lag looms large." Believing that the United States must have a defensive capability that was second to none, Kennedy called for acceleration of the Polaris, Minuteman, and other missiles programs; expansion and modernization of conventional forces; and provision of greater protections for the nuclear retaliatory force so it would not suffer a "knockout blow."[94]

Concluding that "the American people are ready to face the facts and pay the cost" Kennedy reminded his fellow veterans that "the enemy has the power to destroy—but . . . he also seeks, by economic and political warfare, to isolate us. He intends to outproduce us. He intends to outlast us. . . . And the real question now is whether we are up to the task—whether each and every one of us is willing to face the facts, to bear the burdens . . . to meet our dangers."[95]

Although Kennedy's VFW speech attracted national attention, many of the details of his address were overshadowed in the

Michigan papers by other campaign-related stories. For example, the banner headline "AFL-CIO Endorses Kennedy" dominated the front page of the *Detroit Free Press*. Nonetheless, *Free Press* reporter Ray Courage gamely chronicled the details of Kennedy's speech, including Kennedy's specific proposals for strengthening the nation's defenses.[96]

The press coverage was not, however, uniformly positive; the picture *Free Press* editors painted of the Democratic candidate's charges displayed their ambivalence. "Perhaps without intending to, Senator Kennedy in his Detroit speech brought the entire question of national defense down to a final choice," they wrote in an editorial published on the day after the speech. "By stating that 'the harsh facts of the matter are that our security and leadership are both slipping away from us' he put it up to the individual citizen-voter: Are you going to accept the statement of your President to the effect that we are more than holding our own against the Russians, or are you going to follow Senator Kennedy?" Although the editors did not provide an answer to their own rhetorical question, a related editorial cartoon on the same page suggested that Kennedy was playing political football with defense facts.[97]

Skeptical *Free Press* editors aside, Kennedy still had important political allies in Michigan. Several days after the VFW speech, Michigan senator Philip Hart gave the candidate some advice that would be useful during his campaign in the state. According to a memo drafted by members of Hart's staff, unemployment—calculated at 8.9 percent in Michigan and 9.6 percent in Detroit—was the leading issue in the state. "The cause of Michigan unemployment has been a major state political issue since 1957," the memo stated. Although the Republicans had blamed "Governor Williams for fostering an 'unfavorable business climate,'" Hart's staff pointed instead to the "almost complete loss of defense contracts as emphasis on wheeled vehicles" had declined during the Eisenhower administration.

On the question of defense contracts, Hart's staff noted that the Chrysler missile facility at Redstone Arsenal was "laying off workers as the Army production of the Redstone and the Jupiter missiles comes to an end." The memo explained that Secretary of Defense Gates had told Senator Hart that "as far as the Department of Defense is concerned they consider this facility is no longer needed in our national defense effort. This is in *Congressman Jim O'Hara's district,* and at peak employed about 11,000 workers. The failure to utilize this missile production facility—that produced the missile that put the first satellite into orbit—is a point that could *well be mentioned.*"[98]

Kennedy was also advised of the importance of the Detroit Tank Arsenal at Centerline, which had been reactivated to build the M-60 tank. "The community is quite sensitive to the need for the modernization of the army's equipment," the memo concluded, "and it is this type of defense contract that means the most to the Michigan industrial complex."[99]

Cutbacks within particular military spending programs had had an adverse effect on Michigan's economy. A government report issued in 1963 indicated that purchases of weapons, ammunition, tanks and automotive equipment, and production equipment constituted over 50 percent of the goods delivered to the Defense Department in 1953. By 1961, these same goods combined accounted for less than 13 percent of government purchases. Michigan's economic decline was closely tied to these procurement shifts. Over 10 percent of prime contract awards during World War II went to companies in Michigan, and this proportion was nearly equaled during the Korean War. By 1961, however, only 2.7 percent of defense prime contracts were flowing to the state.[100]

Kennedy returned to the home of the nation's auto industry on Labor Day with advice from the Hart memorandum in the front of his mind. During a series of addresses, Kennedy stressed issues of concern to the hundreds of thousands of autoworkers in the state, and he also managed to work in references to foreign policy and defense. In a written statement to commemorate Labor Day, Kennedy explained that "The free labor movement has played, and will continue to play, an important role in stopping Communist aggression."[101] Later, at Cadillac Square in downtown Detroit, Kennedy repeated his charge that Russia was growing while the United States lagged behind. Evidence of this disparity was abundant. "Our workers have seen it in shorter workweeks," he said. "Our steel industry sees it in producing 50 percent of capacity, and Mr. Khrushchev sees it when he promises to bury us." Kennedy argued, "This country's power is unlimited. . . . If the President of the United States will just merely set before us our national goals," the nation would be "willing to bear the burden that must come to reach those goals."[102] Although Kennedy pledged a larger federal role in employment, with full employment as a clear goal, he made no specific mention of defense; nor did he mention using defense contracts to solve employment problems during this Labor Day campaign visit.

On the heels of this visit to Michigan, Kennedy received additional advice from pollster Louis Harris. A poll taken during the first week of September indicated that Nixon had a slight lead in the state. This same poll also showed that the vice president had a particular edge on the issue of "war and peace," which was the leading issue of concern among those surveyed. This was the "chief source of worry for most people" in other states as well, Harris observed, but whereas the issue worked for neither candidate in California and Ohio, Nixon was benefiting from it in Michigan. Accordingly, Harris recommended a two-tiered strategy. First, he wrote, Kennedy "must blunt the edge of the issue by hammering at Republican do-nothingism while Communism has made strides in the underdeveloped countries of the world. Second, he must continue his declarations that America must grow in courage and spirit as well as in material possessions if it is to be the leader of the new free world." Harris called for "a major effort" to "decrease total concern" over the issue. If this could be done, Harris was confident, Kennedy's superiority on other issues would become "much more valuable than it presently is in the shadow of the foreign affairs issue."[103]

Within a month, Kennedy appeared to have turned the corner. Harris's second poll of prospective voters in Michigan, taken during the first week of October, showed Kennedy with a "fair, though not safe, majority."[104] The key appeared to have been Kennedy's ability to carry through on Harris's advice from the preceding month. Harris found that "war and peace" remained the number one concern among 43 percent of respondents, but this was down from the 50 percent of an earlier poll; meanwhile economic issues had risen in importance, with 39 percent of those surveyed now counting this issue as a matter of primary concern.

Attributing much of Kennedy's reversal of fortune to his success during the first televised debate, Harris urged the candidate to stick with familiar themes. The pollster determined that because Kennedy had "almost completely negated Nixon's former advantage on rebuilding prestige," he could now speak freely on this subject. Likewise, Harris found that Kennedy had overcome Nixon's advantage on the subject of dealing with Russia, and he had increased his edge on national defense. Harris predicted, "Just as long as Kennedy can keep Nixon at least neutralized on foreign affairs, he can club him to death with domestic issues." He further emphasized that "foreign and domestic issues must constantly be related to each other by the point that we cannot be strong abroad if we are not strong at home."[105]

Kennedy stressed these points during a day of campaigning in metropolitan Detroit in late October. Following the advice he had received from Senator Hart, and having learned from his recent experiences in upstate New York and Pennsylvania, he made the case for using defense dollars to rectify regional economic distress. In the Macomb County city of Warren, Kennedy focused on several problems alluded to by Hart's staff by demonstrating how local issues related to the global contest. "In your two arsenals," Kennedy noted, "you have seen employment go from 10,000 to 2,000. This area of the State depends on the Jupiter, and the Jupiter missile program may be coming to an end." "We have to find jobs in Michigan," Kennedy promised, "and we have to find jobs in the United States. . . . Unless we have people working we are not able to maintain our position any place around the world."[106]

Kennedy had spoken in general terms of the federal government's role in boosting regional employment during his first visit to Michigan in early September. On this occasion he was more explicit, calling for a revival of Defense Manpower Policy Number 4. His declaration that the nation "could use . . . defense contracts to put people to work as well as make weapons" drew cheers from the crowd. He further recommended that defense procurement be planned on a long-range basis, so "we take advantage not only of the skills of the people in the area, but we also recognize their needs," and he called for passage of an area redevelopment bill to attract industry to the region. He told his audience that he deplored "the overnight cancellation of contracts which leaves thousands of men stranded on the beach."[107]

Kennedy's emphasis on regional unemployment resonated with some local reporters. One story, for example, quoted Kennedy's statement that "those who say we've never had it so good should come to Michigan and talk to its unemployed—some of whom haven't had a job since the 1958 recession."[108] Other press coverage of Kennedy's campaign treks in Michigan, however, afforded relatively little attention to specific issues, opting instead to document the size of crowds. According to one report, "shrieking, shouting teen-agers" greeted Kennedy in Macomb County, and he was "cheered like a football hero" and greeted by signs in Polish, Ukrainian, and English in the Democratic stronghold of Hamtramck.[109]

A majority of the men and women who turned out on Election Day in Michigan cast their ballots for Kennedy. The margin of victory in the Wolverine State was close as a percentage of the total vote, but Kennedy did manage to win by 66,841 votes. As in other states, labor and urban voters were central to the Kennedy win. Wayne County, which includes Detroit, and neighboring Macomb County to the north were the key to his victory statewide. In Wayne County, Kennedy garnered 66 percent of the popular vote en route to a 378,842-vote plurality. By contrast, Stevenson had won less than 58 percent of the vote in Wayne County in both 1952 and 1956. Meanwhile, in Macomb County, Kennedy's appeal to displaced defense workers appears to have paid dividends. Home of the Redstone Arsenal discussed in Senator Hart's memo, Macomb gave Kennedy 62.8 percent of its popular vote, a considerable improvement over Stevenson's 49.1 and 51.7 percent of the vote in 1952 and 1956, respectively. Many years later, Bill Clinton pollster Stanley Greenberg declared Macomb to have been "the most Democratic suburb in America" in the election of 1960.[110] The limits of Kennedy's victory in Michigan are as striking as his ultimate success. He won only thirteen of the state's eighty-three counties; Macomb and Wayne accounted for 52 percent of all the votes cast for Kennedy in the entire state of Michigan.

California—The Land of Missed Opportunity—Kennedy could not depend exclusively on a lopsided urban vote in California. After winning the nomination at the Democratic National Convention in Los Angeles in July, he returned to California as his party's standard-bearer on at least two separate occasions, and he spent over six days campaigning in the state. Kennedy's foray into Nixon's backyard seems unwise if viewed in isolation. Yet it makes sense when viewed through the lens of Kennedy's broader campaign strategy of relating foreign policy and defense issues to the economic concerns of voters.

Although California's nonagricultural employment had risen two-and-a-half times faster than that of the nation as a whole between 1949 and 1959, employment in the aircraft and ordnance sectors in both Los Angeles and San Diego had declined sharply during the Eisenhower administration. An April 1960 report by the California Department of Labor reported that aircraft employment in the state had fallen to its lowest level in over seven years. The declines continued through the summer of 1960. By September the number of people employed in the aircraft industry in Greater Los Angeles alone was down 17.5 percent from the previous year.[111] The situation was even worse in San Diego, where in June the state reported "the most marked reversal of nonfarm employment trends in the first half of 1960 compared with 1959."[112]

These declines carried over to other industries as well. Reflecting continued reductions in the aircraft and ordnance industries, employment in durable goods manufacturing had dropped by 8 percent since the beginning of the year, in contrast to a 3 percent increase during the same six-month period in 1959.[113] Kennedy found fertile ground amidst the anxieties of thousands of displaced workers for his campaign pledge to "get the country moving again." Accordingly, during nearly all of his appearances in the state, but particularly those in southern California, Kennedy focused on the related issues of jobs and rebuilding the nation's defenses.

During a four-day campaign swing through California that took him from the Oregon border to San Diego, Kennedy shifted his message from place to place to address local concerns, but he rarely missed an opportunity to relate local issues to the global struggle with communism. Within the small farming communities of northern California, Kennedy focused on resource development, water and irrigation, and power generation. He then pointed out that the Soviets were quickly gaining on the United States in the development of their hydroelectric capacity.[114] Then, after lingering only briefly in the San Francisco area to deliver a speech in Oakland that stressed the issues of substandard housing, hunger, and unemployment, Kennedy turned inland again with his campaign. In Stockton he said that the United States could do better. In Modesto, Merced, and Madera, he stressed that America could both take care of its own people and serve as the leader of the free world. In each place he continued to hammer away at themes of sacrifice and willingness to accept the burdens of prosperity in order to lead the free world.[115]

Kennedy also put forward his belief that by building more weapons the nation would achieve lasting security. Achieving peace in an era when both the United States and the Soviet Union possessed thermonuclear weapons, he noted, was the one problem facing the entire nation. In Fresno Kennedy confronted directly the view that the Democratic Party was the party of war. He asserted that all Americans wanted to live in peace and security but that the prerequisite for such security was military strength. Only from a position of strength could the United States negotiate with the Soviets toward global disarmament.[116]

Kennedy concluded his train travels through the state's central valley in Bakersfield before boarding a plane to Los Angeles, where he addressed a large crowd in the Shrine Auditorium. Having just traveled over three thousand miles within the state, Kennedy stated his belief that California would be "a good place to settle this election, right here in the Vice President's own backyard." Then he repeated the charges he had made during his train campaign, again blending foreign policy and domestic issues. On everything from agricultural surpluses to economic growth to the training of scientists and engineers, what the United States accomplished had importance not only for the people of this country, but for the people of Latin America, Africa, Asia, and Western Europe as well.[117]

During a brief press conference on the same day, Kennedy was asked what sacrifices were needed in order for the country to wage, and win, the fight for hearts and minds. The candidate reiterated that a "bigger effort in the field of national defense" was required, including a continuation of the draft and the strengthening of conventional forces with new technology. But Kennedy otherwise tried to downplay the burdens on ordinary citizens. For example, although he conceded that his proposals might require higher taxes, he did not rule out the need for deficit spending, arguing that the greater threat at that time was deflation, not inflation.[118]

Kennedy's travels through California took him to San Diego on the fourth and final day of his long tour. The city was home to thousands of workers employed in defense industries, and Kennedy lost no time trying to attract their support. Before a small crowd at Lindbergh Field, Kennedy reminded his audience that "the basic issue which separates the Republicans and Democrats in this campaign is whether we are doing as well as we can do." He explained that Democrats held the view "that while this is a great country, we can do better; while this is a great State, we can do better; while this is a powerful country, it can be stronger," and he predicted that San Diego, a leading place for building "American strength and American force and American vitality," would "lead the Democratic tide."[119]

Later in the day Kennedy focused almost exclusively on the related questions of national defense and employment by recognizing the unique role of military spending in southern California. In San Diego, Kennedy said, "which is particularly dependent upon those industries which serve our national defense, you have seen the effect of a governmental policy which I consider to be shortsighted, and that is a policy which takes risks . . . with our national security." Kennedy made clear that he would embark on a different course. He declared that the nation "should strengthen itself, and I think this city has a particular role to play in that strengthening." The senator committed himself to making "a greater effort in the field of missiles," to expanding the nation's airlift capacity, and finally to strengthening the country's retaliatory capacity with "the traditional manned bomber," and he concluded his remarks with a firm pledge: "I think we can do more, . . . and having known we can do more, I think we should not do less."[120]

Kennedy's bold appeal for the support of defense workers was immediately noticed by local reporters covering his campaign visit. For example, *San Diego Union* reporter Henry Love stressed the prominent role Kennedy had afforded to San Diego in his national defense program.[121] But not everyone welcomed the attention. Kennedy's speech in San Diego combined an explicit pledge to build the nation's defenses with a merely implicit promise to help those seeking employment opportunities in defense industries, but that promise was clear to conservatives who remained unalterably opposed to any federal employment initiatives, defense-related or otherwise. Editors of the *San Diego Union* ridiculed Kennedy's "Campaign of Promises for All" and questioned the wisdom of spending "billions more for the American military machine, thus providing fat overtime checks" for the United Auto Workers "and other industrial hands."[122]

Undeterred by such criticism, Kennedy returned to California late in the campaign. This time he focused his efforts almost entirely on the defense-dependent areas of Los Angeles, Long Beach, and San Diego. During a two-day foray into Nixon's backyard, Kennedy again emphasized foreign policy and defense issues, particularly as they related to the economic well-being of those communities. The local press took note. The *Los Angeles Times* recorded Kennedy's criticisms of the GOP's "arbitrary" budget slashes on aircraft and missile programs. "The Republican decision to cut national defense and defense employment, without regard for either our national security or the needs of our workers," Kennedy argued, "should shock every citizen."[123]

Still, Kennedy realized almost as soon as he arrived this time that his efforts in California may have been misdirected. Although enthusiastic crowds greeted him, Kennedy's appearances in southern California were largely upstaged in the press by news about an important defense contract for a local company.

The B-70 Valkyrie was a new supersonic bomber that was intended to replace the B-52. Weighing over five hundred thousand pounds, powered by six advanced turbojet engines, and constructed with new composite materials, the experimental version of the B-70 was, according to one industry historian, "the most advanced aircraft ever conceived."[124] The Eisenhower administration had awarded the B-70 development contract to North American Aviation Corporation, based in Long Beach, California, in December 1957. But the project had long been a point of contention between Eisenhower and senior air force officers. The president had become convinced of the futility of manned aircraft in the missile age, and he had grown increasingly skeptical of the value of the B-70. He preferred to cancel the program completely, but finally accepted a compromise with the air force. In late 1959 the president approved the expenditure of $150 million for the B-70 for FY 1961, and another $75 million for FY 1962—a reduction of nearly $550 million from previous budgets.[125] Even with the budget reduction, however, the B-70 refused to die. Air force generals including Nathan Twining, Thomas White, Thomas Power, and Curtis LeMay all pushed for continued development of the B-70, directly contradicting Eisenhower's wishes.

North American Aviation employees in southern California followed this debate over the B-70 with increasing urgency, and they implored their elected officials to save their "beloved B-70." The over twenty-seven thousand of the company's workers who were members of Local 887 of the United Auto Workers were particularly vocal during the campaign year of 1960, criticizing the Eisenhower-Nixon administration for its shortsightedness.[126]

Meanwhile, the union celebrated John F. Kennedy's candidacy.[127] The senator repeatedly called for continued funding for the bomber, particularly during his two campaign swings through California in 1960. Other presidential aspirants, including Stuart Symington and Lyndon Johnson, also supported the B-70, and Congress, under the control of the Democratic Party, authorized $265 million for the program in FY 1960, $190 million more than Eisenhower had requested. The president initially refused to spend the additional monies, but when he chose in early November to release over $155 million for the B-70, the local media cheered his apparent change of heart.[128]

Kennedy tried to put his own spin on the president's decision. He charged that Eisenhower's objective was "not to increase national defense" but rather "to increase Republican votes." Kennedy pointed out that the Democratic Congress had twice tried to increase defense spending, but that the economy-minded Eisenhower had blocked these efforts, choosing instead to impound funds that had been appropriated for a number of defense programs. "In short," Kennedy's statement concluded, "while the Republicans are willing to take desperate measures to win votes, they are doing less than the Congress has stipulated in building the Nation's defenses."[129]

Kennedy was also on the defensive in California for his support of Defense Manpower Policy Number 4 and other procurement reforms that might have shifted defense jobs out of the state. In response to charges that he wanted to relocate defense jobs to the East, as he said he would do while campaigning in Pennsylvania, New York, and Michigan, Kennedy stressed that he was for "employment in California and New York and across the nation," whereas his opponent thought that unemployment was "inevitable."[130]

When Kennedy traveled south to San Diego on 2 November, he blasted Nixon for suggesting that the senator would take defense jobs away from Californians. "To show you how desperate and despicable this campaign has become," Kennedy said, the Nixon forces "are handing out outside defense plants a poster which says 'Attention Defense workers: Jack Kennedy is after your job. He urges moving defense industries back east.'" The senator categorically rejected Nixon's claims. "If I were President of the United States," he stressed, "I would represent the United States. . . . The defense plants were put out here for good reason, and they are going to stay here for the same reason. It has not anything to do with whether I come from Massachusetts or California." To further make his case against his rival, Kennedy noted that "California has seen defense plants leave," during Nixon's tenure as vice president.[131]

"I want Mr. Khrushchev to know," Kennedy continued, "that a new generation of Americans . . . is going to fight in the 1960s for the defense of freedom in the United States and all around the world." Kennedy was ready to lead that fight. He emphasized that he had voted to appropriate over $300 million for the B-70 aircraft, and he reaffirmed his determination to build the nation's defenses. As before, San Diegans were assigned a crucial role in that effort. Kennedy exhorted his audience, "I ask you in this community, hard hit, but a basic defense area of the United States, I ask you as citizens of the country, can we entrust the leadership to Mr. Nixon and the Republican Party?" For Kennedy the answer was a clear and resounding no. He said that he wanted to see "this country move again," and he called on the people of San Diego and California to help him "in securing the future."[132]

Contemporary media accounts of Kennedy's final campaign visit to the state varied. On 2 November the *Los Angeles Times* ran a story about Kennedy's visit to the area beneath a huge banner headline in their final edition and included two front-page stories detailing his travels. Lou Fleming of the *Times* noted that Kennedy emphasized full employment and national defense in his final appeal for the voters' support, while another article noted Kennedy's criticisms of the GOP's "arbitrary" slashes of aircraft and missile program budgets.[133]

But at times Kennedy's appeal to southern Californians was hampered by an unsympathetic press. The *San Diego Union*'s story of JFK's visit was overshadowed by a banner headline proclaiming Eisenhower's decision to release funds for the B-70.[134] *Union* reporter Henry Love reported only that the Democratic nominee had "accused the GOP administration of failing to produce defense contracts" in San Diego.[135] Although reporting within these articles were generally favorable, the newspaper's campaign coverage was dominated by Eisenhower and Nixon's visit to New York City and included several editorials that were critical of Kennedy.[136]

Less than one week later, a narrow majority of Californians who went to the polls voted for Kennedy, but the senator had failed to win the support of absentee voters. The Nixon campaign had made a concerted get-out-the-vote effort among absentees, and these efforts paid off. Largely as a result of his strength among these voters, Nixon was ultimately declared the winner in the state, over a week after the election nationwide had already been decided.

Although Kennedy lost the state by a narrow margin, his efforts might have paid off within the grand scheme of the national campaign. The 1958 midterm elections had shattered GOP hopes of an easy victory in the state in the presidential election, and Nixon was forced to expend considerable resources in California in order to secure his narrow victory. The time and money Nixon partisans spent in the vice president's home state might have been better invested in the East, where Kennedy won most of the electoral votes needed to win the election.

In California, and especially in San Diego and Los Angeles, Kennedy tried to tie defense spending to local employment. It is not clear how successful this effort was. At first glance, the Kennedy campaign made gains, especially as compared to Adlai Stevenson's campaigns of 1952 and 1956. For example, 43.3 percent of voters in San Diego County chose Kennedy; the county had given Stevenson only 36.5 and 35.2 percent of the votes in 1952 and 1956, respectively. Kennedy's gains in Los Angeles County were more impressive. Improving on Stevenson's totals by nearly 314,000 votes, Kennedy won a slim majority over Nixon, who was raised in the Los Angeles suburb of Whittier. Statewide, Kennedy improved upon Stevenson's vote totals significantly.

Further analysis reveals, however, that Kennedy's performance in the state was significantly worse than should have been expected. Kennedy professed to have modest expectations for success in California, but recent history suggested that he should have won easily.[137] Democrat Edmund G. "Pat" Brown had won the governor's race in 1958 by a margin of over one million votes, and Democrats outnumbered Republicans in the state by more than one million registered voters. It is true that Kennedy narrowly won Los Angeles County—garnering a plurality of less than twenty-two thousand votes—but his totals ran behind those of local Democratic candidates for the state assembly by two hundred thousand votes.[138] Democrats in other statewide races both before and after the presidential contest of 1960 also did much better than Kennedy.

Perhaps most telling is Kennedy's showing in the one county in the state that was arguably most dependent upon defense spending, and consequently the one that stood to gain the most from Kennedy's pledge to close the missile gap. Kennedy lost San Diego County by more than fifty thousand votes, to the mild surprise of veteran GOP watchers.[139] That Kennedy did not win in California is doubly striking given the negative impact of Eisenhower's New Look on thousands of defense workers throughout the state. Kennedy's appeal for their support ultimately failed to resonate.

Conclusion

John F. Kennedy and his campaign advisers recognized how foreign policy issues might work to the senator's disadvantage during the course of the presidential campaign. Kennedy responded to this challenge by regularly tying foreign policy to domestic issues while on the stump. Such a strategy is conventional, but Kennedy went beyond it with an innovative use of Louis Harris's state-level surveys, which helped him to tailor his message. In some states, Kennedy was advised to downplay foreign policy and defense. In other states, the candidate was urged to hammer away at his opponent's foreign policy. In each instance, however, Harris encouraged Kennedy to connect foreign policy and national security to the local concerns of individual voters.

The central rhetorical vehicle for this message was Kennedy's reference to the country's declining prestige. The country, Kennedy said, could not be strong abroad if it was not strong at home. Unused industrial capacity, regional unemployment, and poorly distributed surpluses were all, in Kennedy's stump-speech scenarios, signs of a nation in decline.

The missile gap was another sign of relative decline. Kennedy referred to a gap, either current or impending, on several occasions during the course of the campaign. Former military officers and defense intellectuals such as James Gavin, Maxwell Taylor, Henry Kissinger, John Medaris, and B. H. Liddell Hart had all argued that the nation's defensive needs had grown while military capabilities had shrunk. Several of these men had discussed the missile gap specifically. Borrowing heavily from their books and articles, Kennedy spoke often of the weakness and vulnerability of the nation's defenses.

Occasionally Kennedy's case was bolstered by criticisms of Eisenhower's defense program voiced by Republicans—including Nelson Rockefeller—and by inconsistent and contradictory statements made by officials within the Eisenhower administration. Kennedy was also aided by Nixon's inconsistent views on economic growth, defense spending, and the missile gap.

Given that criticisms of Eisenhower's defense program and allegations of a missile gap emanated from members of both political parties, what can be said of the political significance of the gap? Was it a decisive issue for Kennedy in his successful campaign for the presidency in 1960? Did Kennedy's allegations that a missile gap existed cause voters to wonder whether President Dwight Eisenhower's defense budgets had left the nation vulnerable to a Soviet nuclear attack? Did Kennedy's promises to close the missile gap by strengthening the nation's defenses win him support among the men and women employed in defense-related industries, many of whom had seen their economic fortunes decline during Eisenhower's tenure in office?

On all of these questions scholars disagree. Former Kennedy national security adviser McGeorge Bundy suggests that "the missile-gap debate was narrow and its resonance limited." He stresses that in the waning days of the presidential campaign, when Kennedy increasingly found himself on the defensive on foreign policy issues, he made only one reference to the missile gap. Bundy concedes that Kennedy's references to declining American prestige worked for him politically. He concluded, however, that "the most respected voice in the country on foreign issues . . . belonged to Eisenhower." "In terms of what actually happened," Bundy wrote, "Eisenhower won the missile gap debate."[140] Careful analysis of the contents of Kennedy's campaign speeches suggests a more complex phenomenon at work. While the term *missile gap* appears only five times in the index to Kennedy's campaign speeches, his repeated references to declining American prestige, of which the perceived missile gap was a crucial component, were a staple of his campaign.

Long before the campaign ever began, Kennedy had linked himself intellectually with some of the Eisenhower administration's most vocal opponents. He was also associated with those who repeatedly argued that the nation was threatened by a missile gap, and by all indications Kennedy himself believed that a gap existed in 1960, not simply that there would be a gap in the future if corrective action were not taken. On at least two separate occasions during the campaign, Kennedy stated explicitly that a gap existed at the present time and that it would loom larger in the future unless dramatic steps were taken to reverse the decline. Special intelligence briefings by officials from the Eisenhower administration failed to alter Kennedy's public position on the missile gap. An analysis of his speeches given before and after these briefings reveals little change in his rhetoric; he continued to refer to the missile gap and the related prestige gap until the very last days of the campaign.

These semantic differences obscure the true meaning of the issue within the broader context. Kennedy's allusions to a missile gap— whether real or impending—referred to the entire defense establishment, not simply missile and rocket forces. Inherent in his charge that the Eisenhower administration was not adequately providing for the nation's defenses were two crucial assumptions: first, that "a greater effort" in national defense was both necessary and wise; and second, that an overreliance on nuclear weapons threatened to undermine the nation's ability to conduct wars in the future. Neither of these assumptions was considered extreme at the time. Respected foreign policy observers from both parties openly challenged Eisenhower's apparent dependence on the threat to use nuclear weapons during international crises, even those crises that did not involve the use of nuclear weapons. They had also questioned Eisenhower's judgment that excessive defense spending threatened the nation's economic security.

The missile gap issue worked for Democrats. And the underlying issues that Kennedy and the Democrats addressed—concerns over declining U.S. prestige and doubts about economic growth—were very real. Kennedy chose to focus on these concerns for his own political gain,[141] but he would soon come to recognize the dangers of this political strategy when, as president, he was forced to contend with the enduring myth of the missile gap—a myth that he had helped to build.

CHAPTER FOUR

The New Frontier and
the Closing of the Missile Gap

"I would like to know ... how we came to the judgment that there
was a missile gap."
   —**President John F. Kennedy to McGeorge Bundy, 11 February 1963**[1]

"I want to be able to demonstrate that there was a military and intelligence lag in the previous administration that started the missile gap."
               —**Kennedy to Bundy, 15 May 1963**[2]

John F. Kennedy's references to the missile gap were integral to a carefully crafted political strategy that included critiques of Eisenhower's economic policies and his strategy for fighting the Cold War. After nearly a
decade of relative prosperity, a number of communities were facing economic decline. Kennedy's promise to spend more on defense in order to
close the missile gap was intended, in part, to address the anxieties of
workers displaced by the New Look. Job losses were particularly acute in
communities dependent on defense spending. In Buffalo, New York, a
single Bell Aircraft plant had seen employment decline from ten thousand at the height of the Korean War to less than two thousand by the
summer of 1960. Detroit, Michigan, had experienced similar declines.
Unemployment stood at 9.6 percent in Detroit, and it was calculated at
8.9 percent in Michigan as a whole, at a time when fewer than 6 percent
of workers throughout the rest of the country lacked a job.

   Kennedy's commitment to increase spending on defense was more
than simply political rhetoric, however; it also reflected Kennedy's
long-held belief—shared with many others in the late 1950s—that the
New Look was an ineffective strategy for dealing with localized, nonnuclear forms of aggression. Here Kennedy's criticisms of the Eisenhower
administration's defense policies also resonated with Americans who did
not stand to gain economically from increases in defense spending.

For many Americans the Cold War was a costly proposition. The maintenance of a large-scale permanent military presence, unprecedented in the nation's history, imposed a substantial tax burden on all Americans and subjected millions of men to the threat of the draft. Still, although John F. Kennedy's missile gap rhetoric may not have been singularly significant during the presidential campaign of 1960, many voters did respond to Kennedy's call for sacrifice. They did so out of a sense of duty combined with a profound anxiety—an anxiety shared by the candidate himself. Kennedy was genuinely fearful that the Soviet Union was racing ahead of the United States—politically, militarily, and economically—and he was convinced that this widening disparity threatened the survival of the United States and the free world.

Kennedy recognized the depths of concern over the state of the nation's defenses, and he correctly gauged his fellow citizens' willingness to sacrifice in order to close the missile gap and to address all that the gap represented, but there was a downside to his use of the issue. Within a few weeks of the election, the new president came to realize the political costs of having focused on the gap during his campaign.

Policy Making in the Kennedy Administration

John F. Kennedy began his presidency as he had begun his campaign for the office—with a pledge to close the missile gap. Ever mindful of his razor-thin margin of victory, Kennedy, in a gesture of bipartisanship, invited a number of Eisenhower administration officials, including CIA director Allen Dulles and Undersecretary of State C. Douglas Dillon, to join his administration. He did not, however, moderate his criticism of the departing president. He was determined to make the changes to the nation's military that he deemed necessary. In early January 1961, prior to his inauguration, Kennedy continued his assault on the Eisenhower administration's defense program. In a published reply to a query from the American Legion, he again called for a "crash" program to secure the nation's nuclear deterrent.[3]

Eisenhower responded in kind. In his final State of the Union message Eisenhower asserted that the nation "must not return to the 'crash program' psychology of the past when each new feint by the Communists was responded to in panic." In particular, the president pointed out that the missile gap, like the bomber gap before it, was a fiction.[4] Less than a week later, in his celebrated farewell address, Eisenhower noted how the military establishment had changed in the years after World War II. At one time few companies in the United States were dedicated full-time to the manufacture of weapons, but the Cold War required "a permanent armaments industry of vast proportions." Eisenhower pointed out that the nation's annual military spending totaled "more than the net income of all United State corporations." The seventy-year-old president who had spent over thirty-five years of his life in uniform was troubled by the implications of this spending, and he warned of the growing influence of a burgeoning "military-industrial complex." He also cautioned that "public policy could itself become the captive of a scientific-technological elite." He warned that "we must never let the weight of this combination endanger our liberties or democratic processes."[5]

When the two men met on the day before Kennedy's inauguration, Eisenhower and Kennedy focused particular attention on recent events in Southeast Asia, but Eisenhower was still nettled by the fallacious missile gap charges. The departing president stressed the overall strength of the U.S. nuclear arsenal relative to that of the Soviet Union. In particular, Eisenhower pointed out that the Polaris weapon system, which had been deployed recently, gave Kennedy an impervious nuclear deterrent.[6] The Republican even offered to support Kennedy's nascent administration in spite of the harsh criticism that had been leveled against him during the campaign if Kennedy would drop his plans to spend more on defense.[7]

But Kennedy did not back off from his commitment to boost military spending. Instead, the new president adopted a hard-line stance against the Soviet Union in his inaugural address. Shaken by Nikita Khrushchev's pledge earlier that month to support "wars of national liberation," Kennedy promised to "pay any price" and "bear any burden" in defense of freedom around the globe.[8] To support such a strategy and to deliver on his campaign promises, Kennedy called, in his first State of the Union address, for an increase in airlift capacity, an acceleration of the Polaris submarine program, and an expansion of "our entire missile program."[9]

Kennedy did not forget his promises to the poor and to those living in the nation's depressed areas. His top legislative priorities—federal assistance for education, medical insurance for the elderly, federal housing legislation, and an increase in the minimum wage—addressed traditional liberal goals harkening back to the days of Franklin Roosevelt's administration.[10] Kennedy's economic advisers, including Walter Heller, whom he named chair of his Council of Economic Advisers, and John Kenneth Galbraith, whom he dispatched to India as U.S. ambassador, advocated a number of programs to boost government spending. In one of his first official acts as president, Kennedy proposed a multifaceted program to reinvigorate the nation's economy. Included within this program was yet another push for an area redevelopment program that had twice been vetoed by his predecessor.[11]

Taken as a whole, however, Kennedy's early efforts to tackle the problem of the sluggish economy are best characterized as cautious. The new president rejected Heller's call for an immediate tax cut and turned aside Galbraith's various proposals for increasing spending on public works. Amidst this chorus of liberal advice, Kennedy often turned to his secretary of the treasury, the Republican C. Douglas Dillon, who was far less inclined to support massive new federal spending. The president was also constrained by the chairman of the Federal Reserve Board, William McChesney Martin. For all Kennedy's charges during the presidential campaign that the "hard money, tight money" policies of the Eisenhower administration had stifled economic growth, his approach to fiscal and monetary policy in these early months was neither soft nor loose. As the historian James Giglio observes, "the financial homilies of the Eisenhower era held sway during the early Kennedy presidency." The liberal economist Seymour Harris was so frustrated by the new president's approach that he referred to the Kennedy administration as the "Third Eisenhower Administration."[12]

There was one important exception to this rule. While Kennedy normatively was fiscally conservative, he exhibited no such tendencies when it came to spending for the nation's defense. The new president's military spending increases in the spring and summer of 1961 pumped over $7 billion into the economy. New spending for domestic programs, by contrast, totaled only $2.3 billion.[13]

Several factors explain this dichotomy in Kennedy's approach to government spending. First, although Kennedy spoke of traditional liberal themes throughout the election year, his personal beliefs toward government spending were more like those of his conservative, businessman father, Joseph P. Kennedy, than like those of liberal academics such as Galbraith, Heller, and Harris. Second, and more important, for Kennedy security concerns took precedence over concern for maintaining fiscal balance. Kennedy might have questioned the merits of public works projects and other liberal pump-priming measures centered on nonmilitary spending, but he was convinced that American national security was threatened. Although he was mindful of the fact that his defense spending increases might boost the economic fortunes of certain communities, he was motivated primarily by his conviction that more must be done to strengthen the nation's military.

There is little evidence that Kennedy had serious doubts prior to his election about the nation's military standing relative to that of the Soviets and the Chinese. Kennedy likely did believe that the United States was falling behind, that there was a missile gap, and that this gap threatened U.S. security. Others who were similarly convinced were advising the president-elect during the period between the election and the inauguration. For example, Kennedy appointed Paul Nitze, author of NSC 68 and the Gaither Report, to chair a transition team assigned to study the nation's defense needs. Nitze's influence during the Kennedy administration continued after he was named assistant secretary of defense for international security affairs under Robert McNamara.[14]

Others hoping to influence the formulation of Kennedy's national security strategy also stressed the importance of the missile gap. Henry Kissinger, a prominent critic of Eisenhower's New Look, stepped forward in early 1961. Kissinger's book *The Necessity for Choice* built upon the criticisms expressed in his earlier works, including *Nuclear Weapons and Foreign Policy* and the Rockefeller Brothers Report. The Harvard professor argued that the nation's "margin of survival" had "narrowed dangerously" under Eisenhower, and he asserted that "there is no dispute about the missile gap as such. . . . It is generally admitted that from 1961 until at least 1964 the Soviet Union will possess more missiles than the United States." He was confident, however, that the trends could be reversed "if we move boldly and with conviction."[15]

Meanwhile, in the January 1961 issue of the journal *Foreign Affairs,* Maxwell Taylor applauded Kennedy's determination to initiate "substantial changes" in the nation's military strategy. He also warned, however, that such changes must be made immediately because "the military trend is running against us and decisive measures are needed to reverse it." The retired general worried that even if the new policy makers were "imbued with the utmost sense of urgency" they would "find many cogent reasons for proceeding slowly" before making any important decisions.[16]

Taylor called for a rejection of the New Look and urged that the new administration adopt instead a "flexible military strategy designed to deter war, large or small, and to assist the West in winning the cold war." He pointed to a number of specific plans on file at the Pentagon that had been shelved "largely for fiscal reasons" and could be implemented immediately. These plans included the creation of an "invulnerable, long-range missile force with a second-strike capability" and modernization and expansion of conventional forces.[17]

Stressing that "complete invulnerability will never be attained," Taylor stepped back somewhat from the most inflated estimates of what would be needed to close the missile gap. Rather than calling for a massive buildup of thousands of missiles, he suggested that a "few hundred" reliable long-range missiles, protected by defensive measures, would stand a "reasonable" chance of surviving a surprise attack. These missiles would constitute a sufficient second-strike force and would provide the nation with a measure of security. This crucial second-strike aspect of Taylor's argument appeared to echo the sentiments of the outgoing president, Dwight Eisenhower. "While we are often inclined to stress numbers in our efforts to close the missile gap," Taylor wrote, "we usually fail to recognize the importance of the defensive elements of a 'second-strike' missile system."[18]

Taylor also considered the economics of a new national security strategy. Arguing that new military spending should be predicated on "verifiable military requirements" so as to "withstand hard scrutiny by the fiscal powers," he predicted that the modernization of the army's forces alone would cost "about $3 billion a year for five years." Comparable plans existed for the air force, navy, and marines. Taylor estimated that, all told, the Department of Defense should "plan on receiving an annual sum approximating 10 percent of the Gross National Product."[19]

Both Kissinger and Taylor advised Kennedy during the early days of his administration, albeit in very different capacities. Kissinger had known Kennedy since 1958, and as a member of the Harvard faculty he was on familiar terms with a number of other Kennedy advisers, including Arthur Schlesinger Jr. Kissinger biographer Walter Isaacson argues that *Necessity for Choice* "read like a manifesto for the Democrats" and that it was "a job application in case the new president decided to seek some fresh thinking from Cambridge."[20] Kennedy praised Kissinger's new book in a meeting with the professor in February 1961, but it is not clear that the new president had actually read the book. After all, fresh thinking was not in short supply in the Kennedy administration.

Although Kennedy had cited Kissinger's writings on several occasions on the floor of the Senate, as well as during the presidential campaign, by February 1961 the president already had a favorite former Harvard faculty member on his staff in the person of McGeorge Bundy, whom he had hired as his special assistant for national security affairs. Denied a more influential role in the new administration, Kissinger accepted a job as a part-time consultant and worked primarily through Bundy.[21] Although Bundy had once aided Kissinger in securing tenure at Harvard, the two clashed during the Kennedy administration. Once in the White House, Bundy jealously guarded his turf against, in Kissinger's words, professors "of comparable academic competence." In the end, Kissinger did not exert great influence within the new administration.[22]

Bundy was not nearly as successful, however, in guarding his turf against the encroachments of Kennedy's favorite former army generals. Unlike Kissinger, Maxwell Taylor did not actively seek a position in the new administration. When Secretary of State Dean Rusk offered Taylor a job as ambassador of France, the retired general politely declined. He had recently accepted a position as head of the Lincoln Center in New York, and he was reluctant to disappoint the center's main benefactor, John D. Rockefeller III. The ambassadorship was then given to retired army general James Gavin, who had advised Kennedy on occasion prior to the election.[23]

Taylor did not remain on the outside for long, however, and he ultimately had far more influence over Kennedy's policy making than did Gavin. Although he had never met Kennedy before the inauguration, Taylor became an integral part of his national security team. He developed a particularly close personal relationship with the president's brother, Attorney General Robert F. Kennedy.[24] Following the failed invasion of Cuba at the Bay of Pigs in April 1961, Taylor was invited to Washington to chair a panel to investigate the debacle. After serving in a number of unofficial advisory roles, he returned to active service and was later selected to serve as chair of the Joint Chiefs of Staff. His friend the attorney general swore him in on 1 October 1962.[25]

Taylor's influence was apparent even before he was summoned to Washington. Kennedy's supplemental defense appropriation for FY 1961, submitted to Congress only weeks after his inauguration, called for a 15 percent increase in military spending. Much of it was directed to the very forces Taylor had called for in his "flexible response" strategy. At least some of this increase was also intended specifically to boost the domestic economy: one preinauguration task force report had pointed to military spending as the primary vehicle for reversing the deepening recession.[26]

Kennedy, McNamara, and the End of the Missile Gap

Kennedy's defense spending increases might have boosted the flagging economy, and they might have been aimed at addressing perceived weaknesses in the nation's conventional forces, but they were not designed to close the missile gap. There was no missile gap. When, in early February 1961, science adviser Jerome Wiesner informed the new president that the missile gap was a fiction, Kennedy greeted the news with a single expletive "delivered more in anger than in relief."[27]

What was the probable reason for the president's anger? Kennedy knew that the true nature of the strategic balance would soon be apparent. Indeed, by February 1961, this truth was emerging on many fronts. In early February, only days after the Wiesner briefing, the president telephoned Charles Hitch, a defense analyst formerly with the Rand Corporation, and conceded that there was no missile gap. Hitch had come to the same conclusion within days of arriving at the Pentagon in January 1961.[28]

The Eisenhower administration had said as much a year earlier, in January 1960, but Kennedy and other critics had assumed that Ike had "cooked the books" for political reasons to show that the United States had an advantage over the Soviet Union. Now the circumstances were reversed and the shoe was on the other foot. Having advocated a major increase in military spending as a candidate, Kennedy could not simply dismiss the missile gap by declaring that the U.S. deterrent was superior to that of the Soviet Union after all. Furthermore, the missile gap still had political value. The new president was committed to expanding U.S. capabilities for fighting limited wars, believing that Eisenhower's all-or-nothing nuclear deterrent strategy was fundamentally flawed. Therefore, he needed the missile gap myth to linger just a little while longer—long enough for him to push through a package of military spending that he deemed crucial whether or not there was a gap. His desire to dampen speculation that there was no gap was almost foiled, however, by a misstep on the part of his newly appointed secretary of defense, Robert McNamara.

McNamara, the former president of Ford Motor Company and a registered Republican, had cast his ballot for Kennedy in the November election. The secretary had had minimal exposure to politics prior to his arrival at the Pentagon in January 1961, but the new president valued McNamara's skills as an administrator, which had earned him the respect of the business community—a critical mind, a perceptive intuition, and a work ethic that valued action over inaction. True to form, the new secretary wasted no time in taking charge of the nation's largest bureaucratic institution, and ever since he has had a larger-than-life historical persona.[29] In his zeal for straight talk and because he lacked knowledge of the ways of Washington, however, McNamara caused problems for the new administration when he met for the first time with a group of Washington reporters.

The secretary's first assignment upon coming to Washington had been to study the missile gap. He had set about this task with typical enthusiasm, assisted by his deputy Roswell Gilpatric, who had been undersecretary of the air force in the Truman administration; General James Walsh, the head of air force intelligence; and others.[30] McNamara's review included an analysis of aerial photography that was held at Strategic Air Command (SAC) headquarters at Offutt Air Force Base in Omaha, Nebraska. SAC had assembled a sophisticated intelligence-gathering and assessment operation. Air force personnel dominated the process, but several navy and army personnel were eventually invited to join the group that was responsible for identifying potential targets for the Single Integrated Operational Plan, or SIOP. The data was considered so sensitive that some individuals hesitated before allowing the secretary to view it, but concerns over his security clearance were quickly cleared up. McNamara found that air force intelligence officers remained convinced that there was a missile gap, but the army and navy personnel and the representatives of civilian intelligence were not so sure. Upon reviewing the data, McNamara sided with the latter, and he began to make preparations to reduce the number of weapons planned for the U.S. stockpile.[31]

At the end of the day on 6 February, his first full day in the office after returning from Omaha, McNamara met the reporters who covered the Pentagon. He was accompanied by Gilpatric, public affairs chief Arthur Sylvester, and Orville Splitt of the Pentagon newsroom. The group of journalists included veteran newsmen John Scali of the Associated Press, John Norris of the *Washington Post,* and Jack Raymond of the *New York Times.* Not surprisingly, one of the first questions concerned the missile gap. McNamara replied that there should be no talk about missile gaps because "There's no missile gap."[32]

The reporters, some of whom had disseminated the story of the gap for the past three years, were taken aback. One pointed out that the gap was understood to include future as well as current missile strength. Another stressed that the gap referred to the Soviet Union's capability to produce missiles, not to the relative strength or the destructive power of the nuclear force presently in existence. McNamara did not budge. Instead, he reiterated that there was no gap, regardless of the terminology used. When the reporters pointed out that this information contravened what "your party" and one of the president's best friends (understood to be Joe Alsop) had been saying for years, McNamara said with a chuckle, "I still manage to keep most people guessing whether I'm a Republican or Democrat so I can speak with ease on this subject." This elicited laughter from the group, and the discussion continued on to other subjects. McNamara left the meeting thinking his first encounter with the Washington press corps had been a success.[33]

He was wrong. Judging from the uproar, he should have avoided the group completely. Contrary to what McNamara asserted in later years, however, the reporters did not break "the damn door down" in their rush to write their stories.[34] The meeting had taken place at the close of the business day, after the afternoon papers had already gone to press, and some reporters were reluctant to immediately file the story. Jack Raymond of the *New York Times* urged his colleagues to hold off until the next day to enable McNamara to explain himself. The United Press correspondent agreed. He also preferred to wait, but he threatened, "If anyone files this tonight, I'll be on the wire . . . before they begin dictating."[35]

The *Washington Post's* John Norris refused to delay, however, saying that he would not be upstaged the following day by the afternoon papers. Although Raymond argued that McNamara would never give another background briefing if he was confronted by the story in the morning papers, the assembled majority disagreed: they would file their stories right away, in time for the morning editions. It was only after this exchange that veteran reporter Raymond made the decision to submit his story on the evening of 6 February.[36]

Raymond's concerns about blindsiding the new secretary were well-founded. President Kennedy first learned of McNamara's encounter with the newsmen when he read Raymond's story on the front page of the *New York Times*. Under the headline "Kennedy Defense Study Finds No Evidence of a 'Missile Gap,'" Raymond's lead paragraph read: "Studies made by the Kennedy Administration since Inauguration Day show tentatively that no 'missile gap' exists in favor of the Soviet Union." Raymond explained that the Soviets had not engaged "in a 'crash program' to build intercontinental ballistic missiles" as some had feared they would, and he predicted that this new information might influence the new administration's decisions with respect to defense.[37]

Although Raymond had avoided citing administration sources in the first story he filed, *Times* editors changed the lead in time for the late city edition after both AP and UP wire-service reports attributed the story to the Kennedy administration. It was the late edition of the *Times* that greeted Kennedy on the morning of 7 February. Kennedy allegedly blasted McNamara over the phone, and McNamara asserted years later that he offered to resign in the wake of his gaffe.[38]

McNamara's intentions at the time of the briefing have become the subject of considerable scholarly debate. The president attributed Mc-Namara's ill-advised remarks to political naïveté, and he quickly moved to put the mistake behind them. McGeorge Bundy and Adam Yarmolinsky both considered the incident to have been a mistake, a consequence of McNamara's inexperience, and they claimed that Kennedy was not seriously upset by the gaffe.[39] Roger Hilsman argues that the first "hard evidence" that the gap did not exist was not made available until June 1961, and he asserted that McNamara's dismissal of it was based simply on a "gut feeling."[40]

Hilsman's interpretation, however, cannot account for other aspects of the McNamara briefing that suggest that the secretary was speaking truthfully and that his characterization of the strategic balance was accurate. For example, Roswell Gilpatric, former undersecretary of the air force and a longtime adviser to Stuart Symington, one of the most vocal of the missile gap's proponents, offered no explanation or qualifying remarks during the briefing. McNamara believed that his deputy had come to the Pentagon convinced that there was a gap and that Gilpatric had emerged from the process of analyzing the intelligence data with the clear sense that there was no gap. Over forty years after the fact, McNamara stands by his original statement—that there was no missile gap and that this was obvious in early February 1961.[41]

But while McNamara spoke with confidence on the basis of his own interpretation of the facts at his disposal, he might have given some thought to the political significance of the missile gap before casually dismissing it as null and void. McNamara's claim that he was ignorant of the potential ramifications of his remarks seems odd, at best. The secretary surely knew that the strategic arms race with the Soviet Union was a hotly contested area of debate. More specifically, even casual observers of the 1960 presidential election realized that the missile gap was a major element of John Kennedy's critique of the Eisenhower administration.

Jack Raymond made several observations about the meeting only days after it occurred that can inform the continuing discussion about McNamara's comments. First of all, he noted that Gilpatric had failed to offer additional information to clarify what McNamara said. Meanwhile, the department's public relations people, Sylvester and Splitt, had also failed to intervene. They had only commented that the secretary's remarks were for background, but not that they were off the record—essentially clearing the way for the information to be published, albeit on a not-for-attribution basis. Raymond concluded, therefore, that the missile gap myth had been debunked as the result of an honest interpretation of the most up-to-date intelligence information, and not because of some misunderstanding or misstatement on McNamara's part.[42]

The White House was determined to convince Raymond otherwise. On 7 February 1961, less than twenty-four hours after the McNamara briefing, White House Press Secretary Pierre Salinger issued a statement saying that the reports about the "end" of the missile gap were "absolutely wrong."[43] Kennedy, during his televised press conference the next day, also brushed aside a discussion of the end of the missile gap. According to the president, McNamara had told him that "no study" had been completed that "would lead to any conclusion at this time as to whether there is a gap or not." Kennedy asserted, therefore, that "it would be premature to reach a judgment as to whether there is a gap or not a gap."[44]

The White House antics troubled Raymond and some of his colleagues in the press. Warren Rogers of the *New York Herald Tribune* concluded that McNamara had lied when he contradicted his earlier comments to reporters. Rogers complained that the new secretary was treating Pentagon reporters like the "tame" Detroit press he had been accustomed to dealing with during his days as an auto industry executive.[45]

Charles J. V. Murphy adopted a different view of the incident. A Time-Life publishing executive and journalist with close ties to members of the military, Murphy was more amused than troubled when he noted in a letter to air force general Lauris Norstad, then serving as commander of NATO forces in Europe, that "Poor McNamara has put his foot into it at his first off-the-record press conference."[46]

Kennedy himself may have once believed that a missile gap threatened the security of the United States, but Murphy called the "gap-no-gap issue . . . the product of political fakery." He thought that McNamara had done the "country a service by disclosing his private judgment." Still, Murphy appreciated the potential cost. What McNamara "did not realize at the time, of course," Murphy wrote: "was that he had exploded one of the major premises on which the Administration had campaigned; he had demolished the Gaither and Rockefeller reports, . . . and had left Symington, Scoop Jackson, Lyndon Johnson, not to mention Ros Gilpatric, . . . and quite a few scientists, in most awkward stances."[47]

Murphy saw an opportunity for effecting major change in the nation's defenses, with or without the missile gap. Referring obliquely to Kennedy's campaign promises to reinvigorate American defenses and to reassert American leadership abroad, Murphy expressed hope that Kennedy and McNamara would "have the wit and the resolution to reestablish confidence of Americans in their own capacity for world action."[48]

Joseph Alsop, whom the reporters had singled out during the McNamara meeting as a central figure behind the missile gap, also registered an opinion on the McNamara briefing. The columnist had had regular contact with Kennedy staffers during the interregnum, and he had maintained his friendship with John Kennedy; indeed, the new president had visited Alsop's home in the early morning of 21 January, just hours after the inauguration.[49] But Alsop had little influence within the Pentagon. In his commentary, which appeared on 10 February, the columnist called the McNamara press briefing "the first bad bobble of the Kennedy Administration," and he suggested that McNamara had been fooled by the intelligence bureaucracy when he concluded that there was no missile gap.[50]

Less than a week later, McNamara seemed to agree. In a letter to Senate Minority Leader Everett Dirksen dated 16 February 1961, the secretary of defense disavowed his earlier statements to the Pentagon reporters.[51] He publicly repeated these denials in a convoluted way when, according to John Norris of the *Washington Post,* he "declared . . . that he neither told the newsmen that the United States is behind Russia in missile power nor that it is ahead."[52]

McNamara's sworn testimony before the House Appropriations Committee in April 1961 clarified the administration's position on the missile gap. In a carefully worded exchange with committee chairman George Mahon, McNamara explained that administration policy continued to be governed by the conviction that the United States lagged behind the Soviet Union in missile development and deployment. Noting that there had been "some confusion" about McNamara's own views on the missile gap, Mahon deftly guided the secretary through his testimony.

With respect to intercontinental ballistic missiles (ICBMs), such as the Atlas, Titan, and Minuteman, and excluding intermediate-range weapons such as the Polaris, Mahon asked, "Is there presently . . . a missile gap?"

McNamara's response was unequivocal: "Based on the intelligence estimates available to me, yes."

Mahon continued. "According to these estimates, was there a missile gap in existence or in anticipation last year?"

Again, McNamara replied in the affirmative. "Based on the estimates I understand were available last year," he testified, "there was indicated a probable missile gap then and for this period."[53]

The congressman then asked whether the missile gap was "estimated to exist up to and through 1963." Here McNamara hedged his response somewhat, but his position did not differ appreciably from what Kennedy's had been on the campaign trail the year before. "Based on the intelligence estimates," McNamara explained, "there is evidence that a missile gap may exist up to and through 1963." He allowed, however, that the U.S. "missile inventory at the end of the fiscal year 1963, or at the end of calendar year 1963, may exceed that of the Soviet Union."[54]

Although McNamara's statements echoed Kennedy's, his comments on the relative strategic significance of the presumed missile gap matched those of senior members of the Eisenhower administration from the previous year. Mahon asked if the missile gap contributed to a "deterrent gap." McNamara said no; there was no deterrent gap at the present time. "The recommendations which the President has made to Congress," the defense secretary continued, "are designed to assure that there will not be a deterrent gap in the future." This factor, the secretary affirmed, was more important "than the more restricted issue of a missile gap."[55]

Mahon then turned to Chairman of the Joint Chiefs of Staff Lyman Lemnitzer, who had accompanied McNamara for his testimony. Lemnitzer replied that current intelligence estimates showed a small difference between the number of ICBMs in the U.S. arsenal and the number held by the Soviet Union. He agreed, however, that there was no deterrent gap separating the two countries and that there would be no deterrent gap during the next two to three years if the administration's "present programs are carried out in the future."[56]

The Kennedy-McNamara Defense Buildup

The language that was entered into the public record as a result of this exchange was intended to ensure that disgruntled Republicans would not charge that Kennedy had deliberately manufactured the missile gap to further his own political ends. The gambit worked, for a time. Such accusations would not resurface for nearly a year.

In March 1961, Bundy advised the president not to mention the missile gap in his special message to Congress on the defense budget,[57] and when Kennedy pressed on with his promised defense buildup in the spring and early summer, he downplayed the significance of the gap in his push for more spending. With the passage in March of the $3.7 billion supplemental defense appropriation, Kennedy's total defense budget exceeded Eisenhower's by 10 percent.

The increases would fund an acceleration of Minuteman and Polaris production, an enhanced alert posture for SAC bombers in the realm of strategic weapons, and expanded airlift and equipment support for conventional forces.[58]

Then, with tensions over Berlin rising in the summer of 1961, Kennedy requested, and Congress approved, over $3 billion in emergency spending in July 1961. The money would be used to increase the size of the army from eleven regular combat-ready divisions to sixteen, and to pay 150,000 reservists who would be called to active duty in the meantime. By year's end, Kennedy's defense budget exceeded that of his predecessor by over 15 percent. Kennedy's spending continued to far outstrip Eisenhower's projections in the following fiscal year. Whereas Eisenhower's budget had projected FY 1962 military spending at more than $43.6 billion, Kennedy's budget for the same period totaled nearly $50 billion, amounting to over 9 percent of projected GNP.[59]

These increases reflected the new administration's view that Eisenhower's efforts to control defense expenditures out of concern for the health of the domestic economy were neither warranted nor wise. One of the leading proponents of this perspective was Paul Samuelson, a renowned economics professor at the Massachusetts Institute of Technology who had periodically advised John Kennedy as the senator rose to national prominence in the late 1950s. Although Samuelson was assigned no formal role within the Kennedy administration, he continued to offer economic advice. His report on the economy, prepared during the interregnum, maintained that defense expenditures ought not "be kept below the optimal level needed for security because of the mistaken notion that the economy is unable to bear any extra burdens."[60] Echoing these themes in his message to Congress on 28 March, Kennedy proclaimed that the nation's "arms must be adequate to meet our commitments and insure [sic] our security, without being bound by arbitrary budget ceilings." Repeating a frequent refrain from his campaign, the president declared, "This nation can afford to be strong—it cannot afford to be weak."[61]

The White House argued that these defense increases were predicated on strategic merit, and Samuelson stated that military expenditures ought not be "the football of economic stabilization." In this same report, however, the economist maintained that "any stepping up" of defense programs "that is deemed desirable for its own sake can only help rather than hinder" the health of the economy.[62] Charles Hitch, serving in the capacity of comptroller of the Pentagon in 1961, agreed. The "requirements for higher military . . . expenditures," he observed, "were in harmony with the Administration's economic policy, and in this case fiscal policy was accommodated to the needs of national security."[63]

Hitch testified before Congress in April 1961 that the Defense Department had accelerated "the placement of contracts for programs already approved" in order to boost the sluggish economy. These actions, he said, were taken "wherever feasible and sensible."[64] Although some questioned the wisdom and efficacy of using defense spending as a Keynesian stimulus, few could argue with the near-term effects of Kennedy's military spending initiatives. The recession eased in February 1961, and the economy slowly rebounded for the remainder of the year. The belief that defense expenditures had stimulated the economy was widespread throughout the Kennedy administration.[65]

Although these attitudes toward defense spending and the economy represented a philosophical shift from the previous administration, Kennedy's decisions relating to specific weapon systems validated many of his predecessor's actions. For example, although Kennedy had pledged during his campaign to strengthen and protect the nation's nuclear deterrent, as president he chose neither to expand the existing Atlas ICBM force nor to accelerate the Titan ICBM program. Although he had promised during a campaign visit to Warren, Michigan, to create jobs for the men and women who had once built the Jupiter intermediate-range ballistic missile, Kennedy did not call for new funding for this project when he assumed the presidency. He also chose not to reverse Eisenhower's earlier decision to cancel development of the B-58 bomber. And although the B-70 bomber limped along for several years as a research and development project, Kennedy was no more enamored of the futuristic plane than was his predecessor, Eisenhower, who had repeatedly questioned the bomber's usefulness.[66]

With respect to long-range missiles, the Kennedy administration tacitly agreed with Eisenhower's earlier contention that a crash program to build first-generation liquid-fueled ICBMs, such as the Atlas and Titan, was unwarranted. In 1958 Joseph Alsop had criticized the Eisenhower administration for "gambling the American future" on the Minuteman missile, given that that weapon, according to Alsop, could not "possibly be ready for operational use before the end of 1963 or early 1964." He was equally dismissive of the Polaris, arguing that a few more Polaris missile submarines would not appreciably alter the balance in favor of the United States.[67] Alsop's friend John Kennedy, however, had supported both programs, both on the floor of the Senate, and as a candidate for the presidency.[68]

In the spring of 1961, Kennedy, McNamara and others in the administration recognized that because the liquid-fueled Atlas, Titan, and Jupiter missiles required advance notice to fuel and launch, they were less reliable than solid-fueled missiles. Early models were deployed above ground in an upright position, and therefore were vulnerable to attack. Thus, these first-generation missiles were not acceptable second-strike weapons because they would not be available in sufficient numbers following a preemptive first strike. In light of this, McNamara and Kennedy seized upon the successful test of a Minuteman rocket in early February 1961 to cancel production of the final two squadrons of Titan II missiles and replace them with additional Minuteman missiles, and they approved no new monies for the Atlas.[69] Even without these weapons, the Minuteman and Polaris missiles combined to make for an effective second-strike force. Although Kennedy retained a first-strike option, he was the first U.S. president to disavow such a strategy in public. In its planning and in its public statements, the Kennedy administration focused on the second-strike aspects of nuclear force, and this approach was embodied in subsequent defense budgets.[70]

Much of the new spending for defense that was initiated during the early months of the Kennedy administration was unrelated to strategic weapons. In addition to accelerating the missile programs, Kennedy also directed much of his attention to implementing a flexible response strategy by expanding the nation's conventional forces. Included within this new push were an increase in the size of the active army and a renewed emphasis on counterinsurgency tactics.[71]

The Long, Slow Demise of the Missile Gap

The president and his administration held the line on the missile gap as they made these changes to the nation's force structure during the spring and summer of 1961. Kennedy made no explicit references to the missile gap in his press conferences and in his public pronouncements during this time, and the public seemed to have little interest in the gap.[72] The administration waited, pondering the additional data they had received, which confirmed what McNamara and others had realized by early February.

Information about the Soviets' weapons programs trickled in from several new sources. The Kennedy administration had access to improved photographic intelligence from reconnaissance satellites first launched during the Eisenhower years. The quality of these early satellite photographs was poor but was steadily improving by the spring and summer of 1961. In addition, the intelligence community had begun to digest information provided by the most senior Soviet defector, Colonel Oleg Penkovsky, an officer in the Chief Intelligence Directorate. Penkovsky asserted that the Soviets lagged well behind the United States in the development of ICBMs. Although he had little direct knowledge of the details of the Soviet missile program, he was confident that Khrushchev's missile claims were highly exaggerated. He told his handlers that the Soviets "did not have the capability of firing even 'one or two' ICBMs," and he backed up these claims in May 1961 by handing over to the CIA three rolls of microfilm that provided a clearer picture of the Soviet missile and rocket programs.[73] Armed with this new data, and anxious following the recent flare-up over Berlin to put the Soviets on notice that they did not possess superiority over the United States, Kennedy authorized his staff to reveal the truth about the missile gap.

After several weeks of intensive behind-the-scenes study and preparation, Deputy Secretary of Defense Gilpatric delivered a speech on 21 October 1961 before a meeting of the Business Council at Hot Springs, Virginia. Gilpatric stated explicitly that the United States now knew that the Soviets had neither a quantitative nor a qualitative superiority in nuclear missile technology. He delineated the diversity of U.S. nuclear forces and explained that a "sneak attack could not effectively disarm" the United States. The U.S. second-strike force, Gilpatric said, "is at least as extensive as what the Soviets can deliver by striking first."[74]

The message from the administration for both foreign and domestic audiences was clear—there was no missile gap. This message was repeated by Secretary of State Dean Rusk during a television interview the following day. In the same week McNamara asserted that the United States had "nuclear power several times that of the Soviet Union." Then, during his press conference on 8 November 1961, President Kennedy further reinforced the administration's new line on the missile gap when he declared that he would "not trade places with anyone in the world."[75]

Observers in the media took note. In the lead to an analytical piece in the *New York Times,* reporter Hanson W. Baldwin said that the missile gap had been "quietly, though unofficially, interred." "Thus," he went on, "an 'issue,' which played a major part in the last Presidential campaign, was finally declared—as many had long claimed—not to be an issue at all."[76] Even the self-described inventor of the missile gap, Joseph Alsop, had accepted the new intelligence information as definitive. A few weeks before the Gilpatric speech, Alsop had acknowledged in his newspaper column that the Soviets had fewer than fifty intercontinental missiles, whereas before he had asserted that they might have had as many as two hundred.[77]

Most historical accounts cite the occasion of Gilpatric's speech in October 1961 as the point at which any lingering doubts about the missile gap were officially dispelled.[78] The controversy, however, continued to simmer. While the issue was clearly on the wane, not all partisans were willing to declare that there was no gap. The trade journal *Missiles and Rockets* chastised the Kennedy administration for allegedly abandoning its promised defense buildup. Gilpatric's words, the editors wrote, might reassure "the casually informed American voter and the even more casually informed camel drivers of the world. But when closely examined, the claims are found to be far less impressive and considerably misleading."[79] Then in February 1962 Missouri senator Stuart Symington, one of the most outspoken of the missile gap propagandists, urged restraint "before we take to dancing in the streets to celebrate the disappearance of the missile gap."[80]

A minor storm erupted once again in March 1962 when Republican Frank Osmers of New Jersey assailed Kennedy on the floor of the House of Representatives for manufacturing a "big lie" during the presidential campaign of 1960. Osmers thought that Kennedy's charge "that the Eisenhower administration had been derelict in permitting a missile gap to develop between Russia and the United States . . . was probably the greatest single factor in his winning the election by a few thousand votes."[81] In that same month, excerpts of Richard Nixon's memoir *Six Crises* began filtering out to reporters, who highlighted Nixon's charge that Kennedy had been fully briefed by the CIA during the campaign. The implication in *Six Crises* was that Kennedy was told the truth about the missile gap, but Nixon refrained from making this charge explicitly. With good reason: Nixon likely knew that there was sufficient ambiguity in the intelligence estimates in the summer of 1960 to prevent even the CIA from declaring that there was no gap. And although Allen Dulles left no detailed accounts of the briefings, given his circumspection in other forums in the summer of 1960, it seems highly unlikely that the CIA director would have told Kennedy that there was no gap.[82]

Intending to quash accusations that Kennedy knew more about the true state of the nation's defenses than he had claimed during the campaign, the White House issued a statement denying that anything of substance had been discussed during the CIA briefings. Dulles further corroborated Kennedy's account of events during the campaign with a memorandum for the record that the White House distributed to the press.[83] This minor controversy focused on what was said or not said about an impending American invasion of Cuba. The missile gap was not mentioned. In subsequent months, the gap faded again from public view.

Nearly a year later, long after the public and the media had lost interest in the missile gap, Kennedy still harbored doubts about his use of the issue during his campaign. His interest in nuclear weapons piqued by the recent Cuban missile crisis, Kennedy asked national security adviser McGeorge Bundy for a "history of the missile gap controversy." "I would like to know its genesis," he continued, including "what previous government officials put forth their views and how we came to the judgment that there was a missile gap."[84] Planning for his own reelection bid, Kennedy wanted to be prepared for any questions that might surface during the upcoming presidential election. With a formal study in hand, Kennedy would have ready answers for those who would charge that he had manufactured the issue solely for political gain.[85]

The Pentagon stepped forward with the first attempt to answer Kennedy's questions. In a formal memorandum for the president, McNamara asserted that there had been "general agreement within the intelligence community" on the Soviets' "ICBM test program . . . but disagreement on the scale and pace of deployment." He surmised, therefore, "that the missile gap was based on a comparison between U.S. ICBM strength as then programmed, and reasonable, although erroneous, estimates of prospective Soviet ICBM strength which were generally accepted by responsible officials." Although the earlier estimates of Soviet ICBM strength had "turned out to be wrong," McNamara hastened to add, they were based on "the best intelligence information available." Ignoring Eisenhower's repeated denials, the secretary alleged that "the anticipated existence of a missile gap . . . was not even a matter of debate."[86]

Further, McNamara believed that the "weaknesses of overall defense policy" were of equal importance to the missile gap. He pointed out that independent observers, including the Gaither and Rockefeller committees, had all expressed the view that the nation's defensive posture was severely in need of strengthening. "The term 'missile gap,'" McNamara explained, "became the symbol of what critics felt to be fundamental flaws in the then-U.S. defense policy." Therefore, even if the missile gap in its "narrower senses" did not materialize, the "overall defense deficiencies . . . very definitely did exist" and were a concern for individuals "of all political views. . . . Whatever may be said (in hindsight) of the reality of the 'missile gap,' there is no question about the reality of a 'defense gap' which required vigorous action by the incoming administration to correct."[87]

Kennedy was dissatisfied with this first attempt to explain the history of the missile gap. The Pentagon version focused too much attention on the period from 1957 to early 1960. The president, therefore, asked for more information, specifically, as Bundy recorded, on "the immediate period when we said there was *no* missile gap—Dec 60–Feb 61."[88] Here Kennedy was referring to the three months between the election and the time of McNamara's press conference, before the administration had submitted its supplemental defense appropriations request. This time frame also coincided with the period when the president himself, along with Jerome Wiesner and Charles Hitch, had privately concluded that there was no gap. McNamara, with Roswell Gilpatric's implicit consent, had made these conclusions public during the press briefing in early February, before the White House was willing to disclose the information.

In response to the president's request for more information, Special Assistant to the Secretary of Defense Adam Yarmolinsky provided additional detail about the disputed gap. While acknowledging that both administrations had now denied its existence, Yarmolinsky argued that the more important issue was Eisenhower's fundamental faith in the adequacy of the U.S. defense posture. By contrast, the Kennedy administration was publicly committed to improving U.S. defenses. "Thus, although there was little difference in what Defense officials *said* about the missile gap before and after January 1961," Yarmolinsky wrote, "there were major differences in what was *done* about the missile gap and the whole range of defense deficiencies which this term had come to symbolize."[89]

The more relevant question concerns how the mistaken belief in the missile gap had led Kennedy and his senior advisers to overstate these alleged defense deficiencies before they moved into the White House and the Pentagon. But the belief in the missile gap was seriously shaken long before the "defense deficiencies" were corrected. McNamara had realized that there was no gap in February 1961 after only a few days of study. Bundy had urged the president to downplay the missile gap in his request for supplemental defense appropriations in March 1961, suggesting that he too had doubts about its existence. Although McNamara had stated in April 1961 during his testimony before the House Appropriations Committee that there *was* a missile gap and that the administration's defense requests would close it, many within the Kennedy administration knew well before that time that the gap was nonexistent.

Faced with an opportunity to rein in the nuclear "overkill" that had begun during Eisenhower's administration, Kennedy chose instead to spend more on nuclear weapons.[90] He also chose to dramatically increase spending on the conventional weapons needed to fight limited, nonnuclear wars. The pressures to spend more were primarily political, and to the extent that they carried over from the promises Kennedy had made during his presidential campaign, they were largely of his own making. In short, Kennedy's unwillingness to suffer the political embarrassment of reversing course on an issue on which he had campaigned led the president in the spring and summer of 1961 to accelerate and expand several weapons programs that were no longer justified in the absence of a missile gap.

Even those individuals working outside of the Oval Office and presumably insulated from politics were mindful of the risks for the president if the missile program fell well short of expectations. During a meeting in February 1961 to discuss the administration's proposed missile force, Herbert York, an adviser to Eisenhower who had remained in the government to assist with the transition, was prepared to argue that the original U.S. force projections could be cut in half—to about five hundred missiles—given what had recently been learned about the Soviet force. Carl Kaysen, along with science advisers Jerome Wiesner and Spurgeon Keeny, believed that the United States needed no more than four hundred ICBMs to deter the Russians but recommended six hundred out of recognition for the political pressures on the president. Several others familiar with these discussions agreed that the final size of the missile force was influenced primarily by political considerations.[91]

In most other instances, the defense bureaucracy—or, more ominously, the military-industrial complex—appears to have exerted relatively little influence over the Kennedy administration's defense policies. McNamara and his so-called Whiz Kids axed a number of weapon systems that were favored by senior military officers and even by a few influential politicians, in a manner that seemed almost blissfully ignorant of the wishes of the Pentagon and their allies in Congress. And although Kennedy and McNamara agreed in November 1961 to call for the construction of 1,200 Minuteman missiles, nearly double the number they believed was necessary, they resisted pressures to build as many as SAC thought necessary (10,000), or even as many as other air force generals deemed essential (3,000).[92]

Nonetheless, by pushing increases in weapon systems that his predecessor had resisted on economic grounds, Kennedy tacitly endorsed the views of those who argued that the economic effects of additional defense spending would not be deleterious and might even be salutary. Kennedy administration officials denied that defense spending increases were intended as an economic stimulus in the spring and summer of 1961, but during his presidential campaign Kennedy had said that the United States could use defense spending both to strengthen the nation and to provide jobs. Although these economic considerations were not the primary motivating factor behind Kennedy's defense policies, they were a factor.

Another factor in Kennedy's decision to spend more on defense was his continued confusion over the nature of the Soviet arms buildup. This confusion might have been resolved by a more careful review of what the intelligence community was—and had been—saying, and by a more critical assessment of the motivations of those who had dissented. The intelligence estimates developed in late 1959 and early 1960 provided little basis for continued faith in the missile gap. Although some individuals questioned these findings, the official NIEs did reflect the majority opinion of those within the intelligence community. After January 1960 many individuals with access to classified information had begun to question the perception that the Soviets were embarked on an enormous missile buildup. By early 1961, a number of individuals within the Kennedy administration who had reviewed the intelligence data compiled during the Eisenhower years had joined the ranks of those who harbored reservations about the need for more ICBMs.

To borrow from the language of the McNamara memo, the "reasonable, although erroneous, estimates" that had counted Soviet ICBMs in the hundreds and thousands had been dismissed by many responsible officials a full year before McNamara's press briefing in February 1961. Apparently, the particular responsible officials to whom McNamara had alluded in his memo were air force officers who had found it necessary to issue a dissenting opinion from that of the intelligence estimates panel because their interpretations were at odds with those of the other services and with civilian intelligence. These dissenting opinions, as shown in chapter 2, were then picked up by many journalists and politicians and thereby became the de facto public estimates of Soviet missile strength.

Kennedy realized the importance of the public perceptions. Therefore, in late March 1963, still not satisfied with the first attempts to explain the missile gap, he returned to the matter of crafting a history of the phenomenon. However, even if Kennedy intended for this study to be an objective history, his repeated requests for more and more information suggest that he was actively searching for a particular interpretation that would reflect most favorably on himself and his administration. He was also seeking ammunition for a looming political battle over the budget. Accordingly, on 30 March 1963 the president again asked about the status of the missile gap study and also requested an "appraisal of the military and space deficiencies which existed in January 1961" to "provide justification for the budget increases required to overcome these deficiencies."[93] Six weeks later, calling the previous report on the missile gap "too superficial," Kennedy told Bundy that he wanted "to be able to demonstrate that there was a military and intelligence lag in the previous administration that started the missile gap."[94]

Paul Nitze's office responded to these requests in late May 1963 in a report titled "But Where Did the Missile Gap Go?" The lengthy memorandum authored by Nitze's assistant Lawrence McQuade judged the concern associated with the missile gap to have been justified; the apparent gap "was a serious phenomena [sic] calling for significant shifts in our defense posture to decrease U.S. vulnerability."[95]

McQuade, like McNamara and Yarmolinsky before him, focused on the competing intelligence estimates of the late 1950s and early 1960s, which consistently overreported Soviet ICBM strength. In considerable detail, McQuade described how each estimate changed certain assumptions that had underlain the previous reports. Each of these revised estimates, McQuade noted, reflected a growing appreciation that the Soviets had not engaged in a crash program to build first-generation ICBMs as originally feared.[96]

While the estimates for the Soviet programs started high and moved lower as new evidence was compiled and analyzed, progress within U.S. weapon programs was often overlooked or downgraded. McQuade pointed, for example, to the findings of Rand analysts and to those of the Gaither Committee, which concluded that the United States "would not change its then existing pattern of defense plans and expenditures so as to be better prepared to meet the potential threat." But the pattern of military spending in the United States was substantially altered, McQuade explained, beginning during Eisenhower's second term and then continuing under Kennedy. In particular, McQuade cited the acceleration of the deployment of Atlas missiles and the successful test and early deployment of the Polaris missile submarines. The Kennedy administration had subsequently boosted the Minuteman program, effectively doubling Minuteman capacity beyond that programmed by the Eisenhower administration. "Clearly the pace of the U.S. missile programs had been moved forward substantially," McQuade explained, "but the impact in terms of ready operational missiles . . . only began to be significant in 1962." The combination of these two factors—the overestimate of Soviet strength and the underestimate of U.S. forces—had led to the mistaken belief in the missile gap. "The phenomenon of the missile gap and its disappearance," McQuade concluded, "were understandable and legitimate in the light of the facts as seen at the relevant time."[97]

McQuade could not, however, answer Kennedy's more direct question about *when* the missile gap was known to be false, or in McQuade's words, "when the potentiality of the missile gap ceased to be meaningful." Because he failed to resolve this question, McQuade could not show that the changes to weapons programs initiated under Eisenhower would have been insufficient to ensure American security well into the 1960s, as Kennedy and others had charged. McQuade concluded that the alarm associated with the missile gap was "amply justified" in part because of the necessity to "allow for a wide range of *possibilities* when there is a dearth of evidence on which to base the required estimates."[98] In effect, McQuade held, as Kennedy had for years, that it was preferable to err on the more pessimistic side of the competing intelligence estimates and to presume that the Soviets were engaged in a crash program to achieve superiority; it was better to risk spending too much money on defense than to risk national security by spending too little.

While McQuade researched and wrote his report, Kennedy grew impatient; on 3 June he again asked Bundy about it.[99] Drafts continued to flow to Bundy's office. Paul Nitze offered his own interpretation on 17 June. In a cover letter to Bundy, Nitze stressed that "Senator Kennedy's statements" on defense and the missile gap in the late 1950s were sensible and responsible." Further, he argued that Kennedy's "program for action made sense whether or not the intelligence on the Soviet ICBM program was accurate."[100]

Then, in a series of appendices, Nitze noted the many instances in which the public record indicated that "responsible people" both inside and outside the government had expressed "concern over the U.S. lag in long-range missiles." On the basis of this research, Nitze argued that there was "a substantial public record during the late 1950s to support a legitimate concern about the lag in the U.S. ICBM program behind that of the Soviets and a concern for the implication of such a lag on our defense posture."[101]

Air force major William Y. Smith, an adviser to both General Maxwell Taylor and McGeorge Bundy, reinforced this view in a memorandum drafted independently of Nitze's. He also argued that concern about the missile gap was reasonable and justified. "There is ample evidence on the public record," he wrote in a 20 June memo, "to substantiate why many people believed that the U.S. was, or would be, behind the USSR in the production and deployment of ICBMs."[102]

Smith cited three pieces of information, "two public and one classified—that would have persuaded a member of Congress in the late 1950s that a missile gap would exist." First, public testimony and statements by government officials were often contradictory. Although the secretary of defense and the chairman of the Joint Chiefs of Staff had both testified in January 1960 that there was no missile gap, CIA Director Allen Dulles had said in February 1960 that "the Russians would have a two-to-one advantage in ICBMs in mid-1960." This "was certainly enough to confirm the mounting suspicions of critics of the Administration's defense policy." Calling administration denials "suspect," because they came from an "Executive Branch committed to hold defense expenditures to a minimum," Smith concluded that "officials of the Eisenhower Administration themselves created the environment and made the case that there was a missile gap—and presented considerable evidence to back it up."[103]

The second major piece of public information about the missile gap came from "knowledgeable defense critics," including James Gavin, Maxwell Taylor, and Henry Kissinger. "These three critics were known to be conservative in their assessments of the importance of massive strategic nuclear power," Smith wrote, "yet each of them saw the U.S. faced with considerable dangers during the early 1960s because of the missile gap." Their case was bolstered, in Smith's view, by their presumed objectivity: "Their views . . . carried much more weight than would have the same call sounded (as it was) by Air Force advocates."[104]

Finally, Smith asserted that inconclusive classified intelligence presented before congressional committees had also contributed to a belief in the missile gap. The CIA briefing to the Senate Foreign Relations Committee in January 1959, for example, estimated that the Russians would have one hundred ICBMs in mid-1961 and the capability to produce five hundred by mid-1962. At that time military planners were projecting a much smaller ICBM force for the United States. A second intelligence briefing in 1960 had estimated that the Russians would possess 250–350 ICBMs in mid-1962, and 350–450 in mid-1963.[105]

Smith also addressed the crucial period of the first few months of the Kennedy administration, as the president had requested. Concerning McNamara's statements of February and April 1961, Smith explained that the secretary had never intended to suggest in early February 1961 that the missile gap no longer existed. This unfortunate but mistaken belief, Smith wrote, developed "because the Secretary wanted to dispel any ideas that the U.S. would no longer be able to defend its vital interests." Kennedy, Smith reminded the president, had said at the time that "he would reserve judgment until a study then under way had been completed." McNamara's public statement in April 1961 before the House Appropriations Committee that the missile gap remained had provided the president with "some maneuver room on the issue about what the Secretary did or did not say in February."[106]

Smith's conclusion was unambiguous: "There were valid reasons which led individuals to accept the existence of a missile gap in the late 1950s." Because his research focused on the administration's public defense for its erroneous belief in the missile gap, he recommended a strategy for "developing a case to remind the public of the then available evidence."[107] Then, over the next three weeks, Smith assembled an extensive collection of public materials to bolster the administration's contention that concern about the missile gap was legitimate in late 1960 and early 1961.

Smith also discussed the possibility of declassifying the CIA briefings that were given before Congress in 1959 and 1960. He noted, however, that the transcripts of the hearings did "not list Senator Kennedy as being present." Although Smith assumed that JFK would have heard about and read the content of the briefings after the fact, he feared that because of Kennedy's absence, emphasis on these briefings could backfire; he advised, therefore, that the White House rely on "published reports for this data" to make their case. Smith also advised against declassifying the Gaither Report because he was confident that the public record would "support the case that a missile gap generally was foreseen." Smith suggested that "in presenting the case from the public record, adroit references could be made to the fact that classified briefings by CIA and DOD to the various committees of Congress and reports to the NSC during this period did nothing to remove doubts but rather served only to confirm them." "In summary," Smith wrote, "I think the case for believing in 1960 that there would be a missile gap can be developed from reliance on (1) the public record before Congress, (2) criticisms from knowledgeable defense critics, and (3) adroit references and innuendos to classified reports and CIA and other classified briefings and testimony before Congress."[108]

The air force major then laid out a plan for developing the case and for releasing, albeit in a surreptitious fashion, classified information on the missile gap. "Rather than declassify any figures," he advised, "it would seem preferable to have several 'authoritative' scholarly, articles, or even a Congressional report quietly floated over the next year which would add substance and perspective to the public record." These articles, Smith predicted, "could confirm any figures deemed necessary to the case that now are available only in classified form."[109]

Finally Kennedy had what he wanted. His repeated requests for a history of the missile gap that demonstrated that there was "a military and intelligence lag in the previous administration that started the missile gap" had been met. The information assembled by McNamara, Yarmolinsky, McQuade, Nitze, and Smith would have provided the president with the ammunition necessary to defend his position during the upcoming presidential campaign. The issue of the missile gap had finally been closed.

Kennedy was never able to make the case that, in Paul Nitze's words, his "statements on defense and the missile gap in the late 1950s were sensible and responsible." During the summer of 1963 the president shifted his attention toward negotiation of a limited nuclear test ban treaty. Then, during the late summer and early autumn, the president was preoccupied by events in Southeast Asia. Despite these distractions, Kennedy continued to look ahead to the upcoming presidential election. His pledge from the 1960 campaign to close the missile gap was on his agenda on the day an assassin ended his life.

Specifically, Kennedy planned to focus on how he had reinvigorated the nation's defenses at a luncheon speech on 22 November 1963 in Fort Worth, Texas, home to thousands of men and women employed in defense industries. The text of the address provides a glimpse into Kennedy's final thoughts on the subject of the missile gap and on the defense buildup of his first years in office. The president was to have explained that his administration had increased the number of Polaris submarines by 50 percent, had boosted the number of Minuteman missiles by more than 75 percent, and had doubled "the total number of nuclear weapons available in our strategic alert forces." Kennedy's text celebrated these efforts: "The strategic nuclear power of the United States has been so greatly modernized and expanded in the last 1,000 days, by the rapid production and deployment of the most modern missile systems, that any and all potential aggressors are clearly confronted now with the impossibility of strategic victory—and the certainty of total destruction."[110]

Crafting the Historical Record

Although John F. Kennedy was never called upon to answer charges that he had manufactured the missile gap issue for political gain, his advisers set about protecting the legacy of the fallen president. In his influential memorandum, Major Smith had suggested that someone publish "authoritative" articles to substantiate Kennedy's version of events with respect to the gap. McGeorge Bundy stepped forward in the spring of 1964 with just such a piece, which was published in the journal *Foreign Affairs*.

In the years after *Sputnik*, Bundy explained, the missile gap "was forecast and feared by responsible and well-informed men both in and out of the government between 1957 and 1961." The Kennedy administration came to office recognizing the need "both for further action and for a reestablishment of confidence." "The new President himself had feared the missile gap and had pressed his concern in the campaign," Bundy explained, and "it was with honest surprise and relief that in 1961 he found the situation much less dangerous than the best evidence available to the Senate had indicated the year before." Bundy professed that the Kennedy administration had then "moved at once to correct the public impression, and thereafter . . . encouraged and supported policies . . . which aimed to ensure not merely that American strategic power was sufficient—but that its sufficiency was recognized."[111]

In his book *The McNamara Strategy*, also published in 1964, William Kaufmann, too, echoed the Kennedy administration's official version of events as crafted by Smith, Nitze, McQuade, and others. "Responsible officials in the Eisenhower administration and other knowledgeable students of the problem," he wrote, "were deeply concerned about the prospective state of the strategic nuclear balance." The missile gap had not materialized largely because the Soviets "had not built as many ICBMs as they were thought to be capable of doing," and for that, "everyone had reason to be thankful."[112]

The question of when the missile gap ceased to be meaningful dominates the historical debate, and rightly so. The wisdom of Kennedy's defense spending increases in the spring and summer of 1961 must be judged against the strategic balance as it was known at that time. This is where Kaufmann differed from Bundy: whereas Bundy declared that the Kennedy administration had "moved at once" to correct the impression that there was a missile gap, Kaufmann allowed that "it was apparent" that the missile gap "had evaporated" by the time of the Berlin Crisis, over four months before Gilpatric's speech.[113]

Arthur Schlesinger Jr. and Theodore Sorensen also differed over the timing of the end of the missile gap. Bundy had stated that the president had learned "in 1961" that there was no missile gap. Sorensen implicitly agreed, reporting in his book *Kennedy*, published in 1965, that the truth about the missile gap "was clear" some time in the summer of 1961.[114] By contrast, Schlesinger's account, also published in 1965, stressed how new intelligence was received in the winter of 1960–1961, between the time of Kennedy's election and his inauguration. It was this new information, Schlesinger argued, and not information available to Kennedy during the campaign, that had enabled McNamara to conclude in February 1961 that there was no gap.[115]

In later years both Sorensen and Bundy altered their estimates of when Kennedy first learned that there was no missile gap. Sorensen suggested in 1972 that the new intelligence from aerial photography obtained in early 1960 showed that the Soviets had not initiated a crash program to build long-range missiles. He added, however, that although the information was available, it had not been provided to Kennedy and other Democrats who "were suspicious of Republican efforts to dampen the issue in a campaign year." Kennedy did not know the missile gap was fake; therefore, there was nothing improper about the campaign's use of the issue throughout the year.[116] Over fifteen years later, McGeorge Bundy implicitly retreated from his earlier claim that Kennedy had immediately revealed the truth about the missile gap when he wrote in his book *Danger and Survival*, published in 1988, that "definitive" intelligence information was received in 1960–1961. Still, Bundy hedged this observation in Kennedy's favor when he argued that the information "became conclusive in the summer of 1961."[117]

The historical debate over the missile gap has not been resolved by the competing accounts of Kennedy partisans, but the record speaks for itself: a number of officials within the Kennedy administration realized in early 1961 that there was no missile gap. Kennedy should have known at least a year earlier, in January 1960, when the Eisenhower administration for the first time presented information to back up Ike's repeated assertions that there was no gap. But Kennedy, along with many Democrats in Congress and even a few Republicans, had either ignored or rejected the president's claims, choosing instead to listen to the counsel of those with a vested interest in perpetuating the missile gap myth.

Kennedy spoke often of the missile gap in his presidential campaign, and this caused problems in the early months of his presidency. When men whom Kennedy trusted told him in early 1961 that there was no gap, the new president was forced to deal with the potential embarrassment of having to admit that he had been badly mistaken. When Robert McNamara prematurely disclosed the truth about the missile gap, the Kennedy administration scrambled to "correct" the impression that the gap was nonexistent. The administration then pushed forward with its promised defense buildup in the spring and summer of 1961. The missile gap was not a major factor behind its push for more military spending, but the threat of a gap provided useful political cover to protect the administration from those who might have opposed the spending increases.

Conclusion

John F. Kennedy's political fortunes were uniquely tied to the missile gap, which was a major factor in Kennedy's rise to political prominence. General unease throughout the United States over the state of the nation's defenses, encapsulated in fears of such a gap, eroded Eisenhower's authority and opened the way for a young and relatively inexperienced politician to become president. Once Kennedy was in the Oval Office, the public's lingering concern over the gap influenced Kennedy's national security policies. Mindful of the public concern for national security and unwilling to suffer the embarrassment of admitting that he had been wrong about the missile gap, Kennedy turned aside recommendations that he postpone or cancel his planned defense buildup. Only after his own administration had put a new defensive posture in motion would Kennedy concede that the gap did not exist.

After he concluded that there was no gap, John F. Kennedy tried to craft a particular version of the missile gap story that would reflect well on himself and his administration. When he asked his advisers to write a history of the gap, he wanted to know how the country— himself included—had come to believe in it. After several abortive attempts were made to answer Kennedy's question, air force major William Smith composed several memoranda in June and July 1963 summarizing what would become the Kennedy administration's official position on the missile gap. This official stance was then publicly repeated in 1964 and 1965 by McGeorge Bundy, William Kaufmann, Arthur Schlesinger Jr., and Theodore Sorensen.

That Kennedy and his staff were interested in developing a coherent explanation for their mistaken belief in the missile gap is clear; not only were Kennedy and his men still concerned about the missile gap issue as late as July 1963, they were also still worried about public perception of the administration's handling of the issue in the months after the 1960 election, before the new administration had completed its work to reshape the defense budget. Kennedy did not want the historical record to show that he had unnecessarily increased defense spending in 1961.

It is not clear how successful Kennedy's attempt to frame the history of the missile gap was. Although elements of the White House reports prepared in 1963 are evident in many historical accounts of the Kennedy administration, several scholars doubt the central contention of the White House's version of the story—that in 1961 the gap was still a legitimate national security concern calling for substantial changes in the nation's military structure.[118]

Kennedy proceeded with a military buildup that was originally designed to close the missile gap in part because he and many of his advisers believed that changes to the nation's military were needed regardless of the presence or absence of a gap and in part because they believed that increased defense spending would have salutary effects on the stagnant economy. But the president was primarily motivated by his desire to avoid the embarrassment of retreating from the promises he made while on the campaign trail in 1960.

The political pressures Kennedy faced were largely of his own making, but they were very real nonetheless. The president was aware that many of the communities that were dependent upon military spending were expecting a boost from the new administration. He also realized that congressional leaders, many of whom represented districts that were home to sizable defense industries, were looking to the new president to carry through on his promises. Kennedy knew that many military leaders—including outspoken air force hawks such as Curtis LeMay and Thomas Power—were expecting more money, more planes, and more missiles. Retired and active-duty army officers were anticipating a reorientation of the U.S. force structure away from massive retaliation and toward larger, more mobile conventional forces. Naval officers were angling for a role in both the nuclear and nonnuclear realms. Ultimately, Kennedy could not satisfy all of these disparate constituencies.

John F. Kennedy's campaign promises related to the economic aspirations of hundreds of thousands of workers who designed and built the weapons that would have closed the missile gap, but after the election, his administration canceled the B-70 bomber program and dumped plans to expand the number of Atlas and Titan ICBMs. Likewise, the administration chose not to revisit Eisenhower's decision to discontinue production of the liquid-fueled Jupiter intermediate-range missile despite the pressures of the Chrysler Corporation and the men and women employed by the project. In contrast, the Minuteman missile program was fully funded and became the central weapon system within the land-based component of the nuclear deterrent force for over thirty years. Most of these changes had already been initiated by the Eisenhower administration.

On the other hand, Kennedy did implement substantive changes to the nation's nonnuclear forces that had been vigorously opposed by his predecessor; most notably, the army grew by nearly 50 percent before most Americans had even heard of Vietnam. Kennedy seemed to have a personal fascination with covert operations and counterinsurgency. He was instrumental in assigning a distinctive uniform item to the army special forces that would set them apart from their peers. Since 1961, this elite group has been popularly known as the Green Berets.[119]

Although defense contracts were most often awarded on the basis of technical factors, politics played a further role in the Kennedy administration's defense policies. There were many instances during the course of the Cold War when political considerations intruded upon the strictly rational calculus of determining defense needs. Just as Eisenhower had diverted funds to the B-70 bomber program late in 1960 to aid Vice President Richard Nixon's presidential campaign in California, Kennedy helped out his own political friends and allies. Workers at Bell Aircraft in Buffalo believed that the plant's receipt of a crucial defense contract in early 1961 was a reward for the city's strong support for Kennedy in the presidential election. It was also widely believed that the Fort Worth facility of General Dynamics secured the contract to build the advanced fighter aircraft known as the TFX the following year in part as a result of the assistance of Vice President Lyndon Johnson, Navy Secretary Fred Korth, and former Navy Secretary John B. Connally—all native Texans.[120]

Kennedy's defense policies were also shaped by economic considerations. It is fashionable to complain about the poor quality of political discourse, but the national security policy debates of the late 1950s reflected major philosophical differences over the effects of defense spending on the economy. Dwight D. Eisenhower and John F. Kennedy were at the center of this debate. Eisenhower believed that military spending was inherently wasteful and unproductive, while Kennedy and many of his advisers viewed such spending as an appropriate and efficacious vehicle for stimulating short-term economic growth.

In a footnote to his biography of the slain president, Arthur Schlesinger Jr. dismissed as a "fake issue" the Democrats' charge that Eisenhower's budget determined defense needs:

The Kennedy Administration proved to be as concerned as the Eisenhower Administration with the balancing of the defense effort against the other demands of the economy, but it believed—correctly—that the balance could be achieved at a much higher level. The two administrations differed, not in their basic attitude toward the idea of budgetary limits on defense spending, but in their estimates as to how much defense spending the economy could stand. As a party used to spending, the Democrats had fewer inhibitions.[121]

Theodore Sorensen expanded on this theme. He insisted that Kennedy "did not believe that the economic health of either the country or any community had to depend on excessive or inefficient armaments," and he praised Kennedy for spending money on "solid and dependable" deterrent forces and for building a military that was "lean and fit."[122]

However, the evidence indicates that Kennedy followed through on some, though certainly not all, of his campaign promises to increase spending on particular weapon systems in part to make good on his promises, and in part to stimulate the flagging economy. Although the empirical evidence is inconclusive, scholars must now question the use of defense spending to boost national or regional economic output. So-called military Keynesianism is neither warranted nor wise. This is increasingly clear in the wake of the Cold War, but there were dissenting voices over fifty years ago, at the beginning of that decades-long conflict, when Leon Keyserling and Paul Nitze first sought to use military spending to boost the economy. Dwight Eisenhower warned of the crowding-out effects of defense spending in his "Chance for Peace" speech in 1953, and he repeated these warnings in his farewell address in January 1961. In early 1964, John Kennedy's successor, Lyndon Johnson, said that the nation's "nuclear defense expenditures can never be justified as a W.P.A. for selected towns and states."[123] Despite these concerns, defense spending was used throughout the Cold War as a vehicle for stimulating economic activity.

Major industries and entire geographic regions within the United States grew dependent on defense spending during the Cold War. The nation, by extension, grew dependent as well. The defense industry served in an indirect way as a surrogate for a more extensive and comprehensive national industrial policy during the Cold War. Historian Diane Kunz goes so far as to declare that "the ongoing funding by the federal government of a significant defense industry . . . made the affluent America of the Cold War era possible."[124] Defense spending after World War II was, in other words, tied to both national security concerns and perceived domestic economic needs.

In this context, workers provided an important impetus to the development of particular military industries within particular geographic regions during the Cold War. The so-called military-industrial complex was not created by sinister men in smoke-filled rooms conspiring to thwart the will of the people; rather, the military-industrial complex *was* the will of the people, and politicians throughout the Cold War era attempted to bend this will to their advantage.[125] It did not always work, and it was almost always messy. The unequal distribution of military industries throughout the United States during the Cold War resulted from a combination of political and economic factors.[126] These same factors placed pressures on politicians and policy makers to sustain a level of military expenditures that had not been seen before in the history of the United States. Such was the nature of the political economy of the missile gap of the late 1950s. Such was the nature of John F. Kennedy's use of the missile gap in the presidential campaign of 1960. And such was the nature of the missile gap in the context of the Kennedy administration's defense policies of the early 1960s.

Epilogue

The Legacy of Cold War Military Spending

"I thought I was supposed to retire from this company. My grandfather did. My dad is getting ready to. I thought it was my legacy to retire from here, like everybody else. Now it's gone. Now I have to start all over again somewhere else."

—**Chip Hogue, former employee of Convair, San Diego, ca 1995**[1]

"San Diego's version of the peace dividend arrived due to the defense engineers and managers diverted, by the loss of their jobs, into entrepreneurial pursuits. . . . These helped the region emerge from the severe economic challenge posed by defense cutbacks at the beginning of the 1990s. Today, San Diego's economy is growing and contains a more diverse set of industries."

—**Michael E. Porter, May 2001**[2]

In the early summer of 1997 I witnessed a dying company breathing its last.

During a visit to southern California in June 1997, on a whim I called the phone number in the telephone directory for the Convair division of General Dynamics. The voice on the other end of the line gave me directions to 3302 Pacific Highway; nothing could have prepared me for what I saw when I pulled up to that address. Inside a paneled construction trailer on the tarmac of San Diego's airport sat Convair's final two employees. Roy Gilmore was one of them.

I knew very little about Convair at that time, so I had a lot of questions. Roy was accommodating. I began by telling him about the nature of my project. I explained how John F. Kennedy had used the missile gap during the presidential campaign of 1960, that Kennedy had promised to build more missiles in order close the gap. Gilmore, who had joined Convair in 1959, was puzzled. He remembered that missiles were being produced in large quantities in San Diego in 1960; employment in the company had more than doubled from 1954 to

1961, and in the early 1960s it was at its highest level since World War II. The policy decisions that had prompted these employment increases had been made before Kennedy's campaign visits in late 1960 and well before Kennedy's supplemental defense appropriations of 1961. Thus began a new line of inquiry into the story of John F. Kennedy and the missile gap.

In the course of my research, I found that Roy Gilmore's recollections were accurate. Convair was booming before John F. Kennedy came into office, then employment fell from over fifty thousand in 1961 to less than thirteen thousand in 1966. Although Convair survived for another thirty years, it is clear in retrospect that the end of the Atlas ballistic missile program portended the end of Convair. Employment at the San Diego company never again rose above thirteen thousand, and it averaged less than ten thousand in the period from 1970 to 1995.[3]

The end had been a long time coming for Convair and for most of the firms that had built aircraft for America's military during the twentieth century. At its peak in 1962 the aerospace industry had accounted for 9.4 percent of U.S. exports.[4] Continued robust spending on defense, in part to support the growing U.S. involvement in Vietnam, continued to pump hundreds of millions of dollars into the collective pockets of the men and women employed in the industry. Spending on space exploration contributed hundreds of millions more. Aerospace was the nation's leading industrial employer in 1967, with over 1.4 million men and women working in the design, development, and manufacture of aircraft, missiles, rockets, and related equipment.

This apparent strength, however, could not mask an underlying weakness. Of the industry's total sales of $27 billion in 1967, $15 billion—over 55 percent—was generated by sales to the government.[5] The industry's attempts to overcome this weakness met with mixed success. Consolidation, considered overdue as far back as the late 1940s, proceeded slowly. The General Dynamics acquisition of Convair in 1954 constituted the only significant merger of the 1950s. Then, from 1960 to 1970, the number of firms actively engaged in developing and producing aircraft and missiles shrunk substantially. There was the McDonnell Douglas merger of 1967, and later that year Rockwell-Standard acquired North American Aviation. Lesser manufacturers were also subject to takeovers, including San Diego–based Ryan, purchased by Teledyne in 1968, and Republic, acquired by Fairchild Hiller in 1965.

In the midst of these changes, management and labor pressed for special government protection, and at the same time the military-industrial complex was becoming the focus of greater and greater scrutiny. Some complained about contracts being awarded to the companies most in need rather than on the basis of merit.[6] Competition for major contracts—indeed the entire weapons acquisition process—became increasingly politicized. According to industry historian Donald Pattillo, "Politically aware bidders for contracts focused increasingly on the selection of subcontractors, or location of production facilities, in economically depressed or labor surplus areas, enabling them to point to the salutary effects of . . . a contract on the local economy." "Defense procurement programs," he concludes, "became de facto social programs."[7]

Since my meeting with Roy Gilmore in June 1997, I have met and spoken with a number of other men who, like him, look back on their years in the aviation and aerospace industry with a mixture of pride and satisfaction. They have few regrets. Each of these men explained in his own way what had happened during the industry's long history.

One of the men is Bill Chana, a flight test engineer who first began working for Consolidated Aircraft, the company that would become Convair, in the summer of 1941. Looking back on the Eisenhower and Kennedy years, Chana remembered the late 1950s as good times for the company. But with the end of the Atlas and other space-related projects in the mid-1960s, he recalled, "times started going downhill."[8] John Lull, an engineer who started working at Convair in 1953, was lured to the West Coast during the height of the Cold War by the desire to contribute to the nation's defense effort, to do good work at a good wage, and to escape the cold winters in upstate New York. Although he had "no idea what the West Coast was like, no idea at all," Lull moved his wife and two children to California and never looked back. "We just lucked out," he said. When I asked if he had any regrets, Lull did not hesitate. "No," he answered, "it was great."[9]

John Lull and Roy Gilmore were both nearing retirement when the end finally came. Other Convair workers were just beginning their careers, many of them following in the footsteps of their parents and, for some, their grandparents. The promising future available to workers during the Cold War years seemed almost impossible to achieve for many men and women as they faced the end of defense industry jobs and uncertainty about new careers.

These were the concerns of many former employees of the General Dynamics Convair division, once San Diego's largest private employer, and developer of some of the most important weapons in U.S. history. When the company closed its doors for good in the summer of 1997, Roy Gilmore watched it all happen from the window of the construction trailer that served as his office. The wrecking balls came a while later and removed the last vestiges of Convair's physical presence in San Diego. The city then made plans to expand the airport onto the land that had been occupied by the old Convair plant.

Gilmore seemed to take all of this in stride. Perhaps he had already come to terms with the fact that the job that he had held for over thirty-eight years would finally come to an end in the next few months. Perhaps he had had time to reflect on the work that he had done at Convair. Perhaps he was grateful to still have a job when thousands of his fellow Convair employees had been dismissed months, even years, earlier. Roy's perspective on what had happened to Convair struck me as philosophical, maybe even detached. He explained that there had been dozens of companies building airplanes in the very early days of aviation. Some had survived and others had thrived during World War II. One by one, however, the names of the early aircraft manufacturers had disappeared. Such was the nature of the business, Gilmore seemed to be saying.

Similar scenes were played out in dozens of communities throughout the United States in the early to mid-1990s. Contraction within the aviation and aerospace industry had been apparent during the whole latter half of the twentieth century, but the process accelerated after the end of the Cold War. In western New York—an area targeted by John F. Kennedy's campaign in 1960—the men and women employed by the company once known as Bell Aircraft were involved in three different mergers in 1995 and 1996. The end for most Bell employees in Buffalo and Niagara Falls came in the late 1990s.

Hugh Neeson witnessed the ups and downs at Bell from close range for over forty years. He was hired by Bell right out of college and went on to a long career with the company, serving in a number of management roles. When I asked him in the summer of 2001 what was left, he told me that the enormous plant that had accommodated the work of Bell employees for nearly sixty years was now home to a handful of subcontracting firms and other small businesses. But most of the space was empty.

Despite the ultimate demise of Bell manufacturing in Buffalo, Neeson looked back proudly on its work and that of other companies in western New York. The area had been home to some of the founding firms of the aviation industry, companies that had produced over forty-five thousand aircraft during World War II and that had employed thousands and thousands of people. Neeson characterized Bell's work from the late 1950s to the 1990s as a "vestige of terribly interesting technical work, and a lot of it very significant," that was made possible "because the company valued very smart people." "It was a great and interesting place to work for," Neeson said as he pondered his long career from the comfort of retirement, "and it's now joined the memory banks."[10]

This point of view reflects the perspective of those who take pride in the work that they have done, but who now have few regrets that the nation seems to have turned away from the massive military spending that gave them their livelihood. Their philosophical attitude toward the rise and decline of the aerospace industry in the United States also reflects the opinion of Dwight David Eisenhower who, over fifty years ago, looked ahead to the days when the world could stop "spending the sweat of its laborers, the genius of its scientists" on the development and manufacture of arms.[11]

Although some lamented the loss of defense jobs in the early 1990s following the collapse of the Soviet Union and the end of the Cold War, the "creative destruction" wrought by the free-market process paid handsome dividends for the nation's economy in the second half of the 1990s.[12] New companies in new industries were built and populated by ambitious engineers and computer technicians who might once have migrated to defense firms. The Bill Chanas, John Lulls, and Hugh Neesons of today ply their skills in telecommunications and biotechnology. Other men and women graduating from the top technical and business schools have created entirely new businesses on the backbone of a once-obscure computer network originally built for the Defense Department and now known as the Internet. Thousands of new businesses have been created in the wake of the Cold War. The American economy may have become dependent on military spending during the latter half of the twentieth century, but that is no longer the case. San Diego, a city that had been built around defense industries, now feels few ill effects from the defense drawdown of the 1990s.[13] As one study of the region concludes, the city's rebirth was aided by a "peace dividend" of hundreds of skilled engineers and managers moving into entrepreneurial pursuits. These men and women created scores of companies that today employ tens of thousands of San Diegans.[14]

John F. Kennedy and the Legacy of the Missile Gap

Aaron Friedberg marvels at the "remarkable degree" to which "the American system has proven itself to be highly resistant to centralized industrial planning," even when faced with a powerful enemy.[15] He is correct to focus on the influence of an enduring antistatist tradition within the United States that shaped U.S. military spending during the Cold War. If indeed a large defense establishment was needed during that era, the character of this military machine, and the means whereby the national security apparatus was maintained, might have been far different under a political system with different traditions. According to Friedberg, "By preventing some of the worst, most stifling excesses of statism," these antistatist tendencies "made it easier for the United States to preserve its economic vitality and technological dynamism."[16]

So how much defense spending is enough? Or, put another way, presuming that some level of military expenditure is necessary to maintain national security, how much is too much? Although critics assailed Dwight Eisenhower in the late 1950s for his fiscal restraint with respect to military spending, a new view of his defense policy and of the Cold War generally gives more mature consideration to the inflationary pressures that government spending imposes on the nation's economy, a concept first postulated in the late 1960s by Milton Friedman and Edmund Phelps.[17] This view inherently challenges the contention made by Eisenhower's critics—including John F. Kennedy—that a defense budget that consumed more than 10 percent of the gross national product would impose no serious burden on the nation's economy. The harmful effects of such high expenditures were evident less than a decade later when spending for a conventional army waging a nonnuclear war in Southeast Asia fueled rapid inflation, impinged on domestic spending, and forced higher taxes.[18] Finally, the new view considers the opportunity costs of defense spending that drew some of the best and the brightest minds away from peaceful pursuits during the decades-long Cold War arms race.

This new perspective on the national security debates of the late 1950s is often associated with the spate of scholarship known as Eisenhower revisionism.[19] Revisionist scholars praise Eisenhower for restraining military spending at a time when many politicians, including John Kennedy, were demanding that the United States spend more. Eisenhower, ever mindful of the harmful economic effects of such spending, attempted to push, prod, and persuade his fellow Americans—including members of his own administration—into agreeing that the wisest course was that of moderation. Believing that the nation's limited resources were best employed by private enterprises, Ike argued that it was better to control government spending in order to secure the nation's economic strength. U.S. economic might, Eisenhower reasoned, was the true source of American power vis-à-vis the Soviet Union.

In the wake of the Cold War, in the late 1990s, politicians fought over what to do with the first budget surplus in a generation. Some scholars, with an eye to the economics of defense spending, concluded that the end of the Cold War and the end of persistent fiscal imbalance were inextricably linked. If this conclusion is correct, they might also have concluded that Eisenhower's New Look was precisely the long view that was needed during the height of the Cold War.

In 1960, however, the nation chose another path. John F. Kennedy pledged to close the missile gap by spending more on defense. The nation's resources were limited only by the imagination of its political leaders. Kennedy said that the nation could not afford to gamble its survival on the assumption that excessive defense spending would do long-term damage to the U.S. economy. It was better, he said, to gamble with dollars than with lives. The voters agreed. They made John Kennedy the youngest man ever to be elected president of the United States.

John F. Kennedy likely believed in the existence of a missile gap in 1960. Indeed, he was embarrassed to learn in early 1961 that he had been badly mistaken. The gap on which he had campaigned only a few months earlier was a fiction. Over two years after he had learned the truth, Kennedy still harbored doubts about his use of the issue.

Kennedy's attempt to write the history of the missile gap ultimately failed to resolve a number of vexing questions. It is not clear, as Kennedy apparently wished to show, that the defense decisions made by his administration in 1961 were justified in the light of what was known and suspected about the strategic balance at that time; nor is it clear that alleged military and intelligence deficiencies inherited from the previous administration had created the belief that there was a missile gap. On the contrary, Eisenhower was convinced that there was no gap. This information was made available to Kennedy before the presidential campaign of 1960, but he refused to believe it. Then, when Kennedy was told in early 1961 that the gap was indeed nonexistent, he nonetheless pressed forward with his promised defense buildup, and he continued to have doubts about the nation's position in the arms race. Kennedy was committed to rebuilding the nation's military, and he believed that international crises, including a particularly tense confrontation over Berlin, demanded a stronger military posture for the United States. These concerns alone, however, cannot explain his actions in the spring and summer of 1961.

The broader missile gap critique, and John F. Kennedy's use of the issue, was about more than just missiles. The missile gap idea was, first and foremost, a critique of the entire defense establishment of the

Eisenhower years. And because this defense establishment had been shaped in part by economic considerations and by Eisenhower's personal determination to hold down defense spending, Kennedy's missile gap rhetoric included a scathing critique of Eisenhower's economic philosophy.

When Kennedy committed himself to a program of expanded government spending, including greater spending on defense, he was not the first politician to promise to spend more money on defense, and he was hardly the last. Military expenditures would likely also have increased under a Nixon administration had Eisenhower's vice president defeated Kennedy in November 1960. Although Nixon muted his criticisms of Eisenhower's defense programs, the evidence suggests that he was also committed to expanding U.S. military spending, and he was less concerned than Eisenhower about the possible detrimental economic effects of such spending.

But John Kennedy, not Richard Nixon, was occupying the Oval Office in January 1961. He was told that there was no missile gap shortly after he became president, but he did little to slow the Cold War arms race during his thousand days in office; indeed, by boosting U.S. military spending at a time when Nikita Khrushchev was surreptitiously trying to restrain Soviet spending, Kennedy inadvertently pressured the Soviet leader to reverse course. The process accelerated still further after Khrushchev's embarrassing diplomatic defeat in the Cuban missile crisis of October 1962. The permanent war economy that Eisenhower had feared seemed even more permanent in 1963 than it had in 1961.

In the mid- to late 1990s, military spending consumed a lower share of total U.S. output than at any time since before World War II. It seemed that the nation might finally have reached the place that Eisenhower was seeking, settling into a peacetime economy after fifty years of hot and cold war. Today there are new threats—as the events of 11 September 2001 dramatically displayed—but they are threats of a very different kind and a very different magnitude. Some voices argue that the "military is simply too small for the missions it must perform" and call for a 15 to 20 percent increase in the defense budget.[20] But we need not return to the permanent war economy of the Cold War years in order to protect ourselves from acts of terrorism. Given the benefits of relative peace and prosperity that the nation enjoyed during much of the 1990s, let us hope that we do not.

Notes

Introduction

1. Quoted in Maxwell Taylor, *Swords and Plowshares* (New York: Norton, 1972), 205.

2. Albert Wohlstetter, "The Delicate Balance of Terror," *Foreign Affairs* 37 (January 1959): 211–34.

3. Statement of Senator John F. Kennedy (Dem.-Mass.), 2 January 1960, in Correspondence, "Kennedy, John F., Speeches—Remarks, Biography 1958–1959–1960" File, Box 11, Abraham Ribicoff Papers, Library of Congress Manuscript Collection, Washington, DC (hereafter cited as AR Papers); Chalmers Roberts, "Kennedy Puts Name into Race: Would Not Accept Nomination for No. 2 Spot, He Says," *Washington Post*, 3 January 1960.

4. "An Investment for Peace," speech by John F. Kennedy (JFK) excerpted from Congressional Record, 2–3, in "Speeches—Misc. JFK 6/7/58–3/18/60," '60 Campaign Issues folder, Box 996, Richard Goodwin Working Papers, JFK Pre-Presidential Papers, John F. Kennedy Presidential Library, Boston (hereafter cited as JFKL).

5. U.S. Department of Labor, Bureau of Labor Statistics, *America's Industrial and Occupational Manpower Requirements, 1964–1975* (Washington, DC: U.S. Department of Labor, 1966), 67.

6. Arnold L. Horelick and Myron Rush, *Strategic Power and Soviet Foreign Policy* (Chicago: University of Chicago Press, 1965), vii.

7. S. Nelson Drew found "no fewer than 50 instances" in which Eisenhower either played down or publicly refuted the existence of a missile gap between the United States and the Soviet Union. See S. Nelson Drew, "Expecting the Approach of Danger: The 'Missile Gap' as a Study of Executive-Congressional Competition in Building Consensus on National Security Issues," *Presidential Studies Quarterly* 19, no. 2 (Spring 1989): 321, 335.

8. William C. Wohlforth, *The Elusive Balance: Power and Perceptions during the Cold War* (Ithaca, NY: Cornell University Press, 1993), especially chapter 6. See also Horelick and Rush, *Strategic Power*.

9. See Ernest R. May and Philip D. Zelikow, eds., *The Kennedy Tapes: Inside the White House during the Cuban Missile Crisis* (Cambridge, MA: Belknap, 1997), 31–32; Michael Beschloss, *The Crisis Years: Kennedy and Khrushchev, 1960–1963* (New York: HarperCollins, 1991), 329–32; and Raymond Garthoff, *Reflections on the Cuban Missile Crisis*, rev. ed. (Washington, DC: Brookings Institution, 1989), 45–46, 183.

10. On the missile gap, see especially Peter J. Roman, *Eisenhower and The Missile Gap* (Ithaca, NY: Cornell University Press, 1995); Edgar M. Bottome, *The Missile Gap: A Study of the Formulation of Military and Political Policy* (Rutherford, NJ: Fairleigh Dickinson University Press, 1971); Robert A. Divine, *The Sputnik Challenge: Eisenhower's Response to the Soviet Satellite* (New York: Oxford University Press, 1993); and John Prados, *The Soviet Estimate: U.S. Intelligence Analysis and Russian Military Strength* (New York: Dial, 1982), especially chapters 7 and 8. See also James C. Dick, "The Strategic Arms Race, 1957–61: Who Opened a Missile Gap?" *Journal of Politics* 34, no. 4 (November 1972): 1062–1110; Drew, "Expecting the Approach of Danger"; Colin S. Gray, "'Gap' Prediction and America's Defense: Arms Race Behavior in the Eisenhower Years," *Orbis* 16 (Spring 1972): 257–74; and Roy E. Licklider, "The Missile Gap Controversy," *Political Science Quarterly* 85, no. 4 (December 1970): 600–615.

11. See, for example, Desmond Ball, *Politics and Force Levels: The Strategic Missile Program of the Kennedy Administration* (Berkeley: University of California Press, 1980), 125–26; Lawrence Freedman, *Kennedy's Wars: Berlin, Cuba, Laos, and Vietnam* (New York: Oxford University Press, 2000), 56–57; and May and Zelikow, *Kennedy Tapes,* 32–33.

12. Dwight D. Eisenhower, *The White House Years: Waging Peace, 1956–1961* (Garden City, NY: Doubleday, 1965), 390.

13. Herbert York, *Race to Oblivion: A Participant's View of the Arms Race* (New York: Simon and Schuster, 1970), 147.

14. See, for example, Thomas G. Paterson, ed., *Kennedy's Quest for Victory: American Foreign Policy, 1961–1963* (New York: Oxford University Press, 1989), 5; and Freedman, *Kennedy's Wars,* 417–19.

15. See, for example, Ethan Kapstein, *The Political Economy of National Security: A Global Perspective* (New York: McGraw-Hill, 1992).

16. See Campbell Craig, *Destroying the Village: Eisenhower and Thermonuclear War* (New York: Columbia University Press, 1998). See also John Lewis Gaddis, *We Now Know: Rethinking Cold War History* (New York: Oxford University Press, 1997), 234; and Richard Immerman, *John Foster Dulles: Piety, Pragmatism, and Power in U.S. Foreign Policy* (Wilmington, DE: Scholarly Resources, 1999), 177–78.

17. Maxwell Taylor, *The Uncertain Trumpet* (New York: Harper and Brothers, 1959), 178. See also Douglas Kinnard, *President Eisenhower and Strategy Management: A Study in Defense Politics* (Lexington: University Press of Kentucky, 1977).

18. For a similar argument, see Aaron Friedberg, *In the Shadow of the Garrison State: America's Anti-Statism and Its Cold War Grand Strategy* (Princeton, NJ: Princeton University Press, 2000), 3–4.

19. James Tobin, "Autobiography of James Tobin," *Nobel Lectures, Economic Sciences, 1969–1980* (Stockholm, The Nobel Foundation, 2000), http://www.nobel.se/economics/laureates/1981/tobin-autobio.html.

20. Richard A. Aliano, *American Defense Policy from Eisenhower to Kennedy: The Politics of Changing Military Requirements* (Athens: Ohio University Press, 1975), 277.

21. John Lewis Gaddis, *Strategies of Containment: A Critical Appraisal of Postwar American National Security Policy* (New York: Oxford University Press, 1982), 242, 261.

1—Eisenhower, the New Look, and Their Critics

1. From NSC 68: United States Objectives and Programs for National Security (14 April 1950), as reprinted in Ernest May, ed., *American Cold War Strategy: Interpreting NSC 68* (Boston: Bedford, 1993), 73.

2. From Eisenhower's 1954 State of the Union address, printed in the *New York Times* (8 January 1954) and quoted in John W. Sloan, *Eisenhower and the Management of Prosperity* (Lawrence: University Press of Kansas, 1991), 75.

3. James Tobin, "Defense, Dollars, and Doctrines," *The Yale Review* 47, no. 3 (March 1958): 330, in "Speech Writings—General 1/2/58–6/5/60" Folder, '60 Campaign Issues, Richard Goodwin Working Papers, Box 996, JFK Pre-Presidential Papers, JFKL.

4. See Craig, *Destroying the Village*.

5. Melvyn P. Leffler, *A Preponderance of Power: National Security, the Truman Administration, and the Cold War* (Stanford, CA: Stanford University Press, 1992), 270–71. See also Jeffrey G. Barlow, *Revolt of the Admirals: The Fight for Naval Aviation, 1945–1950* (Washington, DC: Naval Historical Center, 1994).

6. Leon Keyserling and John Clark to Harry S. Truman, 26 August 1949, Leon H. Keyserling Papers, Box 2, Report File, 1946–1953, Harry S. Truman Presidential Library, Independence, MO, cited in Aaron Friedberg, *In the Shadow*, 107.

7. David Callahan, *Dangerous Capabilities: Paul Nitze and the Cold War* (New York: HarperCollins, 1990), 94.

8. Ibid., 12–15, 29–32; Strobe Talbott, *The Master of the Game: Paul Nitze and the Nuclear Peace* (New York: Alfred A. Knopf, 1988), 23–32.

9. May, *American Cold War Strategy*, 4.

10. Alonzo Hamby, *Man of the People: A Life of Harry S. Truman* (New York: Oxford University Press, 1995), 527–29; David McCullough, *Truman* (New York: Simon and Schuster, 1992), 771–73.

11. May, *American Cold War Strategy*, 73.

12. Ibid., 45, 46.

13. Friedberg, *In the Shadow*, 107–8.

14. May, *American Cold War Strategy*, 15, 106.

15. Paul G. Pierpaoli Jr., *Truman and Korea: The Political Culture of the Early Cold War* (Columbia: University of Missouri Press, 1999), 8–10.

16. Ibid., 136; Robert R. Bowie and Richard H. Immerman, *Waging Peace: How Eisenhower Shaped an Enduring Cold War Strategy* (New York: Oxford University Press, 1998), 27; Friedberg, *In the Shadow*, 111–12.

17. Bowie and Immerman, *Waging Peace*, 27–30.

18. Ibid., 33–34; Gaddis, *Strategies of Containment*, 124–25.

19. Leffler, *Preponderance of Power*, 492.

20. On the origins of the term *New Look*, see Dwight D. Eisenhower, *The White House Years: Mandate for Change, 1953–1956* (Garden City, NY: Doubleday, 1963), 449; and Richard Immerman, "Confessions of an Eisenhower Revisionist: An Agonizing Reappraisal," *Diplomatic History* 14 (Summer 1990): 319–24.

21. Eisenhower quoted in Bowie and Immerman, *Waging Peace*, 44.

22. From U.S. Congress, Senate, *Hearings before the Committee on Foreign Relations and the Committee on Armed Services on S. Con. Res. 8*, 82nd Cong., 1st Sess., 1951, 2, cited in Bowie and Immerman, *Waging Peace*, 96.

23. From State of the Union speech, *New York Times*, 8 January 1954, quoted in Sloan, *Eisenhower and the Management of Prosperity*, 75.

24. Yale sociologist Harold Lasswell coined the term. See Friedberg, *In the Shadow*, 57–58.

25. Eisenhower to Lucius Du Bignon Clay, 9 February 1952, in *The Papers of Dwight D. Eisenhower*, ed. Louis Galambos, 13:963, cited in Immerman, "Confessions," 328. On the Great Equation, see Sloan, *Eisenhower and the Management of Prosperity*, 76–77; and Bowie and Immerman, *Waging Peace*, 44, 47.

26. Gaddis, *Strategies of Containment*, 133.

27. Quoted in David Alan Rosenberg, "The Origins of Overkill: Nuclear Weapons and American Strategy, 1945–1960," *International Security* 7, no. 4 (Spring 1983): 27.

28. Sloan, *Eisenhower and the Management of Prosperity*, 15.

29. In his own memoirs Eisenhower counted the interstate highway system and the St. Lawrence Seaway as among the greatest successes of his first term. See Eisenhower, *White House Years: Mandate for Change*, 574.

30. Sloan, *Eisenhower and the Management of Prosperity*, 154.

31. Ibid.

32. Bowie and Immerman, *Waging Peace*, 108, 192.

33. Sloan, *Eisenhower and the Management of Prosperity*, 77, 144.

34. On the Lubbell proposal see Bowie and Immerman, *Waging Peace*, 113.

35. Dwight D. Eisenhower, "A Chance for Peace," Eisenhower speech to the American Society of Newspaper Editors, 16 April 1953, *Public Papers of the Presidents of the United States: Dwight D. Eisenhower, 1953* (Washington, DC: Government Printing Office, 1960), 182.

36. Figures from Gaddis, *Strategies of Containment*, 359.

37. U.S. Congress, Senate, Select Committee on Small Business, *Impact of Defense Spending on Labor Surplus Areas—1962: Hearings on Effect of Defense Spending on Small Business in Labor Surplus Areas*, 87th Cong., 2nd Sess., 29 August 1962, 26–27.

38. Ibid., 60.

39. William W. Kaufmann, ed., *Military Policy and National Security* (Princeton, NJ: Princeton University Press, 1956). See also Fred Kaplan, *The Wizards of Armageddon* (New York: Simon and Schuster, 1983), 185–200.

40. Henry A. Kissinger, *Nuclear Weapons and Foreign Policy* (New York: Harper and Brothers, 1957), 10, 11–12, 16.

41. Ibid., 19, 34–59, 134, 155, 98.

42. Ibid., 125 (emphasis in original), 129.

43. Robert E. Osgood, *Limited War: The Challenge to American Strategy* (Chicago: University of Chicago Press, 1957).

44. From *New York Times*, 13 February 1956, cited in Kissinger, *Nuclear Weapons and Foreign Policy*, 161.

45. On Eisenhower's reaction see "Memorandum of Discussion at the 280th Meeting of the National Security Council, March 22, 1956," in *Foreign Relations of the United States, 1955–1957*, vol. 19: *National Security Policy* (Washington, DC: Government Printing Office, 1990), 271.

46. See Bowie and Immerman, *Waging Peace*, 97–101.

47. Stewart Alsop, "Successful Soviet Test of ICBM Is Reported," *New York Herald Tribune*, 5 July 1957, cited in Robert W. Merry, *Taking on the World: Joseph and Stewart Alsop—Guardians of the American Century* (New York: Viking, 1996), 315.

48. Merry, *Taking on the World*, 315–16.

49. Stephen J. Zaloga, *Target America: The Soviet Union and the Strategic Arms Race, 1945–1964* (Novato, CA: Presidio Press, 1993), 145.

50. David L. Snead, *The Gaither Committee, Eisenhower, and the Cold War* (Columbus: Ohio State University Press, 1999), 64–69.

51. *Deterrence and Survival in the Nuclear Age (The "Gaither Report" of 1957)* (Washington, DC: Government Printing Office, 1976), (hereafter cited as The "Gaither Report"), 12.

52. May, *American Cold War Strategy*, 101.

53. The "Gaither Report," 23.

54. Drew Pearson, "Gaither Report Release Sought," *Washington Post and Times Herald*, 18 December 1957; Arthur Krock, "In the Nation: A Clue to the Top Secret N.S.C. Report," *New York Times*, 20 December 1957, 26. See also Snead, *Gaither Committee*, 138–41.

55. "International Security: The Military Aspect," published as Report 2 in Rockefeller Brothers Fund, *Prospect for America* (Garden City, NY: Doubleday, 1961), 93.

56. Ibid., 152.

57. Ibid.

58. Ball, *Politics and Force Levels*.

59. Roman, *Eisenhower and the Missile Gap*.

60. Rosenberg, "Origins of Overkill," 66 and passim; Roman, *Eisenhower and the Missile Gap*, 177.

61. Rosenberg, "Origins of Overkill," 66.

62. Roman, *Eisenhower and the Missile Gap*, 192; Bowie and Immerman, *Waging Peace*, 248.

63. Walter Heller, *New Dimensions of Political Economy* (New York: Norton, 1966), 28, 29.

64. Seymour E. Harris, "Taxes and the Economy," *Current History* (October 1956), 207, 208

65. Ibid., 210–11.

66. Leon Keyserling, "The Economy in '58," *New Republic,* 13 January 1958, 13–14, 15. See also Leon Keyserling, "Danger Signs in the Economy," *Washington Post,* 6 February 1958.

67. Leon Keyserling, "The Nonsense about Recession and Inflation," *New Republic,* 10 March 1958, 12.

68. Tobin, "Autobiography of James Tobin."

69. Tobin, "Defense, Dollars, and Doctrines," 324, 328.

70. Ibid., 325.

71. Ibid., 327, 330.

72. Ibid., 328–29.

73. Ibid., 325, 329.

74. Ibid., 333 (emphasis in original).

75. John Kenneth Galbraith, "Emeritus Professor John Kenneth Galbraith's Biography," Department of Economics, Harvard University, <http://post.economics.harvard.edu/faculty/galbraith/cv.html>; John Kenneth Galbraith, *The Affluent Society* (Boston: Houghton Mifflin, 1958).

76. For background on the Democratic Advisory Council, see Robert M. Collins, *More: The Politics of Economic Growth in Postwar America* (New York: Oxford University Press, 2000), 45; and Sloan, *Eisenhower and the Management of Prosperity,* 66–67. On the advisory council as a challenge to Johnson and Rayburn, see Robert A. Caro, *The Years of Lyndon Johnson: Master of the Senate* (New York: Alfred A. Knopf, 2002), 840–41; and Robert Dallek, *Lone Star Rising: Lyndon Johnson and His Times, 1908–1960* (New York: Oxford University Press, 1991), 507–8.

77. Galbraith, *Affluent Society,* 2–3.

78. Ibid., 18.

79. Ibid., 178, 180, 175.

80. Ibid., 351, 352.

81. Ibid., 352, 355.

82. Joint Committee on the Economic Report, *January 1955 Economic Report of the President, Hearings,* 326, cited in Herbert Stein, *The Fiscal Revolution in America,* rev. ed. (Washington, DC: AEI Press, 1990), 284.

83. Matthew B. Ridgway, as told to Harold H. Martin, *Soldier: The Memoirs of Matthew B. Ridgway* (New York: Harper and Brothers, 1956), 325, 328.

84. J. H. Thompson, *Chicago Tribune,* 15 April 1956; J. L. Cross, *Christian Science Monitor,* 23 April 1956, 9.

85. James M. Gavin, *War and Peace in the Space Age* (New York: Harper and Brothers, 1958; Matthew Evangelista, *Innovation and the Arms Race: How the United States and the Soviet Union Develop New Military Technologies* (Ithaca, NY: Cornell University Press, 1988), 89, 98–99.

86. James M. Gavin, "Why Missiles," *Army,* November 1957, 25.

87. Alvin Schuster, "Gen. Gavin, Missile Aide, to Quit; Criticized Joint Chiefs System," *New York Times,* 5 January 1958; "Brucker Promises Gavin 4-Star Rank," *New York Times,* 8 January 1958.

88. "Gavin Retires, Backs Atomic Tests," *New York Times,* 1 April 1958.

89. Gavin, *War and Peace in the Space Age.*

90. Ibid., 4.

91. Mark S. Watson, "Lest We Be Nibbled to Death: A Brilliant Retired General Considers Ways to Meet the Nation's Grave Peril," *New York Times,* 10 August 1958; Orville Prescott, "Books of the Times," *New York Times,* 11 August 1958; J. H. Thompson, *Chicago Tribune,* 10 August 1958.

92. James E. King, Jr., "Arms and Man in the Nuclear-Rocket Era," *New Republic* 139, no. 9 (1 September 1958): 16–17.

93. James A. Smith, *The Idea Brokers: Think Tanks and the Rise of the New Policy State* (New York: Free Press, 1991), 104–6.

94. Committee for Economic Development, *The Problem of National Security: Some Economic and Administrative Aspects* (Washington, DC: Committee for Economic Development, 1958), 2.

95. Ibid., 8–9, 10.

96. Ibid., 11.

97. Ibid., 15, 16.

98. Ibid., 20, 21.

99. Ibid., 23, 26.

100. Ibid., 27, 51, 52 (emphasis in original).

101. Seymour Harris, *The Economics of the Political Parties* (New York: Macmillan, 1962), 175, 177.

2—A Senator Finds His Voice

1. John F. Kennedy, *The Strategy of Peace,* edited by Allan Nevins (New York: Popular Library, 1961), 34.

2. Tobin, "Defense, Dollars, and Doctrines," 334.

3. Kennedy's father played an active role in the publication of *Why England Slept* and reportedly purchased thousands of copies himself. See Ronald Kessler, *The Sins of the Father: Joseph P. Kennedy and the Dynasty He Founded* (New York: Time Warner, 1996), 218–20; and Nigel Hamilton, *JFK: Reckless Youth* (New York: Random House, 1992), 380.

4. Michael E. Meagher, "'In an Atmosphere of National Peril': The Development of John F. Kennedy's World View," *Presidential Studies Quarterly* 27, no. 3 (Summer 1997): 467–81.

5. David Burner, *John F. Kennedy and a New Generation,* edited by Oscar Handlin (Boston: Little, Brown, 1988), 30.

6. Meagher, "'In an Atmosphere of National Peril.'"

7. "Secretary McElroy Reports No Evidence of Soviet Lead on ICBM," *New York Times,* 4 April 1958; "U.S. Missile Lead Seen by Deputy Secretary of Defense Quarles," *New York Herald Tribune,* 14 April 1958, both cited in Paul Nitze to McGeorge Bundy, Memorandum, 17 June 1963, Missile Gap 6/63–7/63 folder, National Security Files (NSF), Departments and Agencies (D&A), Box 298, JFKL (hereafter cited as Nitze to Bundy memo, 17 June 1963), Appendix A, "Statements on the Missile Gap in News Media, April 1958–December 1960."

8. Prados, *Soviet Estimate,* 82; Jerry Miller, *Nuclear Weapons and Aircraft Carriers: How the Bomb Saved Naval Aviation* (Washington, DC: Smithsonian Institution Press, 2001), 215–17.

9. Merry, *Taking on the World*, 35–37, 93–104.

10. Ibid., 318–22, 466–67.

11. Wayne G. Jackson, *Allen Welsh Dulles as Director of Central Intelligence, 26 February 1953–29 November 1961*, vol. 5: *Intelligence Support of Policy*, July 1973, p. 64, National Security Archive, George Washington University, Washington, DC.

12. Joseph W. Alsop, "The New Balance of Power: War and Peace in a Strange World," *Encounter* (May 1958), 7, 6, 4.

13. Ibid., 8 (emphasis in original), 10.

14. Joseph W. Alsop, "Our Government Untruths," *New York Herald Tribune*, August 1, 1958.

15. Ibid.

16. Ibid.; SNIE 11-10-57, "The Soviet ICBM Program," in Donald P. Steury, ed., *Intentions and Capabilities: Estimates on Soviet Strategic Forces, 1950–1983* (Washington, DC: Center for the Study of Intelligence, 1996), 64.

17. Kennedy's research materials on the missile gap include an advance copy of Alsop's "Our Government Untruths" column and a one-page summary of missile numbers drawn directly from that column. "National Defense—Missiles 1/7/58–10/21/59, Undated, and Newsclippings," folder, Senate Files, Legislative Assistants, Background Files, Box 771, JFK Pre-Presidential Papers, JFKL.

18. Merry, *Taking on the World*, 342.

19. *New York Times*, 7 November 1957, 16, cited in Drew, "Expecting the Approach of Danger," 326.

20. Nitze to Bundy memo, 17 June 1963, Appendix B, "Statements on the Missile Gap by Senator John F. Kennedy, 1957–1960."

21. Kennedy, *Strategy of Peace*, 60.

22. Ibid., 70, 66.

23. Ibid., 68–69.

24. Ibid., 69.

25. Ibid., 69–70.

26. U.S. Congress, Senate, *Congressional Record* (14 August 1958), 17574; Herbert S. Parmet, *Jack: The Struggles of John F. Kennedy* (New York: Dial, 1980), 446–48. See also Allan Nevins's footnote in Kennedy, *Strategy of Peace*, 60–61.

27. Ibid.

28. Ibid., 17575.

29. Ibid., 17576. See also U.S. Congress, Senate, *Congressional Record*, 15 August 1958, 16282–283.

30. Joseph W. Alsop, "An Authentic Voice," *New York Herald Tribune*, 17 August 1958.

31. Joseph W. Alsop, "A Very Big Issue: ICBM," *New York Herald Tribune*, 18 August 1958.

32. Joseph W. Alsop to Richard Rovere at the *New Yorker*, 15 August 1958, Box 14, "General correspondence, Aug–Sept 1958," Joseph and Stewart Alsop Papers, Library of Congress, Manuscripts Division, Washington, DC (hereafter cited as JWA and SA Papers).

33. Joseph W. Alsop to Henry Luce at *Time*, 3 September 1958; Luce to Alsop (reply to preceding), 23 September 1958; Alsop to Luce, 3 October 1958, Box 14, "General correspondence, Aug–Sept 1958," JWA and SA Papers.

34. Henry R. Luce, Foreword to *Why England Slept*, by John F. Kennedy (New York: Wilfred Funk, 1961), xvi (emphasis in original).

35. JFK letter to Joseph W. Alsop, 23 August 1958, Box 14, "General correspondence, Aug.–Sept. 1958," JWA and SA Papers; Merry, *Taking on the World*, 342; Joseph W. Alsop with Adam Platt, *"I've Seen the Best of It"* (New York: W. W. Norton, 1992), 411.

36. JFK to Abraham Ribicoff, letter, 30 August 1958, in Correspondence, "Kennedy, John F., Speeches—Remarks, Biography 1958–1959–1960" File, Box 11, AR Papers.

37. JFK, "When the Executive Fails to Lead," *The Reporter* 19, no. 4 (18 September 1958): 14–17.

38. "Address by Sen. John F. Kennedy (D-Mass) at Democratic National Committee Regional Conference, Hotel Dennis, Atlantic City, New Jersey, September 10, 1958," Political Files—Misc. National Political, Box 263, Eugene McCarthy Papers, Minnesota Historical Society, St. Paul, MN.

39. "Missile Lag Danger Seen by Kennedy: Senator Calls for Step-Up To Meet Russian Capabilities," *Baltimore Sun*, 25 September 1958, 5, cited in Nitze to Bundy memo, 17 June 1963.

40. Sloan, *Eisenhower and the Management of Prosperity*, 144.

41. The total number of senators increased in the Eighty-Sixth Congress from ninety-six to one hundred with the addition of members from the newly-admitted states of Alaska and Hawaii. Prior to this change, in the Eighty-Fifth Congress, the Democrats had held forty-nine seats in the Senate to the Republicans' forty-seven.

42. Stephen E. Ambrose, *Nixon: The Education of a Politician 1913–1962* (New York: Simon and Schuster, 1987), 485.

43. Eisenhower, *White House Years: Waging Peace*, 374–82; Thomas M. Gaskin, "Senator Lyndon B. Johnson, the Eisenhower Administration and U.S. Foreign Policy, 1957–1960," *Presidential Studies Quarterly* 24, no. 2 (Spring 1994): 349.

44. Rowland Evans, Jr., "Rep. Mahon Warns U.S. against Cuts in Defense," *New York Herald Tribune*, 23 November 1958.

45. Rowland Evans, Jr., "The New Budget," *New York Herald Tribune*, 23 November 1958.

46. Iwan W. Morgan, *Eisenhower versus "The Spenders": The Eisenhower Administration, the Democrats, and the Budget, 1953–1960* (New York: St. Martin's, 1990), 127–28.

47. Stephen E. Ambrose, *Eisenhower: Soldier and President* (New York: Simon and Schuster, 1990), 472; Fred I. Greenstein, *The Hidden Hand Presidency: Eisenhower as Leader* (New York: Basic Books, 1982), 146.

48. See Craig, *Destroying the Village*, especially 49–50, 64–65; and Richard Immerman, ed., *John Foster Dulles and the Diplomacy of the Cold War* (Princeton, NJ: Princeton University Press, 1990), 9. For Eisenhower's views on Dulles's role within the administration, see Eisenhower, *White House Years: Waging Peace*, 361–62.

49. "Memo of meeting with several others on 7/28/59," in "Eisenhower, Dwight D." File, Box 25, Arthur Krock Papers, Seeley G. Mudd Manuscript Library, Princeton University, Princeton, NJ (hereafter cited as Krock Papers).

50. Eisenhower, *White House Years: Waging Peace*, 407.

51. See, for example, McGeorge Bundy, *Danger and Survival: Choices about the Bomb in the First Fifty Years* (New York: Vintage, 1988), 350; Freedman, *Kennedy's Wars*, 48; and Sorensen, *Kennedy*, 610–11.

52. Thomas R. Phillips, "The Growing Missile Gap," *The Reporter*, 8 January 1959, cited in Nitze to Bundy memo, 17 June 1963.

53. Thomas R. Phillips, "McElroy's Claim on Missiles Distorts Intelligence Reports: Secretary Uses Expression 'Positive Evidence'—No Such Thing in Intelligence Estimates," *St. Louis Post-Dispatch*, 23 January 1959, cited in Nitze to Bundy memo, 17 June 1963.

54. Philip Potter, "Symington Firm in Missile View—Hears CIA—Still Predicts 4–1 U.S. Lag by 1961," *Baltimore Sun*, 5 February 1959; "Eisenhower Doubts Reds on Missiles—Tells Nation to Quit Worrying," *New York Herald Tribune*, 5 February 1959, both cited in Nitze to Bundy memo, 17 June 1963.

55. Senate Joint Hearings on Missile and Space Activities, 30 January 1959, 261, cited in Memorandum, William Y. Smith to McGeorge Bundy, 10 July 1963, "Subject: Missile Gap Materials," Missile Gap 6/63–7/63 folder, NSF, D&A, Box 298, JFKL (hereafter cited as Smith to Bundy memo, 10 July 1963); see also "Von Braun Puts Lag at Five Years," *Washington Star*, 8 April 1959, cited in Nitze to Bundy memo, 17 June 1963.

56. "General Schriever Says U.S. Gains on Russians in Missiles—May Wind Up about Same Time with Operational ICBMs," *New York Herald Tribune*, 23 November 1958, cited in Nitze to Bundy memo, 17 June 1963.

57. NIE 11-5-58, "Soviet Capabilities in Guided Missiles and Space Vehicles," in Steury, *Intentions and Capabilities*, 67.

58. Ibid., 68 (emphasis in original). See also Prados, *Soviet Estimate*, 89.

59. Senate, Joint Hearings, Missile and Space Activities, 29 January 1959, 52f, cited in Smith to Bundy memo, 10 July 1963.

60. Hearings, House Appropriations Subcommittee, *DOD Appropriations for 1960*, 23 January 1959, part 1, page 42, cited in Smith to Bundy memo, 10 July 1963.

61. Hearings, House Committee on Armed Forces 1959, *Military Posture Briefings*, 4 February 1959, 851, cited in Smith to Bundy memo, 10 July 1963.

62. Hearings, House Committee on Armed Forces 1959, *Military Posture Briefings*, 6 February 1959, 909f, cited in Smith to Bundy memo, 10 July 1963.

63. Hearings, House Committee on Armed Forces 1959, *Military Posture Briefings*, cited in Smith to Bundy memo, 10 July 1963.

64. Roman, *Eisenhower and the Missile Gap*, 130–31.

65. McElroy to Mahon cited in Nitze to Bundy memo, 17 June 1963.

66. Hearings, House Committee on Armed Forces 1959, *Military Posture Briefings*, 3 February 1959, 820, cited in Smith to Bundy memo, 10 July 1963.

67. Hearings, House Appropriations Subcommittee, *DOD Appropriations for 1960*, 17 February 1959, 850, cited in Smith to Bundy memo, 10 July 1963.

68. Hearings, House Appropriations Subcommittee, *DOD Appropriations for 1960*, 19 February 1959, Part 1, 983–84, cited in Smith to Bundy memo, 10 July 1963.

69. "Surrender on Missiles," *Boston Herald*, 6 February 1959, cited in Nitze to Bundy memo, 17 June 1963.

70. "The President on the Missile 'Lag,'" *New York Herald Tribune*, 5 February 1959.

71. "Big Fuss about Missiles—These Are the Facts," *U.S. News and World Report*, 6 February 1959.

72. "What Are Missiles For?" *Washington Post*, 6 February 1959.

73. Stuart Symington, "Widening The Missile Gap—It Still Exists," *Space Age News*, 9 March 1959; Ray Cromley, "U.S. Risking Missile Gap," *New York World Telegram*, 24 April 1959; and "Lyndon Johnson Raps McElroy View," *Washington Star*, 27 July 1959; all cited in Nitze to Bundy memo, 17 June 1963.

74. "U.S. Ready If Reds Strike, McElroy Says," *New York Herald Tribune*, 9 March 1959; "B/General A. W. Betts Sees No Gap; Scores Defense Critics," *Armed Forces Management*, 10 April 1959; "Soviet Strength Put at 10 ICBMs by McElroy," *Baltimore Sun*, 27 July 1959; "U.S. Missiles Best, View of McElroy— Doubts Red Lead," *New York Herald Tribune*, 27 July 1959; Jack Raymond, "Eisenhower Cites Gains in Missiles," *New York Times*, 30 July 1959, all cited in Nitze to Bundy memo, 17 June 1963.

75. "Leaders Give Their Views on Defenses—ICBM Lag Hit by Symington— McElroy Cites Rise in Power," *New York Journal-American*, 3 February 1959; "Big Fuss About Missiles—These Are the Facts," *U.S. News and World Report*, 6 February 1959, both cited in Nitze to Bundy memo, 17 June 1963.

76. See, for example, James R. Shepley, "Life and Death Debate over Missile Program: President Sticks to Defense Budget but New Military Generation Wants More Hardware to Combat Blackmail," *Life*, 9 March 1959, 116–24.

77. Neal Stanford, "Two Sides of the Missile Debate—One Group Stresses Missile 'Gap,' Other Emphasizes Total Defense Power," *St. Louis Post-Dispatch*, 24 March 1959.

78. "U.S. Missiles vs. Russia's—How the Race Stands Today," Interview with Dr. Herbert F. York, Director, Defense Research and Engineering, *U.S. News and World Report*, 7 September 1959, 76–79, cited in Nitze to Bundy memo, 17 June 1963.

79. John Finney, "York Sees No Lag by U.S. in ICBMs," *New York Times*, 6 October 1959, 1, 4, cited in Nitze to Bundy memo, 17 June 1963.

80. Joseph W. Alsop, "After Ike, the Deluge," *Washington Post*, 7 October 1959.

81. NIE 11-5-58, 67–68.

82. NIE 11-5-59, "Soviet Capabilities in Guided Missiles and Space Vehicles," in *Foreign Relations of the United States, 1958–1960*, vol. 3: *National Security Policy* (Washington, DC: Government Printing Office, 1996), 327.

83. Alsop, "After Ike."

84. Bernard Brodie, *Strategy in the Missile Age* (Princeton, NJ: Princeton University Press, 1959), 333, 369.

85. Wohlstetter, "Delicate Balance of Terror," 230.

86. Maxwell Taylor, *The Uncertain Trumpet* (New York: Harper and Brothers, 1959); Douglas Kinnard, *The Certain Trumpet: Maxwell Taylor and the American Experience in Vietnam* (New York: Brassey's, 1991), 51; John M. Taylor, *General Maxwell Taylor: The Sword and the Pen* (New York: Doubleday, 1989), 224–27.

87. Taylor, *Uncertain Trumpet,* 121, 128, 178.

88. Courtney Sheldon, "The Nation Will Face a Serious Crisis . . ." *Christian Science Monitor,* 7 January 1960, 13.

89. Max Beloff, "Former Weapons," *The Spectator,* 205:6890 (15 July 1960), 106–7.

90. Raymond quoted in Kinnard, *Certain Trumpet,* 51.

91. Andrew Goodpaster, Memorandum of Conference with the President (MCP), 18 November 1959—Augusta [Georgia], dated 20 January 1960, in White House Office, Office of the Staff Secretary, Subject Series, Defense Department Subjects, Box 4, Folder JCS-8, September 59–May 60, Dwight D. Eisenhower Library, Abilene, KS (hereafter cited as DDEL).

92. Bowie and Immerman, *Waging Peace,* 295n.

93. Goodpaster, MCP, 3 November 1959, dated 6 November 1959, in Nuclear History Series, November 1959 folder, National Security Archive, George Washington University, Washington, DC.

94. Craig, *Destroying the Village,* 69; Bowie and Immerman, *Waging Peace,* 179.

95. Memorandum, 13 January 1960, "Discussion at the 430th Meeting of the National Security Council, Thursday, January 7, 1960," Declassified Documents Reference System (1991) 3345.

96. Goodpaster, MCP, 3 November 1959.

97. Goodpaster, MCP, 18 November 1959.

98. Ibid. See also Roman, *Eisenhower and the Missile Gap,* 166–67.

99. Goodpaster, MCP, 18 November 1959.

100. Goodpaster, MCP, 21 November 1959—Augusta [Georgia], dated 2 January 1960, in White House Office, Office of the Staff Secretary, Subject Series, DOD Subjects, Box 2, DOD Vol. 4-1, January 1960, DDEL.

101. Ibid.

102. Briefing Note for National Security Council Meeting of 6 January 1960, "Atlas, Titan, and Polaris Research," Declassified Documents Reference System (1991) 3340.

103. 430th Meeting of the National Security Council, 7 January 1960, Declassified Documents Reference System (1991) 3345.

104. Roman, *Eisenhower and the Missile Gap,* 145.

105. Geoffrey Perret, *Eisenhower* (New York: Random House, 1999), 578.

106. Prados, *Soviet Estimate,* 86–95.

107. McElroy had based his testimony on NIE 11-4-58, issued in December 1958. Figures from Prados, *Soviet Estimate,* 89.

108. 430th Meeting of the National Security Council, 7 January 1960.

109. Ibid.

110. Ibid.

111. NIE 11-8-59, "Soviet Capabilities for Strategic Attack through Mid-1964," in Steury, *Intentions and Capabilities*, 75.

112. Ibid., 73–74.

113. Ibid., 74, footnote 2.

114. George B. Kistiakowsky, Notes for Meeting with the President, 14 January 1960, Nuclear History Series, January 1960 folder, National Security Archive, George Washington University, Washington, DC.

115. John G. Norris, "U.S. to Expand Missile Program: Ike Backs Polaris and ICBM Plan; $1 Billion Project to Widen Work by One Third," *Washington Post*, 13 January 1960; NIE 11-8-59, 75.

116. Cited in Jackson, *Allen Welsh Dulles*, 107; NIE 11-8-59, 79.

117. Norris, "U.S. to Expand Missile Program"; "Navy Drops Construction of Five Ships," *Washington Post*, 13 January 1960.

118. Gordon Gray, MCP, 13 January 1960, dated 15 January 1960, in Nuclear History Series, January 1960 folder, National Security Archive, George Washington University, Washington, DC.

119. James Giglio, *The Presidency of John F. Kennedy* (Lawrence: University Press of Kansas, 1991), 15.

120. Statement of Senator John F. Kennedy (Dem.-Mass.), 2 January 1960, in Correspondence, "Kennedy, John F., Speeches—Remarks, Biography 1958–1959–1960" File, Box 11, AR Papers.

121. Harris Wofford, *Of Kennedys and Kings: Making Sense of the Sixties*, rev. ed. (Pittsburgh: University of Pittsburgh Press, 1992), 37; Burner, *John F. Kennedy and a New Generation*, 32.

122. Chalmers Roberts, "Kennedy Puts Name into Race: Would Not Accept Nomination for No. 2 Spot, He Says," *Washington Post*, 3 January 1960.

123. Nitze to Bundy memo, 17 June 1963, Appendix B, "Statements on the Missile Gap by Senator John F. Kennedy, 1957–1960."

124. John A. Goldsmith, "Red Power to Attack Discounted: Gates Tells Senate Group of New Data on Soviet Strength," *Washington Post*, 20 January 1960.

125. Thomas S. Power, "Military Problems and Prospects of Deterrence: Protecting Our Heritage until a Truly Lasting Peace Can Be Assured," *Vital Speeches* 26, no. 9 (15 February 1960): 286.

126. Adm. G. E. "Jerry" Miller, USN (Ret.), interview by author, 20 February 2003, at the Army-Navy Country Club, Arlington, VA. See also Miller, *Nuclear Weapons and Aircraft Carriers*, 217; and Prados, *Soviet Estimate*, 81–82.

127. "Gates Sees Narrower 'Gap,'" *Missiles and Rockets* 6, no. 4 (25 January 1960): 24.

128. M.C. Donnelly, to Chief of Staff, USAF, "Reply to Questions on General Power's Speech," 25 January 1960, Nuclear History Series, January 1960 folder, National Security Archive, George Washington University, Washington, DC.

129. John G. Norris, "U.S. Estimating Power of Soviet on Basis of 'Intent,' Gates Says," *Washington Post*, 21 January 1960.

130. John G. Norris, "House Unit Reassured by Gates," *Washington Post*, 23 January 1960; "Johnson Sees Peril in 'Guess' on Reds," *Washington Post*, 24 January 1960.

131. "Secretary of Air Force Discounts 'Missile Gap,'" *Washington Post,* 24 January 1960; Jack Raymond, "Democrats Assail Defense Estimate," *New York Times,* 24 January 1960.

132. Taylor, *General Maxwell Taylor,* 224–25.

133. Gordon Gray, "Memo of Mtg with President, February 3, 1960," dated 8 February 1960, from 1960 meetings with the President, vol. 1 (7), Box 4, White House Office, Office of the Special Assistant for National Security Affairs, Special Assistant Series, Presidential Subseries, DDEL.

134. "Twining Testimony Critical of Those Who 'Degrade' U.S.," *Washington Post,* 24 January 1960.

135. Goodpaster, MCP, 25 January 1960, dated 26 January 1960, in Whitman File, DDE Diary, Box 47, Staff Notes, January 1960–1961, DDEL.

136. Joseph W. Alsop, "Conflicts on 'Missile Gap,'" *New York Herald Tribune,* 25 January 1960.

137. Victor Wilson, "A.F. Secretary Denies Gap in Deterrent Power: Says U.S. Defense Bars Attack Even if Soviets Lead in Missiles," *New York Herald Tribune,* 25 January 1960.

138. Joseph W. Alsop, "The Soviet Missile Arsenal," *New York Herald Tribune,* 26 January 1960.

139. Joseph W. Alsop, "The Missile Gap and Survival," *New York Herald Tribune,* 27 January 1960.

140. Warren Rogers, "Eisenhower Backs U.S. Arms Pace," *New York Herald Tribune,* 27 January 1960.

141. Gerald Griffin, "Intelligence on Russia Improves, President Says," *Baltimore Sun,* 27 January 1960; Howard Norton, "U.S.-Soviet Missile 'Gap' Seen Likely to Get Worse," *Baltimore Sun,* 27 January 1960; Mark Watson "Intelligence Uproar Blamed on Inept Pentagon Handling," *Baltimore Sun,* 27 January 1960.

142. Jack Raymond, "Juggling of Missile Data Is Charged by Symington," *New York Times,* 28 January 1960.

143. Gordon Gray, "Memo of Mtg with President, February 3, 1960," dated 8 February 1960, from 1960 meetings with the president, vol. 1 (7), Box 4, OSANSA, Special Assistant Series, Presidential Subseries, DDEL.

144. "Gates Sees Missile Lag Ending in 1962," *Baltimore Sun,* 1 February 1960.

145. Howard Norton, "Gates Rejects General Power's Red Estimate of 300 Missiles to Wipe Out U.S. Ability to Retaliate," *Baltimore Sun,* 2 February 1960.

146. Thomas S. Power, Memorandum for General White, 11 January 1960, "Subject: B-70 Flexibility," Nuclear History Series, January 1960 folder, National Security Archive, George Washington University, Washington, DC.

147. "Gates Sees Missile Lag Ending in 1962," *Baltimore Sun,* 1 February 1960.

148. Taylor, *General Maxwell Taylor,* 225.

149. Joseph W. Alsop, "Matter of Fact: This Very Reason," *Washington Post,* 8 February 1960.

150. George Dixon, "Washington Scene: Generals Might Take the Fifth," *Washington Post,* 8 February 1960, A15.

151. Goodpaster, MCP, 12 February 1960, dated 18 February 1960. From White House Office, Office of the Staff Secretary, Subject Series, DOD Subseries, Box 4, JCS-8, September 1959–May 1960, DDEL.

152. W. W. Kaufmann to G. K. Tanham, Memorandum, "The Puzzle of Polaris," 1 February 1960; Roscoe Wilson to White, "'The Puzzle of Polaris'—an Informal Memorandum by Mr. W. W. Kaufmann," 17 February 1960; William Kaufmann to White, letter, 18 February 1960, and White to Kaufmann, letter, "Comments on Polaris Weapon System," (plus attachments), 4 March 1960, all in Box 36—File 4-5, "Missiles/Space/Nuclear," Thomas Dresser White Papers, Library of Congress, Manuscripts Division, Washington, DC. See also Miller, *Nuclear Weapons and Aircraft Carriers,* 210.

153. "Air Chief Warns of Russian Gains," *New York Times,* 15 February 1960.

154. Robert S. McNamara, telephone conversation with author, 10 April 2003.

155. Raymond L. Garthoff, personal interview, 15 April 2003, Washington, DC.

156. John Kennedy to Joseph Alsop, 27 February 1960, Box 157, "Subject Files, 'Missile Gap' Pamphlet File," JWA and SA Papers.

157. John F. Kennedy, "An Investment for Peace," speech excerpted from U.S. Congress, Senate, *Congressional Record,* 1, in "Speeches—Misc. JFK 6/7/58–3/18/60" folder, '60 Campaign Issues, Richard Goodwin Working Papers, Box 996, JFK Pre-Presidential Papers, JFKL.

158. Ibid.

159. Ibid.

160. Ibid., 1–2.

161. Ibid.

162. Ibid., 2–3.

163. Ibid., 3.

164. Khrushchev had also pushed for economies in defense, hoping to use a modest nuclear force for deterrence while simultaneously reducing conventional forces. Garthoff interview; Jackson, *Allen Welsh Dulles,* 93.

165. Garthoff interview. In 1959 Garthoff, at the time working in the Office of National Estimates, had explained to a study group for Democratic senators that there was no missile gap. The meeting was organized by Senator Albert Gore Sr. and included Gore, Eugene McCarthy, and Stuart Symington. Garthoff could not persuade Symington, who subsequently questioned Garthoff about his claims in a separate meeting to review intelligence data. Raymond Garthoff, *A Journey through the Cold War: A Memoir of Containment and Coexistence* (Washington, DC: Brookings Institution, 2001), 64. See also Raymond Garthoff, *Assessing the Adversary: Estimates by the Eisenhower Administration of Soviet Intentions and Capabilities* (Washington, DC: Brookings Institution, 1991), 47, footnote 123.

166. Kennedy, "Investment for Peace,"4.

167. Ibid., 4–5.

168. Ibid.

169. Ibid., 6.

170. Fred I. Greenstein and Richard H. Immerman, "What Did Eisenhower Tell Kennedy about Indochina? The Politics of Misperception," *Journal of American History* 79 (September 1992): 581–82.

3 — The Presidential Election of 1960 and the Politics of National Security

1. "Poll #826, The Presidential Election in Michigan, II, 10/13/60 (Harris)," 6, General Subject File, 1959–1960, Robert F. Kennedy Papers, Pre-Administration Political Files, JFKL (hereafter cited as RFK Papers).

2. For an overview of the campaign, see Theodore H. White, *The Making of the President, 1960* (New York: Atheneum, 1961). Concerning the role of religion in the campaign, see Elmo Roper, "Polling Post-Mortem," *Saturday Review* 43:48, 26 November 1960, 11; Angus Campbell, Philip E. Converse, Warren E. Miller, and Donald E. Stokes, *Elections and the Political Order,* Survey Research Center, Institute for Social Research, University of Michigan (New York: Wiley, 1966); Richard M. Nixon, *Six Crises* (1962; reprint, New York: Touchstone, 1990), 307; and Sorensen, *Kennedy,* 218–19.

3. Robert A. Divine, *Foreign Policy and U.S. Presidential Elections, Volume 2, 1952–1960* (New York: New Viewpoints, 1974), 191–92, 285–87.

4. Burner, *John F. Kennedy and a New Generation,* 47–48.

5. From *Ground Support Equipment* (April–May 1960), cited in Nitze to Bundy memo, 17 June 1963, Appendix B, "Statements on the Missile Gap by Senator John F. Kennedy, 1957–1960."

6. "Here's Kennedy's Foreign Policy," *U.S. News and World Report,* 27 June 1960, 64. Reprinted from U.S. Congress, Senate, *Congressional Record,* 14 June 1960, 11630. Also cited in Nitze to Bundy memo, 17 June 1963, Appendix B, "Statements on the Missile Gap by Senator John F. Kennedy, 1957–1960."

7. "Here's Kennedy's Foreign Policy," 64–65.

8. James Bamford, *Body of Secrets: Anatomy of the Ultra-Secret National Security Agency* (New York: Doubleday, 2001), 51–55; Michael Beschloss, *MAYDAY: Eisenhower, Khrushchev and the U-2 Affair* (New York: Harper and Row, 1986), 25–29, 331–32.

9. "The Democrats Care," from "Program for 1960 Democratic Convention," in "Democratic National Committee, Prepared by the" file, Box 12, Democratic Party, California Democratic State Central Committee (CDSCC) Papers, Urban Archives Center, University Library, California State University—Northridge (hereafter referred to as Urban Archives, Cal State—Northridge).

10. "Abram Chayes, International Law Specialist, Dies at 77," 20 April 2000, *Harvard University Gazette,* <http://www.news.harvard.edu/gazette/2000/04.20/chayes.html>; "Oral History Interviews," JFKL Web Site, <http://www.jfklibrary.org/oralhist.htm>.

11. Democratic Platform, in "Democratic National Committee, Prepared by the" file, Box 12, Democratic Party, CDSCC Papers, Urban Archives, Cal State—Northridge.

12. Ibid.

13. "Senator John F. Kennedy's Presidential Nomination Acceptance Speech," Memorial Coliseum, Los Angeles, California, 15 July 1960, JFKL Web site, <http://www.jfklibrary.org/j071560.htm>.

14. Extract, Statement by Governor Rockefeller, New York, 23 July 1960, cited in Smith to Bundy memo, 10 July 1963.

15. Ibid.

16. Joseph W. Alsop interview, conducted 14 June 1972 by John Luter at Columbia University, originally part of the Dwight David Eisenhower Library Oral History, located in Box 268, Subject Files—Oral History Interviews, File: DDEL-OH, DDE Administration Project, Box 14, "General correspondence, Aug–Sept 1958," JWA and SA Papers, pp. 12–13.

17. A poll taken in October 1958 found 60 percent of respondents approving of Eisenhower's record as president, and 29 percent disapproving (Roper Poll, October 1958). Two years later, as Eisenhower prepared to leave office, his approval ratings remained at 60 percent (Gallup Poll, December 1960). Another poll taken at that same time found that 66 percent of respondents thought that Eisenhower would "go down in history" as either a "great" or "good" president (Gallup Poll, December 1960).

18. Joseph W. Alsop interview, 14.

19. Regarding the dates and locations of the various intelligence briefings, see Notes, "Dates of Briefings: Presidential Campaign—1960," Box 89, Re: John F. Kennedy, 1960, Allen W. Dulles Papers, Seeley G. Mudd Manuscript Library, Princeton University, Princeton, NJ (hereafter cited as AWD Papers). On the CIA's briefings of the presidential candidates, see John L. Helgerson, *Getting to Know the President: CIA Briefings of Presidential Candidates, 1952–1992* (Washington, DC: Center for the Study of Intelligence, 1996), 22 May 1996, Central Intelligence Agency, <http://www.cia.gov/csi/books/briefing/>. On speculation regarding what Kennedy was told about plans to overthrow Cuban leader Fidel Castro, see Nixon, *Six Crises*, 354; and Memo to John McCone, director of CIA, 5/20/62, Box 104, JFK, 1960, AWD Papers.

20. See, for example, Richard Reeves, *President Kennedy: Profile of Power* (New York: Simon and Schuster, 1993), 58–59; and Seymour M. Hersh, *The Dark Side of Camelot* (Boston: Little, Brown, 1997), 155–56.

21. NIE 11-8-60, "Soviet Capabilities for Long Range Attack through Mid-1965," in Steury, *Intentions and Capabilities*, 109.

22. Powers was supposed to photograph a suspected ICBM site at Plesetsk. Ironically, this proved to be the only site at which the first-generation Soviet ICBM, the SS-6, was ever deployed, but this was not known until mid-1961. Jackson, *Allen Welsh Dulles as Director of Central Intelligence*, 111–12; Garthoff, *Assessing the Adversary*, 41–42.

23. "Memorandum for the President, 8/3/60," Box 89, Re: John F. Kennedy, 1960, AWD Papers. See also Beschloss, *The Crisis Years*, 26.

24. Wheeler oral history, JFKL, cited in Reeves, *President Kennedy*, 58–59.

25. On Robert Kennedy's role in the campaign, see James W. Hilty, *Robert Kennedy: Brother Protector* (Philadelphia: Temple University Press, 1997); and Arthur M. Schlesinger Jr., *Robert Kennedy and His Times* (Boston: Houghton Mifflin, 1978).

26. Sorensen, *Kennedy,* 16; Burner, *John F. Kennedy and a New Generation,* 32.

27. Richard N. Goodwin, *Remembering America: A Voice from The Sixties* (Philadelphia: Harper and Row, 1988), 63–64.

28. Wofford, *Of Kennedys and Kings,* 39–40.

29. Sorensen, *Kennedy,* 119; Kathleen Hall Jamieson, *Packaging the Presidency: A History and Criticism of Presidential Campaign Advertising,* 2nd ed. (New York: Oxford University Press, 1992), 397.

30. "The 'Catholic Vote'—A Kennedy Staff Analysis," *U.S. News and World Report,* 1 August 1960, 68–72.

31. See Counterattack Sourcebook folder, 1960 Campaign Position and Briefing Papers, Box 991, JFK Pre-Presidential Papers, JFKL.

32. William Atwood, "Memo on the 1960 Campaign," June 1960, in "U.S.-Soviet Military Comparisons 10/59–11/1/60 and Undated" folder, '60 Campaign Issues, Richard Goodwin Working Papers, Box 996, JFK Pre-Presidential Papers, JFKL.

33. Wofford, *Of Kennedys and Kings,* 36–37.

34. Hamilton, *JFK: Reckless Youth,* 691–704, 774, 776; Meagher, "'In an Atmosphere of National Peril,'" 467–81.

35. See Tris Coffin, "Speech Materials Undated" folder; Arthur Schlesinger Jr., "The Big Decision: Private Indulgence or National Strength," in "Speech Writings—General 1/2/58–6/5/60" folder, '60 Campaign Issues; and Ken Galbraith to Sorensen, "Memorandum: Campaign Strategy, 1960," undated, in "U.S.-Soviet Military Comparisons 10/59–11/1/60 and Undated" folder, '60 Campaign Issues, all in Richard Goodwin Working Papers, Box 996, JFK Pre-Presidential Papers, JFKL.

36. "Planning for Peace—The Place of Defense Workers and Defense Industry in a Peacetime World," in "Speech Materials Undated" folder, '60 Campaign Issues, Richard Goodwin Working Papers, Box 996, JFK Pre-Presidential Papers, JFKL.

37. On the use of federal defense contracts to boost regional economies, see Christopher Preble, "The Political Economy of National Security in the Nuclear Age: John F. Kennedy and the Missile Gap" (Ph.D. diss., Temple University, 2002), 334–74.

38. Elizabeth Farmer to Mike Feldman, Memorandum, 4 October 1960, "Subject: Documentation of Decline of U.S. Prestige Abroad," in Briefing Papers, "Crime-Foreign Service" folder, '60 Campaign Issues, Position and Briefing Papers, Briefing Book, Box 993A, JFK Pre-Presidential Papers, JFKL.

39. Burner, *John F. Kennedy and a New Generation,* 37.

40. Walt W. Rostow, *The Stages of Economic Growth: A Non-Communist Manifesto,* 2nd ed. (New York: Cambridge University Press, 1973), 2.

41. "Rostow, Walt W(hitman): CA Interview," *Contemporary Authors,* New Revision Series, 8:429–30.

42. Meagher, "'In an Atmosphere of National Peril,'" 3, 7.

43. Sorensen, *Kennedy,* 118; Divine, *Foreign Policy and U.S. Presidential Elections,* 192.

44. Wofford, *Of Kennedys and Kings,* 40.

45. See Giglio, *The Presidency of John F. Kennedy*, 10.

46. 3 September 1960, Book Review of "Deterrent or Defense" by B. H. Liddell Hart, *Saturday Review of Literature*, in U.S. Congress, Senate, Committee on Commerce, Subcommittee of the Subcommittee [*sic*] on Communications, *Freedom of Communications*, Part I: *The Speeches, Remarks, Press Conferences, and Statements of Senator John F. Kennedy, August 1 through November 7, 1960*, 87th Cong., 1st Sess., 1961, 979 (*Freedom of Communication* cited hereafter as *FOC*).

47. Ibid.

48. On Kennedy's comments to Dulles, see "Memorandum for the Record," 9/21/60, AWD Papers; Kennedy's reference to Medaris is in U.S. Congress, Senate, *Congressional Record*, 29 February 1960, 3803.

49. John B. Medaris, *Countdown for Decision* (New York: Putnam, 1960), excerpted in "Defense: Shots from the Hip," *Time*, 17 October 1960, 26.

50. 18 October 1960, Speech, Miami Beach, FL, American Legion Convention, *FOC*, Part I, 649–50.

51. Ibid., 650, 652.

52. Ibid., 654.

53. Russell Baker, "Kennedy Assails 'Retreat' Charge," and Leo Egan, "Nixon Proposes Cuba Quarantine," *New York Times*, 19 October 1960.

54. Sorensen, *Kennedy*, 213; Lawrence O'Brien, *No Final Victories: A Life in Politics from John F. Kennedy to Watergate* (Garden City, NY: Doubleday, 1974), 93; Kenneth P. O'Donnell and David F. Powers, with Joseph McCarthy, *"Johnny We Hardly Knew Ye": Memories of John Fitzgerald Kennedy* (Boston: Little, Brown, 1972), 211.

55. "First Kennedy-Nixon Debate," JFKL Web Site, 10 September 2001, <http://www.jfklibrary.org/60-1st.htm>. Original text from U.S. Congress, Senate, Committee on Commerce, Subcommittee of the Subcommittee [*sic*] on Communications, *FOC*, Part III: *The Joint Appearances of Senator John F. Kennedy and Vice President Richard M. Nixon and Other 1960 Campaign Presentations*, 87th Cong., 1st Sess., 1961, 73–92.

56. White, *Making of the President*, 330.

57. "Second Kennedy-Nixon Debate: October 7, 1960," JFKL Web Site, 17 June 2001, <http://www.jfklibrary.org/60-2nd.htm>. Original text from *FOC*, Part III.

58. "Third Kennedy-Nixon Debate: October 13, 1960," JFKL Web Site, 17 June 2001, <http://www.jfklibrary.org/60-3rd.htm>. Original text from *FOC*, Part III.

59. "Fourth Kennedy-Nixon Debate: October 21, 1960," JFKL Web Site, 17 June 2001, <http://www.jfklibrary.org/60-4th.htm>. Original text from *FOC*, Part III.

60. "Poll #802: The Presidential Election in Pennsylvania 9/13/60 (Harris)," Box 45, General Subject File, 1959–1960, RFK Papers, Pre-Administration Political Files, JFKL.

61. Ibid., 12 (emphasis in original).

62. 15 September 1960, Statewide TV Speech, Zembo Mosque Temple, Harrisburg, PA, *FOC*, Part I, 250–51.

63. 16 September 1960, Remarks, Lebanon, PA, *FOC*, Part I, 253.

64. Joseph H. Miller, "GOP Foreign Policy Assailed by Kennedy," *Philadelphia Inquirer,* 17 September 1960.

65. "Poll #807: The Presidential Election in Pennsylvania, II, 10/12/60 (Harris)," Box 45, General Subject File, 1959–1960, RFK Papers, Pre-Administration Political Files, JFKL.

66. Ibid., 8.

67. 29 October 1960, Remarks, Philadelphia, PA, Lord and Taylor Shopping Center, *FOC,* Part I, 810.

68. Ibid., 811. Nixon's statement had said, "We entered the space competition some paces behind. . . . Not until President Eisenhower took office in 1953 did the United States begin serious work on the intercontinental ballistic missiles. . . . The Eisenhower administration has just about closed an inherited space gap. We have been hard at work on the related problem—the so-called missile gap—likewise inherited—and we have achieved great success." From 25 October 1960, Statement on Space Exploration, Cincinnati, OH, in U.S. Congress, Senate, Committee on Commerce, Subcommittee of the Subcommittee [*sic*] on Communications, *Freedom of Communications,* Part II: *The Speeches, Remarks, Press Conferences, and Statements of Vice President Richard M. Nixon, August 1 through November 7, 1960,* 87th Cong., 1st Sess., 1961, 761.

69. John S. McCullough, "Throngs Halt Motorcade of Candidate," *Philadelphia Evening Bulletin,* 29 October 1960, from "Kennedy, John F.—Phila. Visits—1960—October—Presidential Collection" file, *Philadelphia Evening Bulletin* Clippings Collection, Urban Archives, Samuel Paley Library, Temple University, Philadelphia, PA.

70. 28 October 1960, Remarks, Pottsville, PA, *FOC,* Part I, 790.

71. "Poll #812: The Presidential Election in Pennsylvania, III, 11/3/60 (Harris)," Box 45, General Subject File, 1959–1960, RFK Papers, Pre-Administration Political Files, JFKL.

72. The final official count gave Kennedy 622,544 votes to Nixon's 291,000, the largest plurality in the city's history. Kennedy's plurality statewide was only 116,326 votes. James M. Perry, "Kennedy Wins in Philadelphia by 326,407," *Philadelphia Evening Bulletin,* 9 November 1960, and *Philadelphia Evening Bulletin,* 25 November, from "Kennedy, John F.—Phila. Visits—1960—October—Presidential Collection" file, *Philadelphia Evening Bulletin* Clippings Collection, Urban Archives, Temple University.

73. 14 September 1960, Speech, New York, NY, Citizens for Kennedy Rally, *FOC,* Part I, 235, 237.

74. 14 September 1960, Speech, New York, NY, Acceptance of Liberal Party Nomination, *FOC,* Part I, 238, 241.

75. "Poll #800: The Presidential Election in New York State 9/19/60 (Harris)," pp. 12, 13, Box 44, General Subject File, 1959–1960, RFK Papers, Pre-Administration Political Files, JFKL.

76. Ibid., 12, 13.

77. Ibid., 13.

78. Preble, "Political Economy of National Security," 322–28.

79. 28 September 1960, Remarks, Niagara Falls, NY, Bell Aircraft Co., *FOC,* Part I, 383.

80. Ibid.

81. Ibid., 384.

82. Ibid.

83. Leo Egan, "Upstate Crowds Cheer Kennedy," *New York Times,* 29 September 1960.

84. 12 October 1960, Speech, Prepared for a Dinner Held by the Democratic National and State Committees, Waldorf-Astoria Hotel, New York, NY, *FOC,* Part I, 574.

85. 19 October 1960, Remarks, City Hall Steps, New York, NY, *FOC,* Part I, 664.

86. 19 October 1960, Remarks, Auditorium, Union Hall, New York, NY, *FOC,* Part I, 666.

87. Peter Kihss, "Big Crowds Here Acclaim Kennedy and Mob His Car, *New York Times,* 20 October 1960.

88. Peter Braestrup, "Kennedy Details Housing Program," *New York Times,* 20 October 1960.

89. "Poll #805: The Presidential Election in New York State II, 10/25/60 (Harris)," pp. 3, 9, Box 44, General Subject File, 1959–1960, RFK Papers, Pre-Administration Political Files, JFKL.

90. 27 October 1960, Remarks, New York, NY, Trade Union Council of Liberal Party, *FOC,* Part I, 773.

91. 27 October 1960, Speech, Queens, NY, Sunnyside Gardens, *FOC,* Part I, 782.

92. "Poll #810: The Presidential Election in New York State III, 11/4/60 (Harris)," p. 7, Box 44, General Subject File, 1959–1960, RFK Papers, Pre- Administration Political Files, JFKL.

93. White, *Making of the President,* 161–62.

94. 26 August 1960, Speech, Detroit, Michigan, VFW Convention, *FOC,* Part I, 50, 51, 971 (verbatim text), 52–53. Kennedy made a departure from the advance release text given to reporters before the speech. In the advance version Kennedy was to have said "The facts of the matter are that we are falling behind—behind in our schedules, behind in our needs, behind the Russians in our rate of progress. The missile lag looms larger and larger ahead." 26 August 1960, Speech, Detroit, Michigan, VFW Convention, *FOC,* Part I, 52.

95. Ibid., 53.

96. "Kennedy Gets Big Greeting in Detroit," *Detroit Free Press,* 26 August 1960; "AFL-CIO Endorses Kennedy," *Detroit Free Press,* 27 August 1960; Ray Courage, "Nominee Urges Arms Hike: He Slaps at Nixon in Speech," *Detroit Free Press,* 27 August 1960.

97. "Indeed Yes, There are—20th Century Armor Chinks," *Detroit Free Press,* 27 August 1960.

98. Emphasis in original. Sen. Philip Hart to Frank Sieverts, 29 August 1960, Memorandum "Kennedy Briefing on Michigan," 1, in "State Briefing Papers, Louisiana-Missouri" File, Box 991, Position and Briefing Papers, 1960, JFK Pre-Presidential Papers, JFKL (emphasis in original).

99. Ibid., 4.

100. *Impact of Defense Spending in Labor Surplus Areas, Report of the Subcommittee on Retailing, Distribution, and Marketing Practices to the Select Committee on Small Business, United States Senate on Government Programs and Policies as They Relate to the Use of Procurement in Redeveloping Distressed Areas and a Compilation of Policy Directives, Statutes, and Regulations Relating to Procurement in Distressed Areas,* 88th Cong., 1st Sess., 19 August 1963, 5.

101. 5 September 1960, Statement, Labor Day message, *FOC,* Part I, 110.

102. 5 September 1960, Speech, Detroit, Michigan, Cadillac Square, *FOC,* Part I, 112, 113.

103. "Poll #825, The Presidential Election in Michigan, 9/12/60 (Harris)," pp. 8, 9, Box 44, General Subject File, 1959–1960, RFK Papers, Pre-Administration Political Files, JFKL.

104. "Poll #826, The Presidential Election in Michigan, II, 10/13/60 (Harris)," p. 1., Box 44, General Subject File, 1959–1960, RFK Papers, Pre-Administration Political Files, JFKL.

105. Ibid., 6.

106. 26 October 1960, Remarks, Warren, Michigan, Tech Plaza Shopping Center, *FOC,* Part I, 760.

107. Ibid., 761.

108. "Kennedy's Michigan Visit a Success?" 27 October 1960, *The State Journal* (Lansing).

109. Willard Baird, "U.S. Must Do More—Kennedy: Democrat Choice Draws Small Crowds Here, Big Throng in Gd. Rapids," *The State Journal,* 15 October 1960, 1, 2.

110. Stanley Greenberg, *Middle Class Dreams: The Politics and Power of the New American Majority,* revised and updated edition (New Haven: Yale University Press, 1995), 25.

111. *California Labor Statistics Bulletin Area Supplement,* April 1960, 2; and September 1960, 2.

112. *California Labor Statistics Bulletin Area Supplement,* June 1960, 3.

113. Ibid.

114. 8 September 1960, Remarks, Dunsmuir, California, rear train platform, *FOC,* Part I, 163; and 8 September 1960, Remarks, Redding, California, rear train platform, *FOC,* Part I, 163.

115. 9 September 1960, Remarks, Stockton, California, rear train platform, *FOC,* Part I, 175; and 9 September 1960, Remarks, Modesto, California, rear train platform, *FOC,* Part I, 176.

116. 9 September 1960, Remarks, Fresno, California, "Pathways to Peace," *FOC,* Part I, 178–79. Harris had directly alluded to the Democrats being perceived as the party of war in his polling reports. See "Poll #800: The Presidential Election in New York State, 9/19/60 (Harris)," pp. 12–13, Box 44, General Subject File, 1959–1960, RFK Papers, Pre-Administration Political Files, JFKL.

117. 9 September 1960, Speech, Los Angeles California, Shrine Auditorium, *FOC,* Part I, 190–91.

118. 9 September 1960, Press Conference, Burbank, California, Lockheed Air Terminal, *FOC,* Part I, 182.

119. 11 September 1960, Remarks, San Diego, California, Lindbergh Field, *FOC*, Part I, 195.

120. 11 September 1960, Remarks, San Diego, California, U.S. Grant Hotel, *FOC*, Part I, 196–97.

121. Henry Love, "Kennedy Asks S.D. Defense Role Boost," *San Diego Union*, 12 September 1960.

122. Robert W. Richards, "Kennedy's Cures Span the Continent: A Campaign of Promises for All," *San Diego Union*, 10 September 1960.

123. Lou Fleming, "U.S. Must Move Ahead, Kennedy Tells Overflow Crowd of 35,000," *Los Angeles Times*, 2 November 1960.

124. Donald M. Pattillo, *Pushing the Envelope: The American Aircraft Industry* (Ann Arbor: University of Michigan Press, 1998), 230. See also Michael Brown, *Flying Blind: The Politics of the U.S. Strategic Bomber Program* (Ithaca, NY: Cornell University Press, 1992), esp. 201–13.

125. Brown, *Flying Blind*, 218; Roman, *Eisenhower and the Missile Gap*, 165–67.

126. "Eisenhower-Nixon and the Missiles Failure," *The Propeller*, 17 March 1960; see also "War Vet Jobless 13 Months; Calls it 'Worse Than Battle,'" *The Propeller*, 28 April 1960, both in Propeller Files, Southern California Labor Newspaper Collection, Urban Archives, Cal State—Northridge.

127. "Kennedy: Urges Step-Up in Missile and Aircraft Production to Fight High Unemployment," *The Propeller*, 20 October 1960, 5, Propeller Files, Southern California Labor Newspaper Collection, Urban Archives, Cal State—Northridge.

128. Roman, *Eisenhower and the Missile Gap*, 167.

129. 2 November 1960, Statement, Development of the B-70, *FOC*, Part I, 1232, 1233.

130. Fleming, "U.S. Must Move Ahead."

131. 2 November 1960, Remarks, San Diego California, Horton Plaza, *FOC*, Part I, 858; 2 November 1960, Remarks, San Diego, California, airport, *FOC*, Part I, 857.

132. Ibid., 860.

133. Fleming, "U.S. Must Move Ahead"; Jack Smith, "200,000 Welcome Kennedy in Downtown L.A. Motorcade: Roaring Reception in Streets," *Los Angeles Times*, 2 November 1960, 1, 2.

134. Lyn Nofziger, "Kennedy Outlines 'Dreams' for U.S.," *San Diego Union*, 1 November 1960.

135. Henry T. Love, "Kennedy Terms California Role Key to Election: Candidate Assails Record of GOP in Address at Downtown Plaza," *San Diego Union*, 3 November 1960; Lyn Nofziger, "Peace Corps Proposed by Kennedy," *San Diego Union*, 3 November 1960.

136. Rembert James, "Isles Test Seen If Kennedy Wins," *San Diego Union*, 3 November 1960.

137. 3 September 1960, Press Conference of Senator John F. Kennedy, San Francisco, California, International Airport, *FOC*, Part I, 96.

138. White, *Making of the President*, 407.

139. GOP Congressman Bob Wilson congratulated the Nixon campaign for its strong showing in the city. Bob Wilson to Herbert Klein, c/o Nixon Party, Western Union telegram, 9 November 1960, Political Affairs series, Richard Nixon File, Box 71, Robert C. Wilson Papers, Center for Regional History, University Library, San Diego State University, San Diego, CA.

140. Bundy, *Danger and Survival*, 344, 345.

141. For a similar argument, see Ball, *Politics and Force Levels*, 22.

4—The New Frontier and the Closing of the Missile Gap

1. Memo for Mr. Bundy, 11 February 1963, Missile Gap 2/63–5/63 folder, National Security Files (NSF), Departments and Agencies (D&A), Box 298, JFKL.

2. JFK, Memorandum for McGeorge Bundy, 15 May 1963, "Bundy, McGeorge, 1/63–6/63" file, Presidential Office Files (POF), Staff Memoranda, Box 62A, JFKL.

3. "What Kind of Defense," text of Mr. Kennedy's response to an American Legion question: "What must we do to regain our strength?" *The New Republic* 144 (9 January 1961), 6; *New York Times*, 12 January 1961, both cited in Bottome, *The Missile Gap*, 147.

4. "Annual Message to the Congress on the State of the Union," in *Public Papers of the Presidents of the United States: Dwight D. Eisenhower, 1960–1961* (Washington, DC: Government Printing Office, 1961), 919.

5. Dwight D. Eisenhower, "NLE Farewell Address," 17 January 1960, Dwight D. Eisenhower Presidential Library Web Site, Dwight D. Eisenhower Presidential Library, National Archives and Records Administration, <http://www.eisenhower.utexas.edu/farewell.htm>.

6. Perret, *Eisenhower*, 600. Eisenhower believed that Kennedy's use of the missile gap issue was a sign of his dishonesty (p. 603).

7. Richard Filipink, Jr., "Old Warrior, New President: The Uneasy Relationship of Dwight Eisenhower and John Kennedy," paper presented at the Society or Historians of American Foreign Relations Annual Meeting, 15 June 2001, Washington, DC.

8. JFK, "Inaugural Address, January 20, 1961," JFKL Web Site, 1 July 2001 <http://www.jfklibrary.org/j012061.htm>. On Khrushchev's speech and its influence on Kennedy's thinking, see William Taubman, *Khrushchev: The Man and His Era* (New York: Norton, 2003), 487–88; and Freedman, *Kennedy's Wars*, 287.

9. Quoted in Ball, *Politics and Force Levels*, 109.

10. Giglio, *The Presidency of John F. Kennedy*, 97.

11. "Special Message to the Congress: Program for Economic Recovery and Growth (17)," 2 February 1961, *Public Papers of the Presidents of the United States: John F. Kennedy, 1961* (Washington, DC: Government Printing Office, 1962), 41–53.

12. Giglio, *The Presidency of John F. Kennedy*, 126–27.

13. Ibid., 127.

14. Douglas Brinkley, *Dean Acheson: The Cold War Years, 1953–1971* (New Haven: Yale University Press, 1992), 114; Callahan, *Dangerous Capabilities*, 190–93; Paul H. Nitze, with Ann M. Smith and Steven L. Rearden, *From Hi-*

roshima to Glasnost: At the Center of Decision—A Memoir (New York: Grove Weidenfeld, 1989), 180–82; Talbott, *The Master of the Game,* 77–78.

15. Henry Kissinger, *The Necessity for Choice: Prospects of American Foreign Policy* (New York: Harper and Row, 1961) 2, 6, 15.

16. Maxwell Taylor, "Security Will Not Wait," *Foreign Affairs* 39, no. 2 (January 1961): 174, 175.

17. Ibid., 176, 177.

18. Ibid., 177–78.

19. Ibid., 176, 178–79, 182. These figures are comparable to Taylor's budget projections in his *The Uncertain Trumpet,* 178–79, and chapter 2 above.

20. Walter Isaacson, *Kissinger: A Biography* (New York: Simon and Schuster, 1992), 105, 106.

21. Ibid., 110.

22. Kai Bird, *The Color of Truth: McGeorge Bundy and William Bundy: Brothers in Arms* (New York: Simon and Schuster, 1998), 142–44; Kissinger, quoted in Isaacson, *Kissinger,* 110.

23. Taylor, *General Maxwell Taylor,* 228–29.

24. Robert and Ethel Kennedy named their ninth child Matthew Maxwell Taylor Kennedy after Taylor; Hilty, *Robert Kennedy: Brother Protector,* 418.

25. Taylor, *General Maxwell Taylor,* 230–45; Kinnard, *The Certain Trumpet,* 53–75.

26. Ball, *Politics and Force Levels,* 121.

27. Quoted in Gregg Herken, *Counsels of War* (New York: Alfred A. Knopf, 1985), 140. This quote was taken from Herken's interview with Wiesner conducted on 9 February 1982 in Wiesner's office at the Massachusetts Institute of Technology. Wiesner recollected that the briefing took place in early February 1961. From Gregg Herken, e-mail message to the author, 25 April 2000.

28. Herken, *Counsels of War,* 148; Herken, e-mail message to author, 25 April 2000.

29. Deborah Shapley, *Promise and Power: The Life and Times of Robert McNamara* (Boston: Little, Brown, 1993), 96–97; William W. Kaufmann, *The McNamara Strategy* (New York: Harper and Row, 1964), 44–46.

30. Robert McNamara, interview by Deborah Shapley and David Alan Rosenberg, 1 May 1985, Washington, DC.

31. Adm. G. E. "Jerry" Miller, USN (Ret.), interview by author, 20 February 2003, at the Army-Navy Country Club, Arlington, VA; McNamara telephone conversation with author, 10 April 2003. See also Herbert York, *Race to Oblivion: A Participant's View of the Arms Race* (New York: Simon and Schuster, 1970), 152–53; Herbert York, *Making Weapons, Talking Peace: A Physicist's Odyssey from Hiroshima to Geneva* (New York: Basic Books, 1987), 204; and Ball, *Politics and Force Levels,* 119.

32. "Memo from Jack Raymond on the McNamara backgrounder, Feb. 6, 1961," 1 (hereafter cited as Raymond memo), Robert McNamara file, Box 40, Krock Papers; John Scali recalled that McNamara did not use the term missile gap, but that he did make clear his interpretation that the United States was well ahead of the Soviet Union. Shapley, *Promise and Power,* 97.

33. Raymond memo, 2.

34. Beschloss, *The Crisis Years,* 65; Robert McNamara, with Brian VanDe-Mark, *In Retrospect: The Tragedy and Lessons of Vietnam* (New York: Times Books, 1995), 20–21.

35. Raymond memo, 2.

36. Ibid.

37. Jack Raymond, "Kennedy Defense Study Finds No Evidence of a 'Missile Gap,'" *New York Times,* 7 February 1961.

38. Raymond memo, 2; Reeves, *President Kennedy,* 58–59; McNamara interview; McNamara, *In Retrospect,* 20–21.

39. McGeorge Bundy, telephone interview by author, 10 April 1996; Adam Yarmolinsky, telephone interview by author, 23 April 1996.

40. Roger Hilsman, "McNamara's War—Against the Truth: A Review Essay" *Political Science Quarterly* 111, no. 1 (Winter 1996): 151–63. Hilsman repeated these claims in his letter to the author of 7 October 1996.

41. McNamara conversation with author, 10 April 2003. On reflection, McNamara admitted that he was puzzled about why historians continue to look past his statements of February 1961.

42. Raymond memo, 3.

43. Ball, *Politics and Force Levels,* 91.

44. John F. Kennedy, *The Kennedy Presidential Press Conferences,* with an Introduction by David Halberstam (New York: Earl M. Coleman Enterprises, 1965), 24.

45. Shapley, *Promise and Power,* 98–99.

46. Charles J. V. Murphy, letter to Lauris Norstad, 11 February 1961, Lauris Norstad Papers, Dwight D. Eisenhower Presidential Library, Abilene KS. Thanks to archivist David Haight at the Library for his assistance in locating this document.

47. Ibid.

48. Ibid.

49. Edwin M. Yoder Jr., *Joe Alsop's Cold War: A Study of Journalistic Influence and Intrigue* (Chapel Hill, NC: University of North Carolina Press, 1995), 167.

50. Merry, *Taking on the World,* 370.

51. Editorial Note, *Foreign Relations of the United States, 1961–1963,* vol. 8, *National Security Policy* (Washington, DC: Government Printing Office, 1996), 32; Bottome, *Missile Gap,* 161.

52. *Washington Post,* 17 February 1961, quoted in Shapley, *Promise and Power,* 98.

53. U.S. Congress, House, Committee on Appropriations, *Hearings on Department of Defense Appropriation for 1962,* 87th Cong., 1st Sess., part 3, April 1961, 59–60.

54. Ibid., 60.

55. Ibid., 60–61.

56. Ibid., 61.

57. Memorandum from the President's Special Assistant for National Security Affairs [Bundy] to the President's Special Counsel [Sorensen], 13 March 1961, in *Foreign Relations of the United States, 1961–1963,* 8:67.

58. Memorandum from Secretary of Defense McNamara and the Director of the Bureau of the Budget [Bell] to President Kennedy, 10 March 1961, *Foreign Relations of the United States, 1961–1963,* 8:56–65.

59. Shapley, *Promise and Power,* 118; Giglio, *The Presidency of John F. Kennedy,* 127; Kaufmann, *McNamara Strategy,* 77.

60. Paul Samuelson, "Economic Frontiers," in *New Frontiers of the Kennedy Administration: The Texts of the Task Force Reports Prepared for the President* (Washington, DC: Public Affairs Press, 1961), 31, quoted in Ball, *Politics and Force Levels,* 258.

61. Quoted in Ball, *Politics and Force Levels,* 259.

62. From Samuelson, "Economic Frontiers," 31, quoted in Ball, *Politics and Force Levels,* 258.

63. Charles J. Hitch in Samuel A. Tucker, ed., *A Modern Design for Defense Decision: A McNamara-Hitch-Enthoven Anthology* (Washington, DC: Industrial College of the Armed Forces, 1966), 43, quoted in Ball, *Politics and Force Levels,* 258.

64. U.S. Congress, Joint Economic Committee, *January 1961 Economic Report of the President and the Economic Situation and Outlook (1961),* 87th Cong., 1st Sess., 1961, 615, quoted in Ball, *Politics and Force Levels,* 260.

65. See Seymour E. Harris, *The Economics of the Kennedy Years and a Look Ahead* (New York: Harper and Row, 1964), 220.

66. Preble, "The Political Economy of National Security in the Nuclear Age," 312–14; Brown, *Flying Blind,* 223–26; Pattillo, *Pushing the Envelope,* 230.

67. Alsop, "Our Government Untruths."

68. Kennedy, "An Investment for Peace"; Kennedy, *The Strategy of Peace,* 69–70; John F. Kennedy, "Here's Kennedy's Foreign Policy," *U.S. News and World Report,* 27 June 1960, 64, reprinted from U.S. Congress, Senate, *Congressional Record,* 14 June 1960, 11630; Book Review of "Deterrent or Defense," *Saturday Review,* in *FOC,* 979; 18 October 1960 Speech, Miami Beach, Florida, American Legion Convention, *FOC,* Part I, 652; "Third Kennedy-Nixon Debate: October 13, 1960," JFKL Web Site, 17 June 2001, <http://www.jfklibrary.org/60-3rd.htm>, original text from *FOC,* Part III.

69. Ball, *Politics and Force Levels,* 122–23.

70. David Alan Rosenberg, "Reality and Responsibility: Power and Process in the Making of United States Nuclear Strategy, 1945–1968," *Journal of Strategic Studies* 9, no. 1 (1986): 44–47.

71. Kaufmann, *McNamara Strategy,* 78–79; Shapley, *Promise and Power,* 118.

72. Robert Dallek, *An Unfinished Life: John F. Kennedy, 1917–1963* (New York: Little, Brown, 2003), 338.

73. Prados, *Soviet Estimate,* 104, 116; Jerrold L. Schecter and Peter S. Deriabin, *The Spy Who Saved the World* (New York: Charles Scribner's Sons, 1992), 102; Jackson, *Allen Welsh Dulles,* 130; Garthoff interview.

74. Gilpatric quoted in Beschloss, *Crisis Years,* 330.

75. McNamara quoted in Beschloss, *Crisis Years,* 330–31. On the Kennedy press conference, see Kennedy, *Kennedy Presidential Press Conferences,* 149.

76. Hanson W. Baldwin, "New Figures Close Missile Gap," *New York Times,* 26 November 1961.

77. Alsop, *"I've Seen the Best of It,"* 413–15; Joseph Alsop, "Facts about the Missile Balance," *New York Herald Tribune,* 25 September 1961; Merry, *Taking on the World,* 370.

78. Bottome, *The Missile Gap,* 165; Ball, *Politics and Force Levels,* 97–98; Reeves, *President Kennedy,* 246–47.

79. James Baar, "Kennedy War Deterrent Remains Marginal," *Missiles and Rockets,* 30 October 1961, 13.

80. Stuart Symington, "Where the Missile Gap Went," *The Reporter,* 15 February 1962, 23.

81. U.S. Congress, House, *Congressional Record,* 21 March 1962, 4701.

82. Nixon, *Six Crises,* 354fn; Peter Grose, *Gentleman Spy: The Life of Allen Dulles* (Amherst: University of Massachusetts Press, 1994), 507–8.

83. Allen W. Dulles to John McCone, 20 May 1962, "JFK, 1960" file, Box 104, Allen W. Dulles Papers, Seeley G. Mudd Manuscript Library, Princeton University, Princeton, NJ; "Nixon Says Kennedy Imperiled Security," *New York Times,* 20 March 1962; E. W. Kenworthy, "White House Denies Charge," *New York Times,* 21 March 1962.

84. Memo for Mr. Bundy, 11 February 1963, Missile Gap 2/63–5/63 folder, NSF, D&A, Box 298, JFKL. There does not appear to have been a single specific episode or event that prompted Kennedy's renewed interest in the gap, but McGeorge Bundy and Adam Yarmolinsky both stated in telephone interviews with me that they suspected that the Cuban missile crisis may have been a factor. The president's first request for information about the missile gap may have come as early as December 1962. See Summary of Tape 65 (Part 2) and Tape 66 (Part 1), 12/5/62 Military Budget for FY 1964, from "Presidential Recordings Available for Purchase," posted on the JFKL Web Site, last accessed 21 February 2003, <www.jfklibrary.org/pres_recordings_available.html>.

85. General William Y. Smith, USAF (Ret.), telephone interview by author, 2 February 2001.

86. Robert McNamara, "The Missile Gap Controversy," 4 March 1963, 4, 5, 1, Missile Gap 2/63–5/63 folder, NSF, D&A, Box 298, JFKL.

87. Ibid, 1.

88. Bundy's handwritten notes on "Memorandum for McGeorge Bundy" from Adam Yarmolinsky, 4 March 1963, Missile Gap 2/63–5/63 folder, NSF, D&A, Box 298, JFKL (emphasis in original).

89. Adam Yarmolinsky, Memorandum for Mr. McGeorge Bundy, 15 March 1963, Missile Gap 2/63–5/63 folder, NSF, D&A, Box 298, JFKL (emphasis in original).

90. Arthur M. Schlesinger Jr., *A Thousand Days: John F. Kennedy in the White House* (Boston: Houghton Mifflin, 1965), 499–500; Ball, *Politics and Force Levels,* 175–78; Raymond Garthoff, *Intelligence Assessment and Policymaking: A Decision Point in the Kennedy Administration* (Washington, DC: Brookings Institution, 1984), 17–18.

91. Herken, *Counsels of War,* 153–55.

92. Kaplan, *Wizards of Armageddon*, 254–55; Freedman, *Kennedy's Wars*, 84–85; Shapley, *Promise and Power*, 100–101.

93. Tazewell Shepard Jr. to McGeorge Bundy, 30 March 1963, "Missile Gap 2/63–5/63" file, NSF, D&A, Box 298, JFKL.

94. JFK, Memorandum for McGeorge Bundy, 15 May 1963, "Bundy, Mc-George, 1/63–6/63" file, Presidential Office Files, Staff Memoranda, Box 62A, JFKL.

95. Paul Nitze to McGeorge Bundy, 30 May 1963, Missile Gap 2/63–5/63, NSF, D&A, Box 298, JFKL; Lawrence C. McQuade to Nitze, "But Where Did the Missile Gap Go?" 31 May 1960, Missile Gap 2/63–5/63 folder, NSF, D&A, Box 298, JFKL.

96. Ibid., 14.

97. Ibid., 19, 23.

98. Ibid., 22, 21 (emphasis in original).

99. Memorandum for Mr. Bundy, 3 June 1963, Missile Gap, 6/63–7/63, NSF, D&A, Box 298, JFKL.

100. Cover letter, Nitze to Bundy memo, 17 June 1963, 2.

101. "The Missile Gap, 1958–1960— The Public Record," in Nitze to Bundy memo, 17 June 1963, 3.

102. W. Y. Smith to McGeorge Bundy, Memorandum, 20 June 1963, "Subject: The Missile Gap," Missile Gap 6/63–7/63, NSF, D&A, Box 298, JFKL, 1.

103. Ibid., 1, 2.

104. Ibid., 2.

105. Ibid.

106. Ibid.

107. Ibid., 3.

108. Smith to Bundy memo, 10 July 1963.

109. Ibid.

110. "Remarks Prepared for Delivery at the Trade Mart in Dallas, 11/22/63," JFKL Web Site, <http://www.jfklibrary.org/j112263b.htm>.

111. McGeorge Bundy, "The Presidency and the Peace," *Foreign Affairs* 42, no. 3 (April 1964): 354.

112. Kaufmann, *McNamara Strategy*, 50.

113. Ibid., 65.

114. Sorensen, *Kennedy*, 610–11.

115. Schlesinger, *Thousand Days*, 317.

116. Theodore C. Sorensen, "The Election of 1960," in *The History of American Presidential Elections, 1789–1968*, vol. 4, ed. Arthur M. Schlesinger (New York: Chelsea House, 1972), 3465.

117. Bundy, *Danger and Survival*, 350.

118. See, for example, Ball, *Politics and Force Levels*, 142, 263; Shapley, *Promise and Power*, 107–9; Bottome, *Missile Gap*, 164, 167; and Garthoff, *Intelligence Assessment*, 4.

119. Reeves, *President Kennedy*, 117; Giglio, *The Presidency of John F. Kennedy*, 47.

120. The notion that the TFX decision was based on politics has since been largely dispelled. In retrospect, the decision appears to have been based on sound technical grounds. See Robert J. Art, *The TFX Decision: McNamara and the Military* (Boston: Little, Brown, 1968); Robert F. Coulam, *Illusions of Choice: The F-111 and the Problem of Weapons Acquisition Reform* (Princeton, NJ: Princeton University Press, 1977); Pattillo, *Pushing the Envelope*, 253–60; and Roger E. Bilstein, *The Enterprise of Flight: The American Aviation and Aerospace Industry* (Washington, DC: Smithsonian Institution Press, 2001), 101–3.

121. Schlesinger, *Thousand Days*, 317.

122. Sorensen, *Kennedy*, 417, 418.

123. Johnson is quoted in Bundy, "Presidency and the Peace," 355.

124. Diane Kunz, *Butter and Guns: America's Cold War Economic Diplomacy* (New York: Free Press, 1997), 2.

125. For a different view, see Paul A. C. Koistinen, *The Military-Industrial Complex: A Historical Perspective* (New York: Praeger, 1980).

126. See Ann Markusen, Peter Hall, Scott Campbell, and Sabina Deitrick, *The Rise of the Gunbelt: The Military Remapping of Industrial America* (New York: Oxford University Press, 1991).

Epilogue

1. *Surviving the Bottom Line with Hedrick Smith,* "Episode Two Transcript, Part II," PBS, January 1998, Hedrick Smith Productions, <http://www.hedricksmith.com/site_bottomline/html/e2_trans2.html#Part2>.

2. Michael E. Porter, *San Diego: Clusters of Innovation Initiative* (Washington, DC: Council on Competitiveness, 2001), 39, 41.

3. See Bill Yenne, *Into the Sunset: The Convair Story* (Lyme, CT: Greenwich Publishing Group, 1995).

4. Pattillo, *Pushing the Envelope,* 251.

5. Ibid., 261.

6. Ibid., 252.

7. Ibid., 248–49.

8. Bill Chana, telephone interview by author, 4 April 2001.

9. John Lull, telephone interview by author, 12 April 2001.

10. Hugh M. Neeson, telephone interviews by author, 11 July and 17 August 2001.

11. Eisenhower, "A Chance for Peace," 182.

12. On "creative destruction" see Joseph Schumpeter, *Capitalism, Socialism, and Democracy,* 3rd ed. (New York: Harper and Brothers, 1950), 81–86.

13. San Diego County boasted an unemployment rate of only 3.3 percent in July 2001, the lowest July rate in the city in nearly twenty years and well below the national average. Michael Kinsman, "Working for a Living," *San Diego Union-Tribune,* 3 September 2001. Nearly two years later, and even after the Internet and technology sectors had fallen from their astronomical heights, San Diego's unemployment rate, at 4.2 percent in April 2003, was still far lower than the national average of 6.0 percent.

14. Porter, *San Diego,* 41.

15. Friedberg, *In the Shadow,* 201.

16. Ibid., 3–4.

17. Milton Friedman, "The Role of Monetary Policy," *American Economic Review* (March 1968): 1–17; Edmund S. Phelps, "Money Wage Dynamics and Labor Market Equilibrium," *Journal of Political Economy* (July–August 1967): 678–711.

18. Bernard Brodie had dismissed as highly unlikely the possibility that defense spending in excess of 10 percent of gross national product would cause inflation "rapid enough to have self-intensifying effects." Brodie, *Strategy in the Missile Age,* 369. On the economic crisis of the late 1960s, see Collins, *More,* especially chapter 3, pages 68–97.

19. See, for example, Immerman "Confessions of an Eisenhower Revisionist," 319–24; and Stephen G. Rabe, "Eisenhower Revisionism: A Decade of Scholarship," *Diplomatic History* 17 (Winter 1993): 97–115.

20. Project for a New American Century, "Letter to Pr esident Bush on the Defense Budget," 23 January 2003, available at http://www.newamericancentury.org/defense-20030123.htm.

Works Cited

Manuscript Collections and Oral Histories

Alsop, Joseph W., and Stewart, Papers. Library of Congress Manuscript Collection, Washington, DC.

California Democratic State Central Committee (CDSCC) Papers. Urban Archives Center, University Library, California State University, Northridge, CA.

Dulles, Allen W., Papers. Seeley G. Mudd Manuscript Library, Princeton University, Princeton, NJ.

Kennedy, John F., National Security Files. John F. Kennedy Presidential Library, Boston, MA.

Kennedy, John F., Pre-Presidential Papers. John F. Kennedy Presidential Library, Boston, MA.

Kennedy, John F., Presidential Office Files. John F. Kennedy Presidential Library, Boston, MA.

Kennedy, Robert F., Papers. Pre-Administration Political Files. John F. Kennedy Presidential Library, Boston, MA.

Keyserling, Leon, Papers. Harry S. Truman Presidential Library, Independence, MO.

Krock, Arthur, Papers. Seeley G. Mudd Manuscript Library, Princeton University, Princeton, NJ.

McCarthy, Eugene, Papers. Minnesota Historical Society, St. Paul, MN.

National Security Archive, George Washington University, Washington, DC.

Norstad, Lauris, Papers. Dwight D. Eisenhower Presidential Library, Abilene, KS.

Philadelphia Evening Bulletin Clippings Collection. Urban Archives, Samuel Paley Library, Temple University, Philadelphia, PA.

Ribicoff, Abraham, Papers. Library of Congress Manuscript Collection, Washington, DC.

Southern California Labor Newspaper Collection. Urban Archives Center, University Library, California State University–Northridge, Northridge, CA.

Wilson, Robert C., Papers. Center for Regional History, University Library, San Diego State University, San Diego, CA.

White, Thomas Dresser, Papers. Library of Congress, Manuscripts Division, Washington, DC.

Personal Interviews and Correspondence

Bundy, McGeorge. Telephone interview by author, 10 April 1996. Tape recording.

Chana, Bill. Telephone interview by author, 4 April 2001. Tape recording and transcript.

Garthoff, Raymond L. Interview by author, 15 April 2003, Washington, DC. Tape recording and transcript.

Herken, Gregg. E-mail to author, 25 April 2000.

Hilsman, Roger. Letter to author, 7 October 1996.

Lull, John. Telephone interview by author, 12 April 2001. Tape recording and transcript.

McNamara, Robert. Interview by Deborah Shapley and David Alan Rosenberg, 1 May 1985, Washington, DC. Transcript.

———. Telephone conversation with author, 10 April 2003. Notes.

Miller, Adm. G. E. "Jerry" USN (Ret). Interview by author, 20 February 2003, Arlington, VA. Tape recording and transcript.

Smith, General William Y., USAF (Ret.). Telephone interview by author, 2 February 2001. Tape recording and transcript.

Yarmolinsky, Adam. Telephone interview by author, 23 April 1996. Tape recording.

Articles, Books, and Dissertations

In addition to the specific references below, articles have been cited from the following newspapers and periodicals: *Armed Forces Management; Baltimore Sun; Boston Herald; Business Week; California Labor Statistics Bulletin Area Supplement; Chicago Tribune; Christian Science Monitor; Detroit Free Press; Encounter; Fortune; Harvard University Gazette; Life; Los Angeles Times; Missiles and Rockets; New Republic; New York Herald Tribune; New York Journal-American; New York Times; New York World Telegram; Philadelphia Evening Bulletin; Philadelphia Inquirer; The Reporter; St. Louis Post-Dispatch; San Diego Union-Tribune; Saturday Review; Space Age News; The Spectator; The State Journal* (Lansing, Michigan); *U.S. News and World Report; Virginia Sun; Washington Post (and Times Herald);* and *Washington Star.*

Aliano, Richard A. *American Defense Policy from Eisenhower to Kennedy: The Politics of Changing Military Requirements.* Athens: Ohio University Press, 1975.

Alsop, Joseph. "The New Balance of Power: War and Peace in a Strange World." *Encounter* (May 1958), 3–10.

Alsop, Joseph, with Adam Platt. *"I've Seen the Best of It."* New York: W. W. Norton, 1992.

Ambrose, Stephen E. *Eisenhower: Soldier and President.* New York: Simon and Schuster, 1990.

———. *Nixon: The Education of a Politician, 1913–1962.* New York: Simon and Schuster, 1987.

Art, Robert J. *The TFX Decision: McNamara and the Military.* Boston: Little, Brown, 1968.

Ball, Desmond. *Politics and Force Levels: The Strategic Missile Program of the Kennedy Administration.* Berkeley: University of California Press, 1980.

Bamford, James. *Body of Secrets: Anatomy of the Ultra-Secret National Security Agency.* New York: Doubleday, 2001.

Barlow, Jeffrey G. *Revolt of the Admirals: The Fight for Naval Aviation, 1945–1950.* Washington, DC: Naval Historical Center, 1994.

Beschloss, Michael R. *The Crisis Years: Kennedy and Khrushchev, 1960–1963.* New York: HarperCollins, 1991.

———. *MAYDAY: Eisenhower, Khrushchev, and the U-2 Affair.* New York: Harper and Row, 1986.

Bilstein, Roger E. *The Enterprise of Flight: The American Aviation and Aerospace Industry.* Washington, DC: Smithsonian Institution Press, 2001.

Bird, Kai. *The Color of Truth: McGeorge Bundy and William Bundy: Brothers in Arms.* New York: Simon and Schuster, 1998.

Bottome, Edgar M. *The Missile Gap: A Study of the Formulation of Military and Political Policy.* Rutherford, NJ: Fairleigh Dickinson University Press, 1971.

Bowie, Robert R., and Richard H. Immerman. *Waging Peace: How Eisenhower Shaped an Enduring Cold War Strategy.* New York: Oxford University Press, 1998.

Brinkley, Douglas. *Dean Acheson: The Cold War Years, 1953–1971.* New Haven: Yale University Press, 1992.

Brodie, Bernard. *Strategy in the Missile Age.* Princeton, NJ: Princeton University Press, 1959.

Brown, Michael. *Flying Blind: The Politics of the U.S. Strategic Bomber Program.* Ithaca, NY: Cornell University Press, 1992.

Bundy, McGeorge. *Danger and Survival: Choices about the Bomb in the First Fifty Years.* New York: Vintage, 1988.

Bundy, McGeorge. "The Presidency and the Peace." *Foreign Affairs* 42, no. 3 (April 1964): 353–65.

Burner, David. *John F. Kennedy and a New Generation.* Edited by Oscar Handlin. Boston: Little, Brown, 1988.

Callahan, David. *Dangerous Capabilities: Paul Nitze and the Cold War.* New York: HarperCollins, 1990.

Campbell, Angus, Philip E. Converse, Warren E. Miller, and Donald E. Stokes. *Elections and the Political Order.* Survey Research Center, Institute for Social Research, University of Michigan. New York: Wiley, 1966.

Caro, Robert A. *The Years of Lyndon Johnson: Master of the Senate.* New York: Alfred A. Knopf, 2002.

Collins, Robert M. *More: The Politics of Economic Growth in Postwar America.* New York: Oxford University Press, 2000.

Committee for Economic Development. *The Problem of National Security: Some Economic and Administrative Aspects.* Washington, DC: Committee for Economic Development, 1958.

Coulam, Robert F. *Illusions of Choice: The F-111 and the Problem of Weapons Acquisition Reform.* Princeton, NJ: Princeton University Press, 1977.

Craig, Campbell. *Destroying the Village: Eisenhower and Thermonuclear War.* New York: Columbia University Press, 1998.

Dallek, Robert. *Lone Star Rising: Lyndon Johnson and His Times, 1908–1960.* New York: Oxford University Press, 1991.

———. *An Unfinished Life: John F. Kennedy, 1917–1963.* New York: Little, Brown, 2003.

Deterrence and Survival in the Nuclear Age (The "Gaither Report" of 1957). Washington, DC: Government Printing Office, 1976.

Dick, James C. "The Strategic Arms Race, 1957–61: Who Opened a Missile Gap?" *Journal of Politics* 34, no. 4 (November 1972): 1062–1110.

Divine, Robert A. *Foreign Policy and U.S. Presidential Elections.* Vol. 2: *1952–1960.* New York: New Viewpoints, 1974.

———. *The Sputnik Challenge: Eisenhower's Response to the Soviet Satellite.* New York: Oxford University Press, 1993.

Drew, S. Nelson. "Expecting the Approach of Danger: The 'Missile Gap' as a Study of Executive-Congressional Competition in Building Consensus on National Security Issues." *Presidential Studies Quarterly* 19, no. 2 (Spring 1989): 317–35.

Eisenhower, Dwight D. "NLE Farewell Address." 17 January 1960. Dwight D. Eisenhower Presidential Library Web Site. Dwight D. Eisenhower Presidential Library, National Archives and Records Administration. <http://www.eisenhower.utexas.edu/farewell.htm>.

———. *The White House Years: Mandate for Change, 1953–1956.* Garden City, NY: Doubleday, 1963.

———. *The White House Years: Waging Peace, 1956–1961.* Garden City, NY: Doubleday, 1965.

Evangelista, Matthew. *Innovation and the Arms Race: How the United States and the Soviet Union Develop New Military Technologies.* Ithaca, NY: Cornell University Press, 1988.

Filipink, Richard, Jr. "Old Warrior, New President: The Uneasy Relationship of Dwight Eisenhower and John Kennedy." Paper presented at the Society for Historians of American Foreign Relations Annual Meeting, 15 June 2001, Washington, DC.

Foreign Relations of the United States, 1955–1957. Vol. 19, *National Security Policy.* Washington, DC: Government Printing Office, 1990.

Foreign Relations of the United States, 1958–1960. Vol. 3, *National Security Policy.* Washington, DC: Government Printing Office, 1996.

Foreign Relations of the United States, 1961–1963. Vol. 8, *National Security Policy.* Washington, DC: Government Printing Office, 1996.

Freedman, Lawrence. *Kennedy's Wars: Berlin, Cuba, Laos, and Vietnam.* New York: Oxford University Press, 2000.

Friedberg, Aaron. *In the Shadow of the Garrison State: America's Anti-Statism and Its Cold War Grand Strategy.* Princeton, NJ: Princeton University Press, 2000.

Friedman, Milton. "The Role of Monetary Policy." *American Economic Review* (March 1968): 1–17.

Gaddis, John L. *Strategies of Containment: A Critical Appraisal of Postwar American National Security Policy.* New York: Oxford University Press, 1982.

———. *We Now Know: Rethinking Cold War History.* New York: Oxford University Press, 1997.

Galbraith, John Kenneth. *The Affluent Society.* Boston: Houghton Mifflin, 1958.

———. "Emeritus Professor John Kenneth Galbraith's Biography." Department of Economics, Harvard University. <http://post.economics.harvard.edu/faculty/galbraith/cv.html>.

Garthoff, Raymond. *Assessing the Adversary: Estimates by the Eisenhower Administration of Soviet Intentions and Capabilities.* Washington, DC: Brookings Institution, 1991.

———. *Intelligence Assessment and Policymaking: A Decision Point in the Kennedy Administration.* Washington, DC: Brookings Institution, 1984.

———. *A Journey through the Cold War: A Memoir of Containment and Coexistence.* Washington, DC: Brookings Institution, 2001.

———. *Reflections on the Cuban Missile Crisis,* rev. ed. Washington, DC: Brookings Institution, 1989.

Gaskin, Thomas M. "Senator Lyndon B. Johnson, the Eisenhower Administration, and U.S. Foreign Policy, 1957–1960." *Presidential Studies Quarterly* 24, no. 2 (Spring 1994): 341–61.

Gavin, James M. *War and Peace in the Space Age.* New York: Harper and Brothers, 1958.

———. "Why Missiles." *Army,* November 1957: 25–29.

Giglio, James. *The Presidency of John F. Kennedy.* Lawrence: University Press of Kansas, 1991.

Goodwin, Richard N. *Remembering America: A Voice from the Sixties.* Philadelphia: Harper and Row, 1988.

Gray, Colin S. "'Gap' Prediction and America's Defense: Arms Race Behavior in the Eisenhower Years." *Orbis* 16 (Spring 1972): 257–74.

Greenberg, Stanley. *Middle Class Dreams: The Politics and Power of the New American Majority,* revised and updated edition. New Haven: Yale University Press, 1995.

Greenstein, Fred I. *The Hidden Hand Presidency: Eisenhower as Leader.* New York: Basic Books, 1982.

Greenstein, Fred I., and Richard H. Immerman, "What Did Eisenhower Tell Kennedy about Indochina? The Politics of Misperception." *Journal of American History* 79 (September 1992): 568–87.

Grose, Peter. *Gentleman Spy: The Life of Allen Dulles.* Amherst: University of Massachusetts Press, 1994.

Hamby, Alonzo. *Man of the People: A Life of Harry S. Truman.* New York: Oxford University Press, 1995.

Hamilton, Nigel. *JFK: Reckless Youth.* New York: Random House, 1992.

Harris, Seymour. *The Economics of the Kennedy Years and a Look Ahead.* New York: Harper and Row, 1964.

———. *The Economics of the Political Parties.* New York: Macmillan, 1962.

———. "Taxes and the Economy." *Current History* (October 1956): 206–11.

Helgerson, John L. *Getting to Know the President: CIA Briefings of Presidential Candidates, 1952–1992.* Washington, DC: The Center for the Study of Intelligence, 22 May 1996. Central Intelligence Agency. <http://www.cia.gov/csi/books/briefing/>.

Heller, Walter. *New Dimensions of Political Economy.* New York: Norton, 1966.

Herken, Gregg. *Counsels of War.* New York: Alfred A. Knopf, 1985.

Hersh, Seymour M. *The Dark Side of Camelot.* Boston: Little, Brown, 1997.

Hilsman, Roger. "McNamara's War—Against the Truth: A Review Essay." *Political Science Quarterly* 111, no. 1 (Winter 1996): 151–63.

Hilty, James W. *Robert Kennedy: Brother Protector.* Philadelphia: Temple University Press, 1997.

Horelick, Arnold L., and Myron Rush. *Strategic Power and Soviet Foreign Policy.* Chicago: University of Chicago Press, 1965.

Immerman, Richard. "Confessions of an Eisenhower Revisionist: An Agonizing Reappraisal." *Diplomatic History* 14 (Summer 1990): 319–24.

———. *John Foster Dulles: Piety, Pragmatism, and Power in U.S. Foreign Policy.* Wilmington, DE: Scholarly Resources, 1999.

———, ed. *John Foster Dulles and the Diplomacy of the Cold War.* Princeton, NJ: Princeton University Press, 1990.

Isaacson, Walter. *Kissinger: A Biography.* New York: Simon and Schuster, 1992.

Jamieson, Kathleen Hall. *Packaging the Presidency: A History and Criticism of Presidential Campaign Advertising,* 2nd ed. New York: Oxford University Press, 1992.

Kaplan, Fred. *The Wizards of Armageddon.* New York: Simon and Schuster, 1983.

Kapstein, Ethan. *The Political Economy of National Security: A Global Perspective.* New York: McGraw-Hill, 1992.

Kaufmann, William W. *The McNamara Strategy.* New York: Harper and Row, 1964.

———, ed. *Military Policy and National Security.* Princeton, NJ: Princeton University Press, 1956.

Kennedy, John F. "Inaugural Address, January 20, 1961." John F. Kennedy Presidential Library Web Site. John F. Kennedy Presidential Library, National Archives and Records Administration. <http://www.jfklibrary.org/j012061.htm>.

[———]. "Oral History Interviews." John F. Kennedy Presidential Library Web Site. John F. Kennedy Presidential Library, National Archives and Records Administration. <http://www.jfklibrary.org/oralhist.htm>.

[———]. "Remarks Prepared for Delivery at the Trade Mart in Dallas, 11/22/63," John F. Kennedy Presidential Library Web Site. John F. Kennedy Presidential Library, National Archives and Records Administration. <http://www.jfklibrary.org/j112263b.htm>.

[———]. "Senator John F. Kennedy's Presidential Nomination Acceptance Speech—Memorial Coliseum, Los Angeles, California, 15 July 1960." John F. Kennedy Presidential Library Web Site. John F. Kennedy Presidential Library, National Archives and Records Administration. <http://www.jfklibrary.org/j071560.htm>.

———. *The Kennedy Presidential Press Conferences.* With an Introduction by David Halberstam. New York: Earl M. Coleman Enterprises, 1965.

———. *The Strategy of Peace.* Edited by Allan Nevins. New York: Popular Library, 1961.

———. "When the Executive Fails to Lead." *The Reporter* 19, no. 4 (18 September 1958): 14–17.

[Kennedy, John F., and Richard M. Nixon]. "First Kennedy-Nixon Debate: [26 September 1960]." *John F. Kennedy Presidential Library Web Site. John F. Kennedy Presidential Library,* National Archives and Records Administration. <http://www.jfklibrary.org/60-1st.htm>.

[————]. "Fourth Kennedy-Nixon Debate: October 21, 1960." *John F. Kennedy Presidential Library Web Site. John F. Kennedy Presidential Library,* National Archives and Records Administration. <http://www.jfklibrary.org/60-4th.htm>.

[————]. "Second Kennedy-Nixon Debate: October 7, 1960." *John F. Kennedy Presidential Library Web Site. John F. Kennedy Presidential Library,* National Archives and Records Administration. <http://www.jfklibrary.org/60-2nd.htm>.

[————]. "Third Kennedy-Nixon Debate: October 13, 1960." *John F. Kennedy Presidential Library Web Site. John F. Kennedy Presidential Library,* National Archives and Records Administration. <http://www.jfklibrary.org/60-3rd.htm>.

Kessler, Ronald. *The Sins of the Father: Joseph P. Kennedy and the Dynasty He Founded.* New York: Time Warner, 1996.

Keyserling, Leon. "Danger Signs in the Economy." *Washington Post,* 6 February 1958.

————. "The Economy in '58." *New Republic,* 13 January 1958: 13–16.

————. "The Nonsense about Recession and Inflation." *New Republic,* 10 March 1958: 11–12.

Kinnard, Douglas. *The Certain Trumpet: Maxwell Taylor and the American Experience in Vietnam.* New York: Brassey's, 1991.

————. *President Eisenhower and Strategy Management: A Study in Defense Politics.* Lexington: University Press of Kentucky, 1977.

Kissinger, Henry. *The Necessity for Choice: Prospects of American Foreign Policy.* New York: Harper and Row, 1961.

————. *Nuclear Weapons and Foreign Policy.* New York: Harper and Brothers, 1957.

Koistinen, Paul A. C. *The Military-Industrial Complex: A Historical Perspective.* New York: Praeger, 1980.

Kunz, Diane. *Butter and Guns: America's Cold War Economic Diplomacy.* New York: Free Press, 1997.

Leffler, Melvyn P. *A Preponderance of Power: National Security, the Truman Administration, and the Cold War.* Stanford, CA: Stanford University Press, 1992.

Licklider, Roy E. "The Missile Gap Controversy." *Political Science Quarterly* 85, no. 4 (December 1970): 600–615.

Luce, Henry R. Foreword to *Why England Slept* by John F. Kennedy. New York: Wilfred Funk, 1961.

Markusen, Ann, Peter Hall, Scott Campbell, and Sabina Deitrick. *The Rise of the Gunbelt: The Military Remapping of Industrial America.* New York: Oxford University Press, 1991.

May, Ernest R., ed. *American Cold War Strategy: Interpreting NSC 68.* Boston: Bedford, 1993.

May, Ernest R., and Philip D. Zelikow, eds. *The Kennedy Tapes: Inside the White House during the Cuban Missile Crisis*. Cambridge, MA: Belknap, 1997.

McCullough, David. *Truman*. New York: Simon and Schuster, 1992.

McNamara, Robert, with Brian VanDeMark. *In Retrospect: The Tragedy and Lessons of Vietnam*. New York: Times Books, 1995.

Meagher, Michael E. "'In an Atmosphere of National Peril': The Development of John F. Kennedy's World View." *Presidential Studies Quarterly* 27, no. 3 (Summer 1997): 467–81.

Medaris, John B. *Countdown for Decision*. New York: Putnam, 1960.

Merry, Robert W. *Taking on the World: Joseph and Stewart Alsop—Guardians of the American Century*. New York: Viking, 1996.

Miller, Jerry. *Nuclear Weapons and Aircraft Carriers: How the Bomb Saved Naval Aviation*. Washington, DC: Smithsonian Institution Press, 2001.

Morgan, Iwan W. *Eisenhower versus "The Spenders": The Eisenhower Administration, the Democrats, and the Budget, 1953–1960*. New York: St. Martin's, 1990.

Nitze, Paul H., with Ann M. Smith and Steven L. Rearden. *From Hiroshima to Glasnost: At the Center of Decision—A Memoir*. New York: Grove Weidenfeld, 1989.

Nixon, Richard M. *Six Crises*. 1962. Reprint, New York: Touchstone, 1990.

O'Brien, Lawrence. *No Final Victories: A Life in Politics from John F. Kennedy to Watergate*. Garden City, NY: Doubleday, 1974.

O'Donnell, Kenneth P., and David F. Powers, with Joseph McCarthy. *"Johnny We Hardly Knew Ye": Memories of John F. Kennedy*. Boston: Little, Brown, 1972.

Osgood, Robert E. *Limited War: The Challenge to American Strategy*. Chicago: University of Chicago Press, 1957.

Parmet, Herbert S. *Jack: The Struggles of John F. Kennedy*. New York: Dial, 1980.

Paterson, Thomas G., ed. *Kennedy's Quest for Victory: American Foreign Policy, 1961–1963*. New York: Oxford University Press, 1989.

Pattillo, Donald M. *Pushing the Envelope: The American Aircraft Industry*. Ann Arbor: University of Michigan Press, 1998.

Perret, Geoffrey. *Eisenhower*. New York: Random House, 1999.

Phelps, Edmund S. "Money Wage Dynamics and Labor Market Equilibrium." *Journal of Political Economy* (July–August 1967): 678–711.

Pierpaoli, Paul G., Jr. *Truman and Korea: The Political Culture of the Early Cold War*. Columbia: University of Missouri Press, 1999.

Porter, Michael E. *San Diego: Clusters of Innovation Initiative*. Washington, DC: Council on Competitiveness, 2001.

Power, Thomas S. "Military Problems and Prospects of Deterrence: Protecting Our Heritage until a Truly Lasting Peace Can Be Assured." *Vital Speeches* 26, no. 9 (15 February 1960): 285–88.

Prados, John. *The Soviet Estimate: U.S. Intelligence Analysis and Russian Military Strength*. New York: Dial, 1982.

Preble, Chris. "The Political Economy of National Security in the Nuclear Age: John F. Kennedy and the Missile Gap." Ph.D. diss., Temple University, 2002.

Project for a New American Century. "Letter to President Bush on the Defense Budget," 23 January 2003. Available at http://www.newamericancentury.org/defense-20030123.htm.

Public Papers of the Presidents of the United States: Dwight D. Eisenhower, 1953. Washington, DC: Government Printing Office, 1960.

Public Papers of the Presidents of the United States: John F. Kennedy, 1961. Washington, DC: Government Printing Office, 1962.

Rabe, Stephen G. "Eisenhower Revisionism: A Decade of Scholarship." *Diplomatic History* 17 (Winter 1993): 97–115.

Reeves, Richard. *President Kennedy: Profile of Power.* New York: Simon and Schuster, 1993.

Ridgway, Matthew B., as told to Harold H. Martin. *Soldier: The Memoirs of Matthew B. Ridgway.* New York: Harper and Brothers, 1956.

Rockefeller Brothers Fund. *Prospect for America.* Garden City, NY: Doubleday, 1961.

Roman, Peter J. *Eisenhower and The Missile Gap.* Ithaca, NY: Cornell University Press, 1995.

Roper, Elmo. "Polling Post-Mortem." *Saturday Review* 43, no. 48 (26 November 1960): 10–12.

Rosenberg, David Alan. "The Origins of Overkill: Nuclear Weapons and American Strategy, 1945–1960." *International Security* 7, no. 4 (Spring 1983): 3–71.

———. "Reality and Responsibility: Power and Process in the Making of United States Nuclear Strategy, 1945–1968." *The Journal of Strategic Studies* 9, no 1. (1986): 35–52.

"Rostow, Walt W(hitman): CA Interview." *Contemporary Authors,* New Revision Series, 8:427–32.

Rostow, Walt W. *The Stages of Economic Growth: A Non-Communist Manifesto,* 2nd ed. New York: Cambridge University Press, 1973.

Samuelson, Paul. "Economic Frontiers." In *New Frontiers of the Kennedy Administration: The Texts of the Task Force Reports Prepared for the President.* Washington, DC: Public Affairs Press, 1961.

Schecter, Jerrold L., and Peter S. Deriabin. *The Spy Who Saved the World.* New York: Charles Scribner's Sons, 1992.

Schlesinger, Arthur M., Jr. *Robert Kennedy and His Times.* Boston: Houghton Mifflin, 1978.

———. *A Thousand Days: John F. Kennedy in The White House.* Boston: Houghton Mifflin, 1965.

Schumpeter, Joseph. *Capitalism, Socialism, and Democracy,* 3rd ed. New York: Harper and Brothers, 1950.

Shapley, Deborah. *Promise and Power: The Life and Times of Robert McNamara.* Boston: Little, Brown, 1993.

Sloan, John W. *Eisenhower and the Management of Prosperity.* Lawrence: University Press of Kansas, 1991.

Smith, James A. *The Idea Brokers: Think Tanks and the Rise of the New Policy State.* New York: Free Press, 1991.

Snead, David L. *The Gaither Committee, Eisenhower, and the Cold War.* Columbus: Ohio State University Press, 1999.

Stein, Herbert. *The Fiscal Revolution in America,* rev. ed. Washington, DC: AEI Press, 1990.

Steury, Donald P., ed. *Intentions and Capabilities: Estimates on Soviet Strategic Forces, 1950–1983.* Washington, DC: Center for the Study of Intelligence, 1996.

Sorensen, Theodore C. "The Election of 1960." In *The History of American Presidential Elections, 1789–1968,* vol. 4, ed. Arthur M. Schlesinger, Jr. New York: Chelsea House, 1972, 3449–562.

———. *Kennedy.* New York: Harper and Row, 1965.

Surviving the Bottom Line with Hedrick Smith. "Episode Two Transcript, Part II." PBS, January 1998. Hedrick Smith Productions. <http://www.hedricksmith.com/site_bottomline/html/e2_trans2.html#Part2>.

Symington, Stuart. "Where the Missile Gap Went." *The Reporter* (15 February 1962): 21–23.

Talbott, Strobe. *The Master of the Game: Paul Nitze and the Nuclear Peace.* New York: Alfred A. Knopf, 1988.

Taubman, William. *Khrushchev: The Man and His Era.* New York: Norton, 2003.

Taylor, John M. *General Maxwell Taylor: The Sword and the Pen.* New York: Doubleday, 1989.

Taylor, Maxwell. "Security Will Not Wait." *Foreign Affairs* 39, no. 2 (January 1961): 174–84.

———. *Swords and Plowshares.* New York: Norton, 1972.

———. *The Uncertain Trumpet.* New York: Harper and Brothers, 1959.

Tobin, James. "Autobiography of James Tobin." *Nobel Lectures, Economic Sciences, 1969–1980.* Stockholm: The Nobel Foundation, 2000, <http://www.nobel.se/economics/laureates/1981/tobin-autobio.html>.

———. "Defense, Dollars, and Doctrines." *The Yale Review* 47, no. 3 (March 1958): 321–34.

Tucker, Samuel A., ed. *A Modern Design for Defense Decision: A McNamara-Hitch-Enthoven Anthology.* Washington, DC: Industrial College of the Armed Forces, 1966.

U.S. Congress. House. Committee on Appropriations. *Hearings on Department of Defense Appropriation for 1962.* 87th Cong., 1st Sess., part 3, April 1961.

U.S. Congress. Joint Economic Committee. *January 1961 Economic Report of the President and the Economic Situation and Outlook (1961).* 87th Cong., 1st Sess., 1961.

U.S. Congress. Senate. *Hearings before the Committee on Foreign Relations and the Committee on Armed Services on S. Con. Res. 8.* 82nd Cong., 1st Sess., 1951.

U.S. Congress. Senate. Select Committee on Small Business. *Impact of Defense Spending on Labor Surplus Areas—1962: Hearings on Effect of Defense Spending on Small Business Labor Surplus Areas,* 87th Cong., 2nd Sess., 29 August 1962.

U.S. Congress. Senate. Committee on Commerce. Subcommittee of the Subcommittee [*sic*] on Communications. *Freedom of Communications, Parts 1–5.* 87th Cong., 1st Sess., 1961.

U.S. Department of Labor. Bureau of Labor Statistics. *America's Industrial and Occupational Manpower Requirements, 1964–1975.* Washington, DC: U.S. Department of Labor, 1966.

White, Theodore H. *The Making of the President, 1960.* New York: Atheneum House, 1961.

Wofford, Harris. *Of Kennedys and Kings: Making Sense of the Sixties,* rev. ed. Pittsburgh: University of Pittsburgh Press, 1992.

Wohlforth, William C. *The Elusive Balance: Power and Perceptions during the Cold War.* Ithaca, NY: Cornell University Press, 1993.

Wohlstetter, Albert. "The Delicate Balance of Terror." *Foreign Affairs* 37 (January 1959): 211–34.

Yenne, Bill. *Into the Sunset: The Convair Story.* Lyme, CT: Greenwich Publishing Group, 1995.

Yoder, Edwin M., Jr. *Joe Alsop's Cold War: A Study of Journalistic Influence and Intrigue.* Chapel Hill, NC: University of North Carolina Press, 1995.

York, Herbert. *Making Weapons, Talking Peace: A Physicist's Odyssey from Hiroshima to Geneva.* New York: Basic Books, 1987.

———. *Race to Oblivion: A Participant's View of the Arms Race.* New York: Simon and Schuster, 1970.

Zaloga, Stephen J. *Target America: The Soviet Union and the Strategic Arms Race, 1945–1964.* Novato, CA: Presidio Press, 1993.

Index

Acheson, Dean, 22
Adams, Sherman, 65
AFL-CIO, 133
Air Force, U.S., 12, 46, 115, 172; and
    B-70 bomber, 78–79, 94, 140; bud-
    gets, 29, 152, 178; and intelligence
    estimates, 54, 82–83, 87, 94–95,
    155, 169; and Minuteman, 168;
    and Polaris, 93–94
Aliano, Richard, 17
Allen, George, 121
Alsop, Joseph, 6, 33, 54–55, 93, 155;
    on Eisenhower, Nixon, and Fifth
    Avenue Compact, 107, 108; and
    intelligence estimates, 56–57, 59,
    73, 90; and Kennedy, 57, 58, 61,
    95–96, 159; and missile gap, 54,
    90, 159, 164–65; and national
    strategy, 55–56, 100; and U.S.
    weapons programs, 56
Alsop, Stewart, 33, 54, 55
American Society of Newspaper Edi-
    tors, 29
Army, U.S., 12, 19, 82, 95, 115, 133,
    134, 155, 187; budgets, 26, 44, 89,
    152; composition and size of, 49,
    64, 76, 161, 163, 178, 179; and na-
    tional strategy, 46, 97, 105; and Red-
    stone rocket, 46; special forces, 179
Atlas (ICBM), 67, 68, 115, 159; and
    Convair (General Dynamics), 183,
    184; force levels of, 80, 162, 170,
    178; Kennedy's support for, 97,
    104, 112; operational shortcom-
    ings of, 37, 163
aviation-aerospace industry, 7, 137, 183

B-52, 47, 140
B-58, 162
B-70, 78–79, 84, 100, 140, 162, 178;
    air force support for, 78–79, 92,
    94; Eisenhower's views of, 79, 140;
    Kennedy's support for, 112, 142;
    politics of, 141–42, 179
Baldwin, Hanson W., 164
Ball, Desmond, 36
Bay of Pigs, 153
Bell Aircraft, 7, 129, 131, 147, 179,
    185–86
Benson, Ezra Taft, 63
Berlin Crisis (1961), 161, 164, 175,
    188
Bohlen, Charles, 24
bomber aircraft, 29, 37, 56, 59;
    Eisenhower's views of, 79;
    Kennedy's support for, 139, 161;
    as part of U.S. deterrent force, 67,
    75, 87, 107. See also B-52; B-58; B-
    70
bomber gap, 10, 80, 91, 148
Bowie, Robert, 77
Bricker, John, 63
Brodie, Bernard, 74, 75
Brown, Edmund G. "Pat," 63, 143
Brucker, Wilbur, 45, 79, 89
Bundy, McGeorge: on history of mis-
    sile gap, 145, 147, 166, 167, 170,
    171, 175, 176, 177; as Kennedy
    adviser, 152–53, 160; on McNa-
    mara and missile gap, 157
Bureau of the Budget, 23–24, 48
Burke, Adm. Arleigh, 78, 79, 93, 94
Burns, Arthur, 27, 37

campaign, 1960 presidential, 11, 99; and Kennedy-Nixon debates, 116–23; and Kennedy's Catholicism 103, 110; and West Virginia primary, 103; and Wisconsin primary, 103. *See also* Kennedy, John F., 1960 presidential campaign

Capehart, Homer, 60

Cater, Douglas, 120

Central Intelligence Agency (CIA), 55, 173; briefings to Kennedy in 1960, 108–9, 165; estimates of Soviet weapons programs, 164. *See also* Dulles, Allen

Chana, Bill, 184, 186

Chayes, Abram, 106

China, 22, 62, 86, 104, 130

Chrysler Corporation, 133, 179

Churchill, Winston, 96

Clark, John, 21

Clinton, Bill, 137

Cold War, 18, 26, 31, 55, 112, 113, 118, 185, 186; arms race, 31; economic burdens of, 51, 148, 187, 188; Eisenhower's views of, 29, 149; Kennedy's views on, 104, 111, 120, 127, 147; and military spending, 14, 15; political economy of, 17–18, 28, 179, 180–81; and roots of conflict, 15; strategy, 15, 19, 21, 22, 46, 151

Committee for Economic Development (CED), 46–47; *The Problem of National Security*, 46, 47–49

Connally, John B., 179

containment, 17. *See also* Cold War, strategy

Convair (Consolidated-Vultee Aircraft) Corporation, 182–85 passim

conventional forces, 5, 114, 151, 178, 187; coercive effects of, 9; Eisenhower and, 8, 26, 29, 49, 50; Kennedy support for expanding, 97, 104, 112, 120, 132, 139, 153, 161, 163, 168, 179; Soviet superiority in, 56, 98. *See also* Flexible Response; limited war

Council of Economic Advisers (CEA), 16, 21, 37, 38, 39, 149

Courage, Ray, 133

Craig, Campbell, 77

Craig, Gordon, 31

Cronkite, Walter, 122

Cuban missile crisis, 12, 166, 189

Daley, Richard, 103

Defense, U.S. Department of, 133, 162, 186; budget, 65, 152; intelligence estimates, 109, 173

defense industry, 111, 129, 130, 136, 180. *See also* aviation-aerospace industry

Defense Manpower Policy Number 4, 112, 127, 130, 136, 141

defense spending, 11, 64, 65, 69, 74, 76, 87, 96, 107, 152; and economy, 8, 25, 35, 48–50, 59, 162, 180, 184, 186; Eisenhower's view of, 7–8, 26, 28–31, 77, 78, 100; increases of, under Kennedy, 150, 160–61; under Truman, 20–25 passim

"The Delicate Balance of Terror" (Wohlstetter), 74–75

Democratic Advisory Council (DAC), 41–42, 105

Democratic Party, 13, 38, 41, 61, 62, 63, 64; in California, 143; National Convention of 1960, 6–7, 99, 106, 137; platform in 1960, 106, 107, 121

deterrence, 19–20, 80, 148, 149; Eisenhower's views on, 26, 78; strategic shortcomings of, 8, 44, 49, 98, 50, 105

deterrent gap, 67, 88, 90, 160

Detroit Tank Arsenal, 134

Dillon, C. Douglas, 148, 150

Dillon, Read and Company, 22

Dirksen, Everett, 159

DiSalle, Michael, 103

Divine, Robert, 102
Dixon, George, 93
Dodge, Joseph, 28
Douglas, James, 71
Drummond, Roscoe, 120–21
Dulles, Allen, 84, 114, 148, 172; and
briefings to Kennedy, 109, 165–66;
and intelligence estimates, 81, 82
Dulles, John Foster, 26, 55, 65–66

eastern establishment, 65
Eastern Europe, 13, 104
economy: and military spending, 5,
20, 28, 153, 162; recession of, 5,
38, 63. *See also* defense spending,
and economy
Eisenhower, Dwight D., 63, 64, 95,
124, 152; and B-70 bomber, 78–79,
92, 140–41; and cabinet, 38, 64,
66, 84; and "Chance for Peace"
speech, 29, 30, 41, 180, 186; and
collapse of Paris summit, 104–5;
compared to Kennedy, 9, 13–14,
150; criticisms of, 6, 10–12, 14, 16,
31, 55–56, 59, 68; on defense
spending and economy, 5, 7–8, 15,
28–30, 48, 50–51, 77–78, 146, 179,
187; economic philosophy of, 26,
27, 65, 189; and farewell address,
148–49, 180; and fears of a garrison state, 26, 47, 49; and the
"Great Equation," 33; and intelligence estimates, 69, 81–82, 84, 91;
and meeting with Kennedy, 149;
on military officers supporting
chain of command, 5, 76–77,
89–92, 100–101; and missile gap, 9,
72, 166, 176; and national security
strategy, 3, 4, 13, 15–16, 19–20; and
response to Fifth Avenue Compact,
107; and response to Gaither Report, 35, 36; and State of the Union
Address of 1954, 25; and State of
the Union Address of 1961, 148
elections, midterm: 1950, 23; 1958,
61, 63, 143

Evans, Rowland, 64
extended deterrence, 31. *See also* deterrence

Fairchild Hiller, 183
Federal Reserve Board, 63, 120, 150
Fifth Avenue Compact, 107
Fisk, James, 36, 37
Flexible Response, 3, 5, 9, 15, 17, 75,
153, 163. *See also* conventional
forces; limited war; Taylor,
Maxwell
Ford, Gerald R., 71
Ford Motor Company, 154
Forrestal, James, 21, 22
Frankfurter, Felix, 110
Friedberg, Aaron, 23, 186–87
Friedman, Milton, 187

Gaddis, John (Lewis), 17
Gaither, H. Rowan, 34, 115
Gaither Committee, 34, 99, 166, 170.
See also Gaither Report
Gaither Report, 38, 43, 45, 119, 158,
173; compared to NSC 68, 34–35,
151; drafting of, 34–35; economic
arguments of, 35; and similarities
with Rockefeller Brothers Report,
36–37. *See also* Eisenhower, Dwight
D., and response to Gaither Report;
Gaither Committee
Galbraith, John Kenneth: *The Affluent
Society,* 41, 42–43; as Kennedy ad-
viser, 9, 113, 149, 150; as propo-
nent of New Economics, 6, 41, 49
Garthoff, Raymond, 94–95
Gates, Thomas S., 84, 133; and intelli-
gence estimates, 86–88 passim, 90,
91, 92; as Secretary of Defense, 80
Gavin, James, 6, 49, 76, 99, 114, 115,
119, 144, 172; as ambassador to
France, 153; and Revolt of the
Generals, 101; *War and Peace in the
Space Age,* 45–46, 58
General Accounting Office, 83
General Dynamics, 179, 182–84

Giglio, James, 150
Gilmore, Roy, 182–83, 184–85
Gilpatric, Roswell A., 36; as Kennedy campaign adviser, 110; and McNamara missile gap controversy, 155, 157, 158, 167; and October 1961 speech to Business Council, 164, 165, 175
Goldwater, Barry, 63
Goodpaster, Andrew, 89
Goodwin, Richard, 110
Gray, Gordon, 84
Great Britain, 53
Green Berets, 179
Greenberg, Stanley, 137
Greenstein, Fred, 101

Hansen, Alvin, 39
Harris, Louis, 102, 110, 144; and Michigan voter polls, 134–35; and New York voter polls, 128–29, 131; and Pennsylvania voter polls, 125, 126, 127
Harris, Seymour Edwin, 38–39, 43, 49, 150
Hart, Philip, 133, 135–36, 137
H-bomb, 97
Heller, Walter, 6, 9, 38, 43, 150; as Council of Economic Advisers chairman, 149; as Kennedy adviser, 113
Herter, Christian, 66
Hilsman, Roger, 31, 157
Hitch, Charles, 154, 161–62, 167
Hoover, Herbert, 112
Horelick, Arnold, 9
Humphrey, George, 28, 65
Humphrey, Hubert, 41–42, 85–86, 103

Immerman, Richard, 77, 101
intelligence estimates of Soviet weapons program, 13, 80–83, 86–87, 108–9, 163–64, 166, 169, 172; criticisms of, 68, 73, 88–89; speculative nature of, 54, 57, 67–69, 70, 94–95, 100. *See also* National Intelligence Estimates

intercontinental ballistic missiles (ICBMs): and comparisons of U.S. and Soviet programs, 70–73, 90, 100, 166; first-generation vs. second-generation, 7, 37, 67; Soviet, 3, 9, 15, 33, 81, 84, 88, 169, 170, 175; U.S., 36, 37, 59, 80, 159, 169. *See also* Atlas; Minuteman; SS-6; Titan
intermediate-range ballistic missiles (IRBMs), 36, 67, 88, 159, 162. *See also* Jupiter
interstate highway system, 27
Isaacson, Walter, 152

Jackson, Henry M. "Scoop," 59, 89, 158
Johnson, Louis, 21
Johnson, Lyndon B., 41, 52, 59, 94, 179; and B-70 bomber, 141; on defense spending and economy, 180; on intelligence estimates, 88–89; and missile gap, 72, 158; and national security strategy, 17, 101; presidential aspirations of, 74, 85, 87
Joint Chiefs of Staff: and B-70 bomber, 79, 100; criticized, 45; policy role of, 89, 94. *See also* Lemnitzer, Gen. Lyman L.; Taylor, Gen. Maxwell D.; Twining, Gen. Nathan F.
Jupiter (IRBM), 133, 136, 162, 163, 178–79

Kaplan, Morton, 31
Kaufmann, William W., 49, 94, 177; *The McNamara Strategy,* 175; *Military Policy and National Security,* 31
Kaysen, Carl, 168
Keeny, Spurgeon, 168
Kefauver, Estes, 42
Kennan, George F., 22
Kennedy, John F.: and Joseph Alsop, 54, 57, 61, 95–96; compared to Eisenhower, 9, 14; and criticism of Eisenhower's policies, 20, 52, 70, 108; and defense budget, 60, 97,

100, 150, 153, 160–61; and "The Delicate Balance of Terror," 75; and Democratic Advisory Council, 42, 105; economic philosophy of, 117, 120, 150; and inaugural address, 149; and intelligence briefings during presidential campaign, 108–9, 145, 165; and McNamara's comments on missile gap, 158; and national security strategy, 3, 5–6, 12, 16–17, 97, 104, 114; on need for sacrifice to defeat communism, 118, 123, 132, 134, 138–39, 148; and personal interest in foreign policy and defense issues, 53, 111; and preinaugural meeting with Eisenhower, 149; *Profiles in Courage,* 53, 113; and State of the Union Address of 1961, 149; *The Strategy of Peace,* 114; on U-2 incident, 105; *Why England Slept,* 53, 61, 111

—on defense spending and economy, 16–18, 187; as economic stimulus, 129, 130, 161, 169, 179

—on defense spending and employment, 8; and concerns of defense workers, 111, 129–30, 135–36, 137, 178; and distribution of defense jobs, 130, 141–42, 147. *See also* Defense Manpower Policy Number 4

—and missile gap: effect on policies, 153–54, 174, 188; misconceptions, 97, 98, 151, 188; politics, 4, 7, 10–11, 61, 64, 74, 100, 116, 169–70; warnings, 58–60, 62, 86, 96–99, 103–4, 115, 132

—1960 presidential campaign: in California, 137–44; and candidacy announcement, 85; foreign policy as issue in, 102; and Kennedy-Nixon debates, 116–23; in Michigan, 132–37; in New York, 127–31; in Pennsylvania, 124–27; and speech to American Legion, 115–16; and

speech to Democratic Convention, 106; and speech to Veterans of Foreign Wars, 132

Kennedy, Joseph P., 53, 150
Kennedy, Robert F., 110, 153
Keynes, John Maynard, 40, 42
Keynesian economics, 27, 40, 52, 113, 162, 180
Keyserling, Leon: as Council of Economic Advisers chair, 21, 22; and criticisms of Eisenhower's policies, 39, 43; on defense spending and economic growth, 23, 25, 48, 180; and Democratic Advisory Council, 41
Khrushchev, Nikita: and collapse of Paris summit, 104–5; and Eisenhower, 78, 80, 95; and "kitchen debate" with Nixon, 123, 126; and Soviet weapons programs, 87, 89, 98, 164, 189; and support for "wars of national liberation," 149
Killian, James, 36, 37
Killian Committee, 99
King, James E. Jr., 46
Kinnard, Douglas, 76
Kissinger, Henry: as adviser to Kennedy, 152–53; and criticisms of Eisenhower's policies, 46, 49; influence of, on Kennedy, 6, 58, 144; on missile gap, 151, 172; *Necessity for Choice,* 151, 152; *Nuclear Weapons and Foreign Policy,* 31–32; and Rockefeller Brothers Report, 35–36
Kistiakowsky, George, 83
Knowland, William F., 63
Korean War: defense spending and, 22, 23, 48, 134; and postwar cuts, 44, 129, 147
Korth, Fred, 179
Krock, Arthur, 53, 65–66
Kunz, Diane, 180

Lawrence, David, 124
Leach, W. Barton, 70
LeMay, Gen. Curtis, 140, 178

Lemnitzer, Gen. Lyman L., 78, 160
Liberal Party (New York), 128, 131
Liddell Hart, B. H., 114, 144
limited war, 32, 45, 46, 74; and danger of escalation, 15–16, 20, 32, 50, Eisenhower's views on, 26; Kennedy's views on, 62, 98, 104, 112, 168. *See also* conventional forces; Flexible Response
Lincoln, George, 34, 36
Lindbergh, Charles, 131
Love, Henry, 139
Lubell, Samuel A., 29
Luce, Henry R., 37, 61
Lull, John, 184, 186

M-60 tank, 134
Maginot Line, 32
Mahon, George, 64, 71, 159–60
Marine Corps, U.S., 64, 105
Martin, William McChesney, 150
massive retaliation: and army, 44, 178; criticized, 14, 31, 46, 50, 55; Kennedy's views on, 58, 98; origins of, 26. *See also* New Look
McCullough, John S., 127
McDonnell Douglas, 183
McElroy, Neil H.: and defense budget, 77; and intelligence estimates, 68, 70, 72, 81, 86; and missile gap, 54, 67, 69, 71, 72; replaced as Secretary of Defense, 80
McNamara, Robert: on air force and missile gap, 94; and assertion of U.S. strategic superiority, 164; background of, 154; and February 1961 missile gap briefing, 154–59 passim, 173, 177; on missile gap history, 166–67, 174
McQuade, Lawrence, 170–71, 174, 175
Meagher, Michael E., 113
Medaris, John B., 114–15, 144
military-industrial complex: during Cold War, 14, 181, 183–84; Eisenhower's warning concerning, 149; and Kennedy's defense policies, 168

Minuteman (ICBM): advantages of, 37, 163; criticisms of, 56, 115, 162; Kennedy's support for, 59, 97, 104, 112, 114, 115, 120, 132, 162; as part of U.S. nuclear deterrent, 159, 168; program accelerated, 161, 170, 174
missile. *See individual missiles by name*
missile gap: as critique of Eisenhower's policies, 4, 6–9, 10–11, 20, 49, 51, 55, 64, 145–46, 147, 188–89; debate over, in Congress, 52, 54, 60, 71–72; defense buildup legitimized by, 8, 11, 45, 46, 112, 152, 154; economics of, 7, 17–18, 143, 181; Eisenhower's attitude toward, 69, 80, 95, 100, 148, 149; examined by Kennedy administration, 164, 166–74; fears of, 3, 11, 148, 175, 177; Gilpatric's speech on, 164, 175; and intelligence estimates, 4, 13, 54, 66–68, 81, 84, 88; in Kennedy's 1960 presidential campaign, 3, 7, 99, 100, 109–10, 124, 143; Kennedy's warnings of, 58–60, 62–63, 86, 96–99, 103–4, 115, 132; legacy of, 186–89; and McNamara briefing, 154–59 passim, 173, 177; as myth, 9, 146, 153–54, 177; as political issue, 51, 53–54, 57, 61–63, 100, 144–45, 157, 160, 168, 175, 177, 178, 181; referenced in 1960 Democratic Party platform, 106; and U-2 program, 80–81, 104–5
Morgan, Edward, 118
Murphy, Charles J. V., 158–59

National Guard, U.S., 79
National Intelligence Estimates (NIEs), 67–68, 73, 81, 83; NIE 11-5-58, 68–69, 73; NIE 11-4-59, 81; NIE 11-5-59, 73; NIE 11-8-59, 81, 82, 109; NIE 11-8-60, 109; SNIE 11-10-57, 57. *See also* intelligence estimates

National Security Council (NSC):
Eisenhower and, 33, 78, 80–82;
Kennedy and, 9; policy debates
within, 66, 83; and press leaks, 84.
See also individual NSC documents
Navy, U.S., 12, 39, 82, 95, 105, 115,
155; budgets, 21, 26, 152; and Polaris, 94; and ship construction,
84; and *Vanguard*, 46
Neeson, Hugh, 185–86
New Deal, 27
New Economics, 6, 13, 16, 17, 38, 39
New Frontier, 16, 102, 106
New Look, 37, 54, 75, 93, 151; blamed
for job losses, 7, 30–31, 144, 147;
criticisms of, 4, 10–11, 12, 26, 37,
41, 44, 45, 46, 51, 55, 66, 74, 100,
147; economic theory of, 15, 19–20,
25, 38, 41; and military force structure, 16; and nuclear deterrence, 6,
8–9, 12, 20, 31, 98; refinements to,
4; and restrictions on defense
spending, 5, 98; supplanted by Flexible Response, 3, 14, 151
Nike-Zeus antiballistic missile, 83
Nitze, Paul, 21–22, 170, 175; and
Gaither Report, 34–35, 151; on
history of missile gap, 171, 174; in
Kennedy administration, 151; and
NSC-68, 22–23, 24, 25, 151, 180
Nixon, Richard, 12, 102, 116, 124,
130, 142, 189; and association
with Eisenhower's policies, 6, 9,
64, 108, 111, 118, 144; and defeat
in 1960 presidential election, 3;
on economic growth, 117, 119–22;
and Fifth Avenue Compact, 107–8;
on intelligence estimates of missile gap, 81–82, 84; Kennedy's criticisms of, 86, 127, 135; and
"kitchen debate" with
Khrushchev, 123, 126; and
midterm elections of 1958, 64;
and presidential campaign in California, 137, 140, 141–43, 179; *Six
Crises*, 165

Norris, John G., 83, 84, 88, 155, 156, 159
Norstad, Lauris, 158
North American Aviation Corpora-
tion, 140, 141, 183
North Atlantic Treaty Organization
(NATO), 114, 158
Nourse, Edwin, 21
NSC 68: budgetary policies called for
in, 22–23, 50; compared to
Gaither Report, 34–35, 151; Eisen-
hower's views of, 25; origins of,
21; significance of, 23
NSC 135/3, 24
NSC 141, 24
NSC 162/2, 4, 25. *See also* New Look
Nuclear "overkill," 168
nuclear war, 16, 20, 32, 77, 114. *See
also* World War III
nuclear weapons. *See specific weapon
systems*

Office of National Estimates, 94–95
O'Hara, Jim, 133
ordnance missile command, 114
Osgood, Robert E., 32, 49
Osmers, Frank, 165

Paris summit, 104–5
Pattillo, Donald, 184
Penkovsky, Oleg, 164
Phelps, Edmund, 187
Phillips, Thomas R., 68
Pierpaoli, Paul, 23
Polaris (SLBM), 56, 107, 115, 159; and
air force, 93–94; Burke's advocacy
of, 93, 94; Kennedy's support for,
59, 97, 104, 112, 114, 115, 120,
132, 149, 162; operational advantages of, 37; program accelerated,
80, 149, 161, 170, 174; and U.S.
nuclear deterrent, 149, 163
Power, Gen. Thomas S., 90, 93, 95,
99, 101, 178; as advocate of B-70
program, 92, 140; and challenge
of intelligence estimates, 94; and
warnings of U.S. vulnerability, 87, 88

Powers, Francis Gary, 105, 109
Preparedness Committee, 89

Quarles, Donald, 54

Radford, Adm. Arthur, 28
Rand Corporation, 74, 154, 170
Rayburn, Sam, 41
Raymond, Jack, 76, 155; on McNamara and missile gap, 156–58
Redstone rocket program, 46, 133, 137
Republican Party, 39, 54, 60, 63, 111
Reuther, Walter, 132
Revolt of the Admirals, 21
Revolt of the Generals, 44–46, 101
Ribicoff, Abraham, 61
Ridgway, Matthew: as advocate for army, 77, 94, 98; and criticisms of Eisenhower's policies, 46, 49, 76, 99, 115, 119; resignation of, as army chief of staff, 44, 75; and Revolt of the Generals, 101; *Soldier,* 44–45
Roberts, Chalmers, 86
Rockefeller, John D., III, 153
Rockefeller, Nelson: and criticisms of Eisenhower's policies cited by Kennedy, 108, 115, 119, 121, 144; elected governor of New York, 63, 128; and Fifth Avenue Compact, 107, 120
Rockefeller Brothers Fund, 35. *See also* Rockefeller Brothers Report
Rockefeller Brothers Report, 38, 45, 119, 158, 166; cited by Kennedy, 99; compared to Gaither Report, 36; findings and recommendations of, 35–36, 43; and limited influence on policy, 37
Rockwell-Standard, 183
Rogers, Warren, 90, 158
Roosevelt, Franklin D., 54, 127, 149
Rostow, Walt Whitman, 112–13, 119
Rovere, Richard, 61
Rush, Myron, 9
Rusk, Dean, 153, 164
Russell, Richard, 87, 91

Salinger, Pierre, 158
Samuelson, Paul, 113, 161
Saulnier, Raymond, 27
Scali, John, 155
Schlesinger, Arthur M. Jr., 110, 152, 176, 177, 179–80
Schriever, Gen. Bernard, 68
Security Resources Panel. *See* Gaither Committee
Sharp, Dudley, 90
Single Integrated Operational Plan (SIOP), 155
Sloan, John, 26, 27
Smith, Al, 127
Smith, Howard K., 116
Smith, Steve, 110
Smith, Walter Bedell ("Beetle"), 25
Smith, William Y., 171–74, 175, 177
Social Security, 27
Sorenson, Ted, 53, 110, 114, 176, 177, 180
Southeast Asia, 14, 15, 17, 149, 174, 187. *See also* Vietnam War
Soviet Union. *See* Union of Soviet Socialist Republics
Spivak, Alvin, 119
Splitt, Orville, 155, 157
Sputnik (satellite), 3, 4, 10, 33, 38, 43, 45, 64, 75, 108, 113, 175
Sputnik II (satellite), 34
SS-6 (ICBM), 67
Staebler, Neil, 132
stagflation, 16
State, U.S. Department of, 66, 122; Policy Planning Staff, 22
Stevenson, Adlai, 38, 41, 85, 110, 131, 136, 143; and criticisms of Eisenhower defense spending cuts, 39
St. Lawrence Seaway, 27
Strategic Air Command (SAC): and B-70 bomber, 94; and enhanced readiness, 36, 59, 161; and intelligence assessment, 87, 155; and Minuteman, 168; and Polaris, 93–94

Strategy in the Missile Age (Brodie), 74
Stratton, Samuel, 70
submarine-launched ballistic missiles (SLBMs), 36, 37. *See also* Polaris
Sylvester, Arthur, 155, 157
Symington, Stuart W., 69, 88, 92, 158; and B-70 bomber, 141; and criticisms of Eisenhower's policies, 59–60, 87; and Democratic Advisory Council, 42; and disputes of intelligence estimates, 68, 72, 91; and missile gap, 72, 157, 165; and presidential aspirations, 74, 85, 87

Taylor, Gen. Maxwell D., 33, 94, 95, 114, 120, 144, 171; as adviser to Kennedy, 152; as advocate of Flexible Response, 9, 75, 151; as chairman of Joint Chiefs of Staff, 153; cited by Kennedy, 99, 115; and criticisms of Eisenhower's policies, 6, 16, 92–93, 172; Eisenhower's views of, 77, 89; military career of, 75; and Revolt of the Generals, 101; *The Uncertain Trumpet*, 75–76, 77; on U.S. nuclear deterrent, 152
Technical Capabilities Panel. *See* Killian Committee
TFX (advanced technical fighter), 179
Titan (ICBM): criticized, 115; Kennedy's decision not to expand program, 162, 163, 178; operational shortcomings of, 37, 163; as part of U.S. nuclear deterrent, 159; program accelerated, 80
Tobin, James: and criticisms of Eisenhower's policies, 40–41, 43, 49; "Defense, Dollars, and Doctrines," 40–41, 52; on economic growth and national security, 48; education and upbringing of, 39–40; as Kennedy adviser, 113; and New Economics, 6, 9, 16
Treasury, U.S. Department of. *See* Dillon, C. Douglas; Humphrey, George

Truman, Harry S., 38, 39, 49, 70, 155; and criticisms of Eisenhower's policies, 89; and defense spending, 20, 22, 24, 50; and fiscal policies, 21, 23; and NSC 68, 22, 24; policies of, compared with Eisenhower's, 19, 25, 27
Twining, Gen. Nathan F.: as advocate of B-70 program, 92, 140; congressional testimony of, scrutinized, 89, 90; on defense budgets, 78; on intelligence estimates, 70, 72

U-2 program: and aircraft shot down over Russia, 104–5; and intelligence estimates, 81, 109. *See also* Paris summit; Powers, Francis Gary
Union of Soviet Socialist Republics (U.S.S.R.): and Cold War, 16, 33, 186, 187; and defense spending, 23, 29, 47, 123; and economic performance (presumed and actual), 26–27, 39, 40, 47, 112–13, 121, 126; fears of, 3, 13, 63, 148; intelligence assessments of, 54, 57, 60, 67–69, 73, 81–83, 94, 95, 100, 109; and military capabilities (presumed and actual), 4, 6, 12, 19, 20, 31–32, 34, 37, 43, 56, 58, 67, 97, 126, 151; and missile programs, 3, 9, 33, 45, 46, 55, 59, 70, 72, 86–87, 104–5, 159–60; and nuclear weapons, 8, 22, 36, 50, 55–56, 78, 98, 138, 149, 164; and space program, 3, 11, 33–34, 45, 52, 122; threat from, 15, 24, 44, 49, 57, 62, 66, 70, 85, 88, 107, 108; and U-2, 104–5
United Auto Workers, 132, 140, 141
United States Information Agency (USIA), 121, 122
United States Intelligence Board, 82
United States Strategic Bombing Survey (USSBS), 22
United States Strategic Command. *See* Polaris

Vanguard (satellite), 34, 46
Vietnam War, 16, 17, 101, 179, 183.
   See also Southeast Asia
von Braun, Wernher, 46, 68, 72

Walsh, Gen. James H., 101, 155; and
   intelligence estimates, 82, 83, 94
Wheeler, Gen. Earle, 109
White, Gen. Thomas D., 71, 88; as ad-
   vocate of B-70 program, 78–79, 92,
   94, 140; and Polaris, 94; and Re-
   volt of the Generals, 101
Whiz Kids, 168
Wiesner, Jerome, 153, 154, 167, 168
Wiley, Alexander, 60
Williams, G. Mennen, 132, 133

Wilson, Charles E., 33, 44, 65, 68
Wilson, Woodrow, 127
Wofford, Harris, 110, 111, 114
Wohlstetter, Albert, 74–75
World War II, 48, 115, 123, 134, 149,
   180, 183, 189
World War III, 20, 92. *See also* nuclear
   war

Yarmolinsky, Adam, 110, 157, 167,
   170, 174
York, Herbert, 13, 72, 79, 168

Zhukov, Marshal Georgi Konstantinovich, 98